itizenship
beyond the state

Citizenship
beyond the state
John Hoffman

SAGE Publications
London • Thousand Oaks • New Delhi

First published 2004

SAGE Publications Ltd
1 Oliver's Yard
55 City Road
London EC1Y 1SP

SAGE Publications Inc.
2455 Teller Road
Thousand Oaks, California 91320

SAGE Publications India Pvt Ltd
B-42, Panchsheel Enclave
Post Box 4109
New Delhi 100 017

British Library Cataloguing in Publication data

A catalogue record for this book is available
from the British Library

ISBN 0-7619-4941-0
ISBN 0-7619-4942-9 (pbk)

Library of Congress Control Number: 2003112271

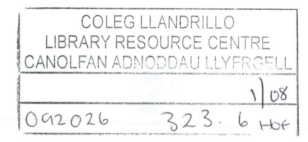
Typeset by C&M Digitals (P) Ltd., Chennai, India
Printed in Great Britain by Athenaeum Press, Gateshead

To Keith Faulks, whose idea this book was, and whose work has been a great inspiration to me

Contents

Acknowledgements

Chapters One, Three, Four and Eight were drafted while on study leave, and I am very grateful to the Department of Politics and the University of Leicester for this sabbatical.

I would like to thank Keith Faulks particularly for reading the book in its entirety. His feedback and comments proved invaluable, and as the reader will see, I have drawn heavily upon his work on citizenship. I would also like to express my gratitude to Gillian Youngs and Audrey Osler for reading particular chapters. While writing this book, I have also been helped by Rose O'Toole who promised that she would read the book when it was produced!

I am also grateful to my partner, Rowan Roenisch, who supported and encouraged me, and my son and daughter, Fred Hoffman and Frieda Roenisch, who expressed an interest in the book.

Introduction

Citizenship has become a fashionable concept and the literature on this subject is now enormous. It has always been central to liberal discourse but what is distinctive about the last ten years or so is the extent to which the concept of citizenship has been taken up by feminists, multi-culturalists, new social movement theorists and those generally critical of the liberal tradition.

During the 1960s and 1970s radicals on the left found the term too 'bourgeois' and, of course, the notion initially signalled one who had a propertied stake in the community. Citizenship was identified with legal and political rights and appeared to ignore the way in which those with wealth could exercise informal power over the property-less and the vulnerable. Yet the term should not be frozen in this way. Citizenship is a concept that is sensitive to historical change; the fact that it offers universal status – rights that everyone is entitled to exercise – makes it an important term to reconstruct and 'reclaim'. Although the liberal view of citizenship is a necessary condition for this process of reconstruction, it is certainly not sufficient, for the liberal view of citizenship still contains exclusionary clauses (even if these are now implicit) that favour certain kinds of people over others.

What is the justification for yet another book on citizenship? Crucial to the argument developed here is the question of the state. This work seeks to challenge the assumption – almost universally held – that citizenship involves the membership of a state. Citizens, it is argued, are French, British or German – and even where citizens are considered to be European or even global the notion is still state-focused. I want to argue that the state is actually a barrier to the notion of citizenship, defined here as a set of entitlements which include *everyone*.

Rowan Williams, the new Archbishop of Canterbury, delivered a Dimbleby lecture on 19 December 2002, which explored many of the themes tackled in this book. My differences with Williams are as instructive as the ground we share in common.

Citizenship and the State

Williams argues – and this was the aspect of his lecture headlined in *The Times* (27 December 2002) – that 'we are witnessing the end of the nation state' (2002: 1). He rightly argues that we need to do some hard thinking about what these changes mean for being a citizen. These changes are, he argues, 'irreversible' (2002: 2). Williams' contention is that the nation state is in decline – a position I would agree with – but he takes the view that the nation state is giving way to something he calls the 'market state'. Although he is critical of the latter, I want to suggest that the state itself, in all its forms, is the problem.

Rousseau urges his reader to be aware of the poverty of language and be prepared to 'wait' (1968: 74) and I am conscious of using words in an unconventional way. My book stands or falls as an attempt to separate the concept of citizenship from that of the state. I define the state in a definition taken from Max Weber as being an institution that claims a monopoly of legitimate force for a particular territory. I seek to 'deconstruct' (i.e., criticize) the notion of the state in terms of Weber's definition, by arguing that the state is a contradictory institution which claims a monopoly that it does not and cannot have. This is true both of its claim to have a monopoly of force and a monopoly of legitimacy.

The state can only claim a monopoly of force because it has competitors (terrorists, criminals, etc.) who use force against the state and society. Hence its monopoly of force is a fiction! The same is true of its claim to have a monopoly of legitimacy. It is because terrorists explicitly and criminals implicitly – not to mention those who are dissidents – challenge the legitimacy of the state that this monopoly is claimed. The state which *actually* had a monopoly of legitimate force would be linked to a society without terrorists or criminals, and hence would not need to exist. These are the implications of Weber's own definition even though we readily concede that they are not implications which he himself acknowledged.

It is this critique of the state that challenges the standard view of citizenship as denoting membership of a state. For how can one be a citizen when laws are passed and functionaries exist, whose authority is underpinned by this claim to exercise a monopoly of legitimate force? Even when force is authorized, it still prevents the recipient of this force from exercising rights and duties that are crucial to citizenship and it means that those against whom such force is not directly exercised, live in its shadow. They know that the laws they obey can be 'enforced', so that the absence of fear which is central to citizenship cannot be proven to exist in a society that centres around the state.

It is the role of the state to impose solutions by force when faced with divisions and conflicts of interest which cannot be tackled through arbitration and negotiation. A person who is not free is not a citizen. It may be objected that the state does not simply use force, but claims – in the celebrated definition that is central to my argument – a monopoly of *legitimate* force.

But this is not a convincing argument since legitimacy implies limits, whereas force, in my view, cannot be limited (however hard authorities might try). Legitimate force is thus a contradiction in terms, and the state, therefore, is an institution seeking to achieve the impossible. Williams argues that the state can no longer protect citizens, given the existence of intercontinental missile technology (2002: 2), but the state's mechanism for protecting 'its' subjects has always been contradictory and paradoxical.

This critique of the state is central to the argument of the book. It explains why we must develop a notion of democracy that goes beyond the state. Years ago I described the concept of the 'democratic state' as an oxymoron (1991: 342) since it is impossible that an institution that claims to have a monopoly of legitimate force can be compatible with the rule of the people. The distinction between nationality and nationalism rests upon this critique of the state, since my argument is that whereas nationalism is a state-centred or statist concept, nationality is not. People have one nationality or many nationalities because it is impossible to be an individual without the language and culture that is central to national belonging. Nationalism, conversely, privileges one nationality above others, and is tied to the fact that the state cannot seek to claim a monopoly of legitimacy in the abstract: it must provide cultural symbols that make its claim plausible and relevant.

States are not only contradictory, oppressive and nationalistic, but among the identities they privilege, is that of masculinity. Many feminists speak critically of the state, and argue for a woman-friendly polity. But women cannot be citizens in any meaningful sense as long as they live under the shadow of the state. In a patriarchal or male dominated society, women are the targets of violence. They are necessarily underrepresented in the state, and the public/private divide works against their participation in the political process. This divide, even as interpreted in the liberal tradition, assumes that women are not really suited to 'public' activity and should confine their activities to the 'private' or domestic sphere. The monopolistic identity of the state – the exaltation of the principle of 'oneness' – works against the interests of women.

Williams argues that the 'market state' is 'here to stay' (2002: 5), but not only is this overly pessimistic, but it points to a meaningless separate identity. The nation state itself has been a 'market state' as long as capitalism and the market have been around. These systems create divisions of interests that make interventions of the state necessary. Capitalism divides society into those who have independent resources, which they can use as capital, and those who have to work for others. Although these divisions are more complex than classical Marxism has assumed, inequality is crucial to the existence of the state since the challenge of the monopoly of the state comes from those who have either too much or too little. Capitalism is inconceivable without a state, even if other forms of exploitative society also necessitate states as well. As for the market, it masks the real power that people exercise and although markets can exist without capitalism, markets ultimately generate the kind of structural inequalities that create a need for the state.

Williams argues that the market state is accompanied by 'a disturbingly high percentage of younger people failing to vote' (2002: 5). The state has always been an elite institution, incompatible with meaningful and widespread participation. Apathy and inequality reinforce one another, so that those who are targets of the force of the state are drawn in part from that section of the population who do not participate in the making of laws. They are 'subjects' who must obey laws without formally authorizing them. Moreover, the notion of the state is incompatible with a meaningful concept of community, and however much communitarians applaud the latter, their arguments are often weakened by an uncritical view of the state.

This is the challenge faced by globalization. Williams' market state (which he takes from Bobbit) presupposes what I describe as 'pseudo-globalization'. By this I mean a 'globalization' which divides rather than unites, so that inequalities are deepened, and states remain necessary. The problem with Ohmae's market-fundamentalist version of globalization is that it rests firmly within a state-centric framework. He sees the nation state giving way to the regional state, and his acknowledgement that market forces aggravate rather than reduce inequalities, means that the state and statism remain central to his notion of globalization. Such is the tyranny of the state concept that some see the United Nations as a world state, and regard global (or even European) citizenship as only intelligible in terms of the state.

States generate particular ways of thinking, which I call 'state-centric' or 'statist' in character. Thus the notion of emancipation is either applauded or (more recently) attacked, since it is assumed that it has to be tied to the absolutism of the state. It is true that the classical liberal concept of the 'rational state' saw emancipation as a state of affairs in which individuals obeyed lawful acts of force which they had prescribed for themselves. But this problematic situation – captured memorably in Rousseau's notion of a legitimate state forcing people to be free – arises from the state, not from the concept of emancipation. Postmodernists are often tempted to blame the concept of emancipation for the absolutism and historical insensitivity that derives from the state. A statist mentality is not simply one that admires the state: it may involve (as with classical Marxism and anarchism) critiques of the state but these are critiques which ensure that divisions continue and states remain in business. Naive optimism is not really preferable to naive pessimism: both express philosophical attitudes tied to a fatalist acceptance of the state.

Coercion and Force: State and Government

But is it possible to envisage life beyond the state? Deeply rooted in our psyche (with 5,000 years of theory and practice to mould and reinforce it) is the notion that the state is part of civilization, and that without the state, we will have chaos and destruction.

In fact humanity has lived for most of its life without a state. While the domestic societies of 'early' peoples cannot constitute a model to which we should return, they are of great interest to political theory in demonstrating that humans can order their lives without a state. Crucial to my argument is the distinction between force, on the one hand, and coercion and constraint, on the other. This distinction enables us to challenge the proposition that order is impossible without the state.

What early stateless societies demonstrate, as does international society – which is also stateless in character – is that order can only be established through sanctions which are social rather than statist in character. Stateless societies maintain order through non-statist sanctions, economic and moral pressures, ostracism, etc., even if some of the sanctions employed in early stateless domestic societies are archaic and no longer meaningful in character. What these sanctions demonstrate is the need to distinguish between coercion (and constraint) on the one hand, and force on the other. It is interesting that Mill refers to a 'moral coercion', which he sees as distinct from the force of the state, and even notes the punitive character of what he calls 'natural penalties' – spontaneous social pressures that arise simply because we interact with one another (Mill, 1974).

Of course, coercion has a 'negative' ring in our liberal culture, and one can preserve some of this negativity by making a distinction between coercion, on the one hand, and constraint, on the other. Coercion can be characterized as a deliberate intervention intended to inflict harm on a recipient through pressures that fall short of force, whereas constraints arise unintentionally and have a much less formal character. They may indeed simply constitute natural and social structures, which cause people to do things they otherwise would not do.

The point about both coercion and constraint is that they are unavoidable. They arise simply because we live in a society and they are inherent in relationships. Both are a condition of freedom, even though the more people can regulate their lives through constraint rather than coercion (other things being equal), the better. It is particularly important to distinguish between coercion and force, since force disables agency in a way that coercion does not. Even when extreme coercion is used and force is threatened, it is not coercion that is the problem, but the credibility of the force threatened. A two-year-old who 'threatens' you with a plastic water pistol is very different from a hardened criminal who produces a sawn-off shotgun! Coercion is unpleasant, but it leaves a person's capacity to exercise choice intact in a way which force does not.

I argue for a concept of force that is broad but is basically physicalist in character. What makes abuse an act of force is that it creates physical harm for the recipient, whereas an adverse moral judgement, for example, need not. Obviously, it can be difficult to distinguish extreme coercion from force, but in my view, it is a crucial distinction to make, since the use of coercion allows for a rule- and law-governed society and the employment of sanctions. Force, on the other hand, actually undermines order since it suppresses agency and creates a desire for revenge, making it ineffective in the long term as a sanction.

Is force never justifiable? I make a distinction between what is justifiable in the short-term and what is legitimate. Force is never legitimate since, as argued above, legitimacy implies limits whereas force always goes to extremes. Force, however, can be justified when (and only when) it is used to create a breathing space enabling non-statist sanctions to operate. I do not make any distinction between force and violence (as some writers do) on the grounds that the distinction is not a practical one as the hapless recipients of force can readily testify. By problematizing force, it becomes necessary to identify the conditions in which force arises, and when it can be avoided. My position is rooted in the argument that force can be avoided where common interests exist between parties to a dispute. This does not mean that common interests presuppose an absence of conflict but rather that conflict arises (and is inevitable) simply because people are different from one another, but this kind of conflict can be resolved through compromise, negotiation and arbitration.

Where common interests do not exist, force comes into play, and the use of force is not only a defeat for negotiation, but it can only suppress or manage conflicts of interest – it can never resolve them. The position adopted here is not a pacifist one – that force should always be avoided – but it sees force as undesirable, dangerous and only to be justified on the grounds that a present act of force makes a future one unnecessary. Force can be justified if it is the only way to enact policies that cement common interests.

The force/coercion (and constraint) distinction translates into a distinction between state and government. Government, in my view, involves resolving conflicts of interest through sanctions that are inherent in social relationships and fall short of force. Williams makes it impossible to look beyond the state when he follows the common pattern of using government and state as synonyms (2002: 1). In stateless societies, governments exist without the state, but in state-centred societies, the distinction is more difficult to make, but it still exists – logically if not empirically. This is not only true in terms of domestic state-centred societies; in international society, the participants are often states whose behaviour is a complex mixture of the statist and what I call the governmental. While I write, the conflict in Iraq is being waged in a way that is depressingly statist in character, although talk of a future reconstruction involves (some) reference to governmental measures as well. It is also true that, in some instances, British troops have been trained to blend the governmental with the statist to a much greater extent than American troops, who appear to regard the Iraqis as enemies to be killed, and not human beings to be empowered.

States can act governmentally, as in situations in which they seek to resolve conflicts through negotiation and compromise. When they do, they are, strictly speaking, dissolving away statism, and changing themselves into something else. Indeed, the disappearance of the state can only occur in this way. This is why I regard citizenship as a governmental and not a statist concept, since people can only become citizens when their agency is acknowledged and they are not subject to force.

The distinction between force and coercion (and constraint), and state and government, is central to a critique which makes it possible to look beyond the state in both a utopian and a realist way. It also means that a democratic society is not one without laws, rules and discipline: rather it is a society governed by coercion and constraint, and not force. Democracy is certainly governmental and political, in that it seeks to resolve conflicts of interest in ways that preserve the agency (and thus capacity for self-government) of parties to a dispute. Citizenship and democracy are contradicted by the use of force. The use of force is incompatible with the idea of self-government (which I see as central to the concept of democracy), even if this force is deemed legitimate because it has been explicitly authorized. I am critical of Held's model of a cosmopolitan democracy because he argues that a cosmopolitan democracy needs to be sanctioned by force. Of course, cosmopolitan institutions may need to use force in the short-term, but this indicates that they still have some distance to go before they can be described as democratic.

If democratic nationalism is a contradiction in terms, a democratic nationality is not. Such a nationality respects and learns from others who are different – both those in their midst and those who live in other countries. What aspects of a national culture are unacceptable? Aspects that harm others and are intolerant of difference. In a democracy, these harmful practices can only be dealt with through non-statist sanctions. In societies yet to be democratic, force may have to be used in situations where social pressures aren't powerful enough to prevent harmful practices.

The tension between force and coercion is well exemplified in terms of the struggle for women's equality. Clearly men (or partners) who are so brutalized that they cannot respond to mere coercion, may have to be suppressed through force, but thoughtful women recognize that, for example, the use of force against rapists must be linked to policies that address the hatred and insecurity of the rapist. Codes of practice that empower women and advance their interests can only really be implemented through coercion and constraint: to rely upon force (though it may be provisionally necessary) can easily become counter-productive.

It is tempting, but wrong, to argue that the very distinction between public and private should be abandoned. The public equates with the political. An issue becomes public when it involves the existence of conflict, which needs to be resolved. Although the distinction is a complex one, what is private refers to a sphere in which conflict is imperceptible or embryonic, so that political mechanisms are not called into play. This 'sphere' is not static since an arena of privacy may become public in character when conflict breaks out. It is important to remember that conflicts can not only be tackled without the use of force, but many conflicts of interest can be resolved by what Mill refers to as natural penalties – spontaneous social pressures that do not even require moral judgements or focused sanctions to be effective. The public/private divide is better characterized as a public/private difference, given the fact that divisions imply conflicts of interest that generate force.

The formal exclusion of women from citizenship was historically premised on the assumption that only those who could fight for their country could be citizens. It is true that women can now enter the armed forces in some societies, and although this is a necessary step in dissolving away naturalistic prejudices, the use of violence remains a statist and patriarchal practice, incompatible with emancipation and citizenship.

Capitalism demonstrates, as Marx's analysis testifies, a distinction between coercion, which compels people to work for an employer and force, which is state-centred. Although Marx makes it clear that the coercion involved in the labour contract is unacceptable, he also indicates that coercion and constraint (a realm of 'necessity') is unavoidable in any society. Making the relationships, which markets obscure, transparent still involves coercion since, to echo Mill, there cannot be too much government helping people to help themselves. Regulations, which prevent harm to others or to oneself, are essential to the governing process. Williams speaks of the market state deregulating in order to 'clear a space for individuals or groups to do their own regulating' (2002: 3), but deregulation is only justifiable when it reduces harm.

The argument for a basic income could not be brought about without a good deal of moral pressure – upon both those who see themselves as having to pay disproportionately for such a measure and those who would benefit from it. The attack on the welfare state has (somewhat demagogically) focused on the paternalistic and authoritarian character of much welfare provision and it has to be said that the welfare state has often and in part provided charity for the vulnerable rather than rights for all. The welfare state is an amalgam of what I would call the statist and the governmental; empowering people but often through a leadership that is elitist and divisive.

The use of quotas to increase participation from those who have been excluded must be handled carefully and sensitively so that these quotas do not perpetuate a zero-sum mentality, which takes the view that in order to include, one must exclude. There is also a problem of voting, although, as the recent protests against the war on Iraq have shown, participation in politics can take other forms. The argument that I advance for compulsory voting is an argument which assumes that formal political processes themselves become more meaningful and although in the short-term compulsory voting may require a small measure of statism, in general it seems to me that the implementation of such a measure would require social pressures of a governmental kind.

Globalization involves the restructuring of the international order as a process that must surely be governmental in character – with the exception of rogue states who will not respond to non-statist sanctions. Global governance or government should be conceived in two ways. First, as a gradual process in which regulatory activities formerly exercised by states, are taken over by global bodies, and second as a process in which global activities do not suddenly vanquish states, but gradually make them redundant. It is crucial that we do not pose the issue in terms of a modernist divide between global government *or* the state, for that assumes that one monopolistic institution replaces another. The point is that states will remain as long as conflicts of interest exist which cannot be settled through negotiation – and that, alas, will be for a long time!

Coercion, constraint and government bring about progress and change as education and socialization alters, but force – like the state – is a static concept and practice which must be phased out as the struggle for emancipation develops. It is a central problem with anarchism that it fails to distinguish coherently between force, coercion and constraint, and between state and government, and hence is utopian without being realist. Marxism's contribution to the realization of an inclusive citizenship is weakened by the fact that the act of revolution can only polarize so that common interests become difficult, if not impossible, to cement.

To realistically envisage a citizenship beyond the state, it is crucial to challenge the collapse of force and coercion (and constraint) and that of state and government which is promoted in the liberal tradition. Few liberals today would regard the state of nature as a meaningful concept, and yet they analyse freedom and force as though it were possible for individuals to exist without relationships.

A Relational Approach

Why can't some be citizens while others are subject to force? Underpinning my argument is what I call a 'relational' approach, which means that we only identify ourselves through others, and when these others are deprived of their freedom, we have no freedom either. Although force particularly harms those who are targeted, the perpetrators of force also lose their autonomy, so that unless everyone is a citizen, no-one is a citizen.

Williams argues that the 'button pushing model' of the market state is 'not the ideal of democratic life but a parody of it' (2002: 7). The 'market state', as Williams describes it, promotes an atomism which denies that individuals must be seen in relationships to one another. The idea that societies calling themselves democratic may be oppressive wrongly assumes that a majority can be free at the expense of minorities. This rests upon a non-relational view of individuals. It takes the view that some can be free while others are dominated.

The critique of patriarchy advanced here is relational in that it argues that men cannot be free while women are subordinated. It is true that in a patriarchal society, men enjoy privileges which make them 'victors', but patriarchy oppresses *everyone* (albeit in different ways). Men have begun to realise that patriarchy not only strips them of involvement in child rearing, but subjects them in particular to the violence of war. Engels admirably captured the relevance of the relational approach to the national question when he argued that no nation can be free that oppresses another, and it is clear that colonialism doesn't merely brutalize and degrade its victims, it also limits the so-called beneficiaries as well.

There is, it seems to me, a tension in Marx's critique of capitalism between a relational view of class around the concept of alienation and the zero-sum logic of a class war. Central, however, to the argument in *Capital*, is the concept of abstraction. Abstraction involves a denial of relationships – an atomistic approach – and abstraction, for Marx, means not 'unreality' but rather mystification. Commodities are perfectly real, but what makes them mystifying (and hence abstract) is the abstract labour embodied in them. This conceals the underlying relations of production which have made them what they are, so that (in the famous phrase) relations between people appear as relations between things.

Appearances are part of reality, but to understand reality more profoundly, Marx argues that a process of concentration needs to be grasped. I assume the process of 'concentration' to involve the highlighting of the social relationships that abstraction conceals, and the problem with Marx is that this 'dialectic of abstraction and concentration' (as I rather grandly call it) is not carried far enough. People do not simply concentrate their interests in economic terms. These classes also take a gender, national, religious form, etc., so that class expresses itself in a specific and culturally particularistic way. The way people experience oppression is crucial to the kind of change they struggle for. It is vital that we make relationships transparent, for the notion of the 'individual' can conceal, as feminists have pointed out, a dominant male identity, and the notion of a 'woman' may only represent females who are rich and well educated.

In fact, it is through regulation that capitalism is transformed and the equality and inclusiveness essential to citizenship, obtained. This is why it is helpful to stress the need for 'post-market' as opposed to 'anti-market' measures. The former seek to realise the dynamism and diversity that the market theoretically extols, but which, through its penchant for abstraction, it actually undermines.

Nothing demonstrates the erosions of the logic of capitalism by new liberal reformism more dramatically than the New Right reaction to this reformism that took place in the 1980s. It is crucial to emphasize that the neo-liberalism of the New Right is not only shorn of the egalitarian character of the classical liberal tradition, but freedom is seen as the antirelational capacities of an elite. What makes the notion of a 'right to be unequal' problematic, is the fact that a right implies an egalitarian relationship (of some kind) between individuals – precisely the point that the

New Right deny. Rights arose historically as part of liberal or modernist discourse, and a society which grants people abstract 'rights' is clearly preferable to a society that grants no rights at all. But the point still remains, that rights need be grasped in a concrete fashion i.e., in a way that is not abstracted from correlative duties or obligations. Rights can only be exercised by individuals, but once we see individuals in relational terms, it is clear that individuals can only identify themselves through collectivities or groups. Groups or collectivities exist in plural and multiple terms so that not only do rights involve an individual having many identities, but no right can exist that harms the individual or his or her associates. A right that does not empower is not a right: the atomistic notion of a 'right' to exploit or be violent has to be rejected.

The literature on globalization warns us of the dangers of assuming that we can study movements and countries in isolation from one other. If the inhabitants of wealthy countries find that the number of refugees and asylum seekers have dramatically increased over the last few years, then they will be compelled to reflect on the global consequences of the North/South divide. Unless we see globalization as a process extending social justice to all, we should not be surprised at the numbers of people who move out of poorer countries in search of a 'better' life.

The so-called realists who, following World War II, describe democracy as a system in which people choose those who rule over them, rested their case for a non-participatory democracy upon the logic of atomism and abstraction. The minority of active decision makers was seen as quite unrelated to the irrational and 'primitive' mass of the population whose temperament and skills left them unsuited to political involvement. Macpherson's argument for greater participation in *The Life and Times of Liberal Democracy* adopts a relational argument in his search for what he calls loopholes within a vicious circle in which apathy and inequality reinforce each other. His argument is that people cannot be effective consumers when the environment deteriorates and job insecurity and inflation set in, so that the formerly apathetic feel compelled to participate. Each increasingly finds that they must relate to others through conscious political participation as the condition of the 'atomistic consumer' becomes increasingly untenable.

The case for compulsory voting that I make is linked to compulsory community service: both can only help to instil in the individual a sense of social responsibility and indebtedness to others. What disrupts the relational approach of many communitarians and republicans is their failure to see that the use of force is incompatible with the mutuality of relationships.

A relational view of the individual underpins the case for a citizenship that excludes no-one. It is essential to isolate those who are staunchly opposed to extending citizenship whether on misogynist, racist or nationalist grounds or because they are so privileged that they cannot identify with others. A critique from within makes it as difficult as possible for the intransigent to gain adherents. As the hapless inhabitants of a Hobbesian state of nature, all who live in state- and market-dominated societies have a vested interest in living in a world in which differences can be celebrated and conflicts of interest resolved through negotiation rather than by force. The well-being of each depends upon the well-being of all.

What undermines the capacity of anarchism and Marxism to assist in moving towards an inclusive citizenship is the way in which both ultimately undermine a relational position. Anarchism treats individuals abstractly, and substitutes a liberal spontaneity for the coercive and constraining discipline of a relationship. Marxism, for its part, is saddled with notions of class war, revolution and dictatorship, which weaken a relational attitude towards contending parties in a dispute.

It is important that we evaluate all differences positively. Although it is likely that the struggle for an inclusive citizenship will be pursued by those who are the victims rather than the beneficiaries of the market and state, people with education and status are (or can be), less subject to prejudice based upon ignorance; 'outsiders' are more likely to see the need for integrating in an open-minded way rather than being bludgeoned into assimilating to dominant norms. The need for self-government affects *everyone*, for even the well-to-do are vulnerable to problems in the social and natural environment.

Momentum Concepts

Crucial for the arguments in this book is the idea of the *momentum concept*. Momentum concepts are those which are infinitely progressive and egalitarian: they have no stopping point and cannot be 'realized'. Static concepts, by way of contrast, are repressively hierarchical and divisive. The latter must be discarded whereas the former have an historical dynamic which means they must be built upon and continuously transcended. The state, patriarchy and violence are examples of static concepts; freedom, autonomy, individuality, citizenship and emancipation are examples of momentum concepts. Tocqueville famously formulated democracy as a momentum concept – a concept that has no stopping point. However, his account is marred by static and 'foundational' features, whereas momentum concepts, as I formulate them, seek to avoid this inconsistency by being infinite in their egalitarian scope. It is crucial to avoid the kind of inversion of modernity that leads some into a scepticism and relativism that simply echoes a Humean empiricism (which is after all still modernist in character).

Curiously, conservatives have sensed that democracy is a 'momentum concept' and have opposed it historically for this reason. But if democracy is a momentum concept, this is not true of liberalism, which is a creed linking individual freedom to the ownership of private property. The classical liberal theory of natural rights is a device for justifying (and authorizing) the need for a state, however many conservatives may protest at the subversive implications of liberal abstractions of the individual, freedom and equality.

In his critique of the market state, Williams argues his relational case in terms of a relation to the eternal, to God (2002: 8). The concept of God needs, however, to be seen as a momentum concept – a God who is always becoming more God – rather than as a static ideal that contrasts tragically with a fallen world. This would mean arguing that God is not dead, but needs to be reconstructed conceptually as being not a person, a supernatural creator, a spiritual force or an object of worship but simply a philosophical principle of infinity – of infinite matter in motion. The notion of 'reconstruction' is tied to the idea of a momentum concept since in criticizing old ideas, we need to consciously (where they have an egalitarian and relational potential) reconstruct them.

In what way is citizenship a momentum concept? In three ways. First, the struggle for citizenship can be developed even by those who seek only limited steps forward and are oblivious of a more wide-ranging agenda. Second, citizenship involves a process of change that is both revolutionary and evolutionary – it is important that we do not privilege one over the other – and third, citizenship is an on-going struggle with no stopping point. It is not that the ends of an inclusive citizenship are not important: it is rather that achieving one, enables us to move to the next, ad infinitum. So-called 'thick' citizenship (a citizenship which gives people real power over their lives) is desirable, but 'thin' citizenship (in terms of formal legal and political entitlements) is better than no citizenship at all. The right to self-rule is important and central to citizenship: but it becomes absurd and paradoxical when placed in the context of the state.

This is why the case for an inclusive citizenship makes it essential that we look beyond the state, and I have tried to outline in this introduction the notions of coercion and constraint; government and relationships; abstraction and momentum which make it possible to present a utopianism that is thoroughly realistic at the same time.

Part One
Definitions and Debates

1

The State

Citizens have been traditionally seen as members of the state. It will be argued that a universal and emancipatory notion of citizenship is only possible if we detach citizenship from the state, and this requires us to set out the logical and empirical problems afflicting the state concept. The state, this chapter will contend, is a contradictory institution that seeks to secure the 'common good' through the ability to resort to violence. The state is a monopolistic institution, which necessarily includes some and excludes others – it polarizes rather than unites. The state, therefore, poses insoluble problems for citizenship that as a concept seeks to embrace all and exclude no-one.

The Statist Tradition in Citizenship Concepts

Traditionally citizenship has been conceived in *statist* terms (Oliver and Heater, 1994: 26; Turner, 1994: 159; Janoski, 1998: 12; Barbalet, 2000: 101). Indeed, Oommen argues that the term is meaningless unless it is anchored to the state and that notions of 'global' or 'world' citizenship cannot be authentic until we have a world or global state. Thus European Union citizenship, he insists, will only become a possibility when the union becomes a multi-national federal state (1997: 224). Although Carter is critical of those who reject cosmopolitanism, she takes it for granted that global citizenship requires a global state (2001: 168).

The problem with the cosmopolitan argument is precisely this. It seeks to extend its reach beyond the nation state while, as it were, leaving the nation state intact. But the state involves a process of 'othering' which does not simply occur between states: it occurs within the state itself. The ideal of cosmopolitan citizenship is, Linklater argues, the condition in which all human beings have equal recognition as co-legislators within a 'global kingdom of ends' (Linklater, 1999: 56). But this is to invite the citizens of existing nation states to broaden their horizons in an idealistic fashion. The problem, as we shall see, lies with the fact that statism naturalizes violence and division both within communities and between them, so that the whole concept of the state itself has to be challenged.

This statist formulation does, it will be argued, frustrate the egalitarian potential of citizenship as a notion that includes everybody. As Dahrendorf puts the matter pithily: 'Exclusion is the enemy of citizenship' (1998: 17). We cannot assume that citizenship is itself an inherently statist concept. This is why Soysal's argument is curiously uncritical, for she assumes that the identity of personhood stressed in human rights discourse goes beyond both citizenship and the state as though if we transcend one, we must transcend the other (1994: 165). National and citizenship identities are, in her view, unthinkable without the state.

Defined in post-statist terms (i.e., in terms that go beyond the state), the concept of citizenship must not only be extended in a horizontal sense so that it embraces all adults in society. The concept of citizenship also needs to be 'deepened' and qualitatively transformed so that it is underpinned by new concepts of freedom, autonomy, community, etc. The logic of citizenship must, in a word, be *relational* rather than *atomistic*, postliberal rather than simply liberal in character. These terms will become clearer as the argument proceeds.

It has been frequently noted that citizenship was first explicitly formulated in a context in which its exclusive nature is clearly and painfully apparent. With Aristotle, citizens are a privileged minority of free, Greek, resident males. Slaves, women and foreigners were explicitly excluded. It is true that citizens enjoy important attributes that must form part of more developed definitions of the concept. Citizens are free, active, participatory and sociable and it is interesting to note that Voet argues for a 'revitalisation' and extension of the Aristotelian ideal of citizenship as the alternation of ruling and being ruled (Voet, 1998: 137). But the positive attributes of ancient Greek theory are undermined by the fact that they express themselves through gender, ethnic and (it should not be forgotten) imperial hierarchies. Citizenship traditionally has been a statist concept, and even when slavery was challenged by a liberal view of humanity, the concept of citizenship has remained limited and exclusive.

It is revealing that Rousseau insists that the 'real meaning' of citizenship is only respected when the word is used selectively and exclusively (1968: 61). Citizens have property, are national (in their political orientation), are public and male. Even the classical liberal opposition between citizenship and slavery is weakened by Rousseau's astonishing comment that in unfortunate situations (as in ancient Greece) 'the citizen can be perfectly free only if the slave is absolutely a slave' (1968: 143).

Classical liberalism injects a potential universalism into the concept of citizenship by arguing that all individuals are free and equal. Yet the universalism of this concept is undermined by support for patriarchy, elitism, colonialism – and as Yeatman has recently reminded us in the case of Locke – by an acceptance of outright slavery (Hoffman, 1988: 162; Yeatman, 1994: 62). What makes citizenship an emancipatory concept is that it compels us to regard exclusionary attitudes as incompatible with its universalist 'promise' and egalitarian potential.

It is not enough, however, to simply broaden the concept so that it *includes* women, minorities, the poor and those generally oppressed. This extension can only be coherently sustained if the concept itself is deepened in the sense of being qualitatively transformed. Citizenship needs to be underpinned with new formulations of freedom and autonomy. At the heart of this transformation lies a challenge to the notion of citizenship as a statist concept. By defining citizens simply as members of the state, we cramp the scope and arrest the egalitarian logic of citizenship. Liberal theory, as Bankowski and Christodoulidis have argued, sees the state in the same abstract way that it views the possessive individual (1999: 101).

There is now a general recognition that, historically, the concept of citizenship has been associated with what has been called the politics of closure (Hall and Held, 1989: 174). At the same time there is a reluctance to identify this 'politics of closure' with the state. This is why it is crucial to (a) define the state and (b) explain why it is incompatible with an emancipatory notion of citizenship (Faulks, 2000: 30, 44). Yuval-Davis is right to argue that we should not assume that the community of which citizens are members are simply states. Citizenship involves the membership of a series of communities: 'local, ethnic, national, state, cross- or trans-state and supra-state' (cited by Squires, 2000: 46). But we need to go further and seek to conceptualize citizenship in a way which looks beyond an institution that claims a monopoly of legitimate force and, which is, therefore, ill-disposed to 'share' citizenship with other communities. If we want an inclusive concept of citizenship, we need to contest the link between citizenship and the state.

Can the State be Defined?

Squires has complained that much of the work on citizenship, even in the case of feminist critiques, has operated with an 'unhelpfully unified conception of the state' (Squires, 2000: 36). She identifies Watson's emphasis upon the complexity of the state as a 'positive development' (2000: 45).

But this positive development has a potentially paralysing downside. The 'complexity argument' (Hoffman, 2001: 74), takes the view that the state is too diverse, abstract, problematic and contradictory to define. Pringle and Watson have contended that definitions of the state tend to be dogmatic and arbitrary – absolutizing the particular dimensions of a diverse institution (1992: 54). The state, they argue, is too complex and heterogeneous to be evoked as an entity or a united institution. If the state is too complex to be defined, then clearly it would be impossible to present the case for an inclusive citizenship that transcends the divisive institutions of the state. In order to detach citizenship from the state, the latter has to be both definable and defined.

In Ashley's view, it is impossible to 'decide what the state is' (1988: 249). What makes the state 'undecidable' is its heterogeneous and diffuse character, so that all generalizations inevitably caricature and vulgarize. Pringle and Watson take a less absolutist position, echoing Foucault that to place the state above or outside society, is to imply a homogeneity that is not there (1992: 55). Certainly, the state is, indeed, heterogenous and complex, but it does not follow that this makes it indefinable. When Foucault describes the state as 'a mythical abstraction whose importance is a lot more limited than many of us think' (Hoffman, 1995: 162), he is right to stress the slippery and pretentious character of the state, but wrong to suggest that these important attributes mean that we should not try to define the state.

As I have argued elsewhere, if states exist – as they do – then we need to define them. What is the point of characterizing the state in critical fashion, if it does not actually exist? Like Foucault, Ashley has the problem of trying to dismiss the existence of an institution that is awkwardly and abstractly there.

Some argue that while the state might exist, it is of no particular interest. Thus, Allen takes the view that whereas a number of concepts are relevant (in her case to a feminist critique) – concepts like 'law', 'bureaucratic culture', 'the body', 'subjectivity', 'violence', 'power', 'paternalism' and 'misogyny' – the state is not one of them. It is, she contends, too abstract, unitary and unspecific to be of use in addressing the disaggregated, diverse, specific or local sites that require our attention (Allen, 1990: 22).

Whether the argument for indefinability is put explicitly or is merely implied, the logical problems noted above will present themselves. If the state is complex, unspecific, abstract, etc., these points need to be woven into a definition both critical and comprehensive. States exist and they do not go away simply because we refuse to define them. Pringle and Watson take the view that we should not *ignore* the state: it is simply too complex to evoke as an entity. There are many varieties of the state, spatially as well as historically. It will be argued that the state is, indeed, a contradictory institution, congenitally unable to practise what it preaches.

The dilemmas of the 'complexity argument' emerge clearly in Brown's detailed critique of the state. She speaks of the state as 'multiple and contradictory': it is not monolithic but is 'deconstructible'. The state, she argues, 'is not a thing, system or subject but a significantly unbounded terrain of powers and techniques, an ensemble of discourses, rules and practices, cohabiting in tension-ridden, often contradictory relation with one another' (1992: 12–13). These are all valid points. But the same point applies: why can't we meet the understandable concern of the complexity argument by defining the state in a way that embraces complexity and diversity (Hoffman, 2001: 77)? For, and this is the point that the proponents of the complexity argument find particularly unpalatable, the state can only be defined if we refuse to allow its undeniable complexity and diversity to overwhelm us. The state, nevertheless, exists (and no-one has ever denied this), and it can only be defined if, in some sense, it exists as a 'unity' or an 'entity' and has the 'homogeneity' and 'sameness' which makes it possible to identify it as an institution with definable features.

Why should we assume that because an institution is diverse, it is not also unified? The critics of the state have unwittingly saddled themselves with the view that because something is abstract, it cannot at the same time concretely exist. The complexity argument falls into what is a dualist trap. It assumes that because an institution is complex, diverse, 'erratic and discontinuous', it cannot be evoked as an entity or a unity. Citizenship is invariably defined as membership of the state. If this identification is to be challenged, it is essential that we define the state, since it is not possible to detach citizenship from that which is indefinable. The state is a barrier to an inclusive notion of citizenship. Indeed, the fact that it is contradictory and divisive in character, can only be demonstrated if we define it.

In Defence of Max Weber

Max Weber has defined the state as an institution that claims a monopoly of legitimate force for a particular territory. This is the definition which we propose to adopt. It commands a wide consensus among scholars and admirably serves to emphasize the exclusive and partial nature of the state. If we are to argue that it is impossible to have an emancipatory concept of citizenship *within* the state, this is the definition from which it is essential to begin.

Weber's definition will be drawn upon without accepting the positivist and conservative gloss which he placed upon his view. Guibernau points out that not only was Weber a positivist and a statist, he was also a liberal imperialist, who viewed the influx of 'inferior' Slavs into eastern Germany with considerable dismay (1996: 37). Gellner broadly identifies with Weber's argument but in a way which suppresses rather than highlights the latent paradox that the definition contains. Thus, Gellner defines the state as that institution or institutions 'specifically concerned with the enforcement of order' (1983: 4).

Yet, as we shall see, the use of violence as a mechanism for tackling conflicts of interest does not create order – it undermines it. Gellner is right to speak of the police forces and the courts as central to the state, but there is no suggestion in his argument that these specialized order-enforcing agencies can only create chaos when they act in a statist fashion. Oommen defines the state as a 'legally constituted institution, which provides its residents with protection from internal insecurity and external aggression' (1997: 19). Of course, this is what states *seek* to do. But to suggest that the use of violence to tackle conflicts of interest provides protection against insecurity and aggression, is, in our view, merely naive. States require (and aggravate) insecurity and aggression as part of their *raison d'être*.

The state has always been a troubled institution. What has happened with the rise of supra-national and sub-national institutions, is that implicit problems have become explicit. The definition of the state was never accurate if it was taken to mean that states actually achieved the monopoly of legitimate force that is their defining attribute. To imagine otherwise is not to understand the contradictory nature of the conception of the state.

Although Weber distinguishes between politics and the state, he does not do so in a way that challenges the necessity for domination and repressive hierarchy. The great merit of his definition, however, is that it does enable us to make distinctions that are crucial to the development of what we call an emancipatory or non-exclusive notion of citizenship – a citizenship beyond the state.

The Centrality of Force

It is revealing that Weber was influenced by Treitschke who saw the state as the only entity capable of maintaining a monopoly of violence. If we return to Weber's notion that the state is an institution that claims a monopoly of legitimate force for a particular territory, then we can make a distinction between what this or that state may do, and what is essential (as it were) to the nature of the state. The state, as we see it, is an institution that seeks to regulate conflicts of interest through the use of superior force.

It is true that Weber does not reduce the state to force. The state asserts a monopoly of legitimate force for a particular territory. Territory, monopoly and legitimacy are also involved along with force: an institution that is unable to credibly claim a monopoly of force would not be regarded as a state, just as an institution that does not claim that its force is legitimate or territorially focused would likewise not be a state. Nevertheless, it does not follow that there is simply an analytical parity between the four discrete elements that make up the state: monopoly, territory, legitimacy and force.

Force is central to the state, whereas the other factors are subsidiary (Hoffman, 1995: 36–7). Force, it can be said, is the content; monopoly, legitimacy and territory are the forms. But what is the basis of arguing this? It is that the other factors can exist outside the state, whereas force cannot exist as a method of tackling conflicts of interests except in the context of the state. Force has to be monopolistic. One 'will' must prevail over the other – otherwise force cannot be said to be used. It is this that distinguishes force from conflict (Nicholson, 1984: 40). Force is always concentrated. For this reason a territorial focus only becomes exclusive (as an aspiration) if force is used, while central to the state's problematic character, is the combination of legitimacy and force – two mutually exclusive attributes. Legitimacy implies limits; force on the other hand, is limitless. Force is impossible to contain or limit: whatever effort is made to moderate it, it always goes to extremes.

Indeed, it is the centrality of force in the Weberian definition that renders the state so problematic for citizenship. Citizenship requires choice and freedom, whereas force negates will. Of course, force is often naturalized: it is seen as part of a timeless human nature and thus unavoidable. To argue, as Oommen does, that the attribute of legitimate force is valid only in the case of the democratic state (at least as an ideal) (1997: 25), is to ignore the way in which force undermines the capacity to exercise choice by those against whom this force is targeted.

In fact, force as a method of resolving conflicts of interest is relatively new. Humans have lived for most of their history in stateless societies. In these societies, conflict is not resolved through force but through moral pressures, the invocation of tradition, etc. – sanctions that may strike us as archaic (particularly when these sanctions involve supernatural spirits or ancestor cults), but the point is that throughout most of their history, people have settled their conflicts of interest without resorting to the use of force.

Of course, the concept of force itself is subject to many definitions, but the term here is used to mean harm to a person resulting in physical consequences. Force, as so defined embraces abuse since abuse (even where it is not in itself physical) leads to depression, anxiety and low self-esteem – and these are problems expressed as real physical pain. We are defending a physicalist concept of force on the grounds that if the concept of force is used too broadly, it becomes synonymous with coercion. As such, the argument of Bourdieu, that violence can be symbolic or 'structural' (1998: 40, 98), is resisted. Clearly, verbal and other forms of non-physical aggression are *linked* to violence, but to distinguish between the causes of violence and violence itself is preferable. Crucial to the argument advanced here is that force and coercion need to be rigorously distinguished from one another.

Force, Coercion and Constraint: Why These Distinctions Matter

Were people asked how to resolve conflicts of interest without the use of the state, force and coercion could not be treated as though they were synonyms. In societies without a state, pressures are employed that are certainly coercive in character, but they do not amount to force. By coercion, I mean pressures that cause people to do things they would not otherwise do. It does not follow, however, that people do things *against* their will when they are coerced, since the notion that individuals can inhabit a world free of negative constraints of any kind, belongs to classical liberal mythology. The argument here seeks to tease out the implications of the proposition that humans are social beings.

Two writers in particular stress the distinction between coercion and force, although they regard both as undesirable. Marx speaks of the worker under capitalism as 'coerced' by market circumstances but not normally subject to direct force (Marx, 1970: 737), while Mill argues that we are subject to the moral coercion of public opinion as well as to the force of the state. The two are quite distinct and indeed Mill (wrongly) regards the former as more sinister than the latter (Mill, 1974: 68). In both cases, however, the question as to whether *any* society can avoid coercion is only dealt with implicitly. Nevertheless, the implication of both Marx's and Mill's position is that coercion is unavoidable even in a free society – which would be classless in Marx's case and marked by an absence of tyranny in Mill's argument. Not only does Marx accept that all subject to the market are coerced (beneficiaries and victims alike), but he assumes that people enter into relations 'independent of their will' (Hoffman, 1984: 107–14). By this, he means not that people are automatons who have no will, but rather that what people intend to happen, is not the same as that which actually occurs. In other words, they find themselves doing things they had not intended to do: i.e., they are coerced and constrained!

Mill speaks of individuals being subject to 'natural penalties'. By this, he means that everything we do affects others, although it does not necessarily *harm* them. When others react (as they must), this constitutes a pressure upon us, causing us to respond. Either we persist with our original line of action i.e., renew our effort, or we adopt a different form of behaviour, but in either case we do something we had not intended to do. Hence we are being *coerced*, not as an infringement of our freedom, but as a condition of being free at all. To reiterate an example that has been given elsewhere (Hoffman, 2000: 9), if I am religious and you are an atheist, your lack of belief *affects* me and may cause me to avoid socializing with you, but your views cannot be said to harm me (although I disapprove of them), unless they prevent me from worshipping as I wish to.

It is true that coercion can be identified in an infinity of different forms and I would make a distinction between coercion as a negative pressure and constraint as a positive pressure. This highlights the fact that coercion is more painful than mere constraint. When constraints cause a person to doubt their self-esteem, they have been coerced. Coercion can appear to be very close to force as in the example where you are given a choice under duress – 'your money or your life'. But, strictly speaking, even here you are free to comply (the attribute of coercion). Indeed, what bothers you, in this grisly and well-worn example, is not the coercion, but the force that is credibly threatened! It is force, not coercion, which prevents us from exercising agency. We would naturally accept that the more we can rely upon (positive) constraints rather than (negative) coercion, the better (other things being equal), but it would be foolish and naive to imagine that a society without coercion and constraint is possible. Coercion and constraint arise from our relationships with others. Conversely, force actually prevents us from having relationships, since it involves treating people as things – as objects rather than as subjects.

The distinction is often drawn between force and violence on the grounds, for example, that states use force while terrorists use violence (see Johnston, 1993: 16). There is a case perhaps for distinguishing between force as a relatively structured violence and violence as something that is more spontaneous and indiscriminate. But this is not, arguably, a useful distinction to make, since it is in the nature of force (however much states seek to regulate it) that it erodes limits and is uncontrollable. To suggest that force is preferable to violence reflects a statist prejudice since such a view downplays the stark reality of the way the state itself seeks to settle conflicts of interest.

Whereas citizenship is made problematic by force, it is compatible with coercion and constraint. The kind of rights and responsibilities that citizenship requires are supremely relational. They involve a recognition that one's own identity depends upon and is linked to the identity of others, so that coercion and constraint are essential to citizenship in the way that force is not.

State and Government

Citizenship is intensely political. The idea that citizenship could be reduced to a pre-political status (Delanty, 2000: 14) only makes sense if we identify politics with the state, so that the activities of individuals are deemed non- or pre-political where they relate to the pursuit of self-interest. Such an atomistic conception of the political will be resisted here.

I define politics as (a) the recognition of difference and (b) the attempt to resolve the conflicts of interest that arise from this difference. Ironically, the use of force undermines politics so that the state becomes an institution which is anti-political in that states suppress conflicts – they never really resolve them (Hoffman, 2000: 2). Citizenship is also governmental. Government involves the resolution of conflicts and all societies have governments. Gellner argues that the state has become inescapable in industrial societies (1983: 5). This is essentially a Hobbesian argument: without the state, government cannot exist! Gellner's contention that a national educational and communications system requires the state (1983: 52) spectacularly ignores the state/government distinction and misses the point that education and communication are in fact threatened by an institution that resorts to violence as a method of tackling conflict. Both communication and education rest upon negotiation and arbitration as methods for resolving disputes. The notion that the state enshrines the freedom of the individual (Guibernau, 1996: 23) grotesquely confuses state and government and conjures up Rousseau's absurd contention that a person can be forced to be free.

As has been argued elsewhere (Hoffman, 1995: 42–6), government often appears to be part of the state as in contemporary polities where the term 'government' is taken to mean the elected section of the executive. The distinction between government (as conventionally regarded) and the state is important in liberal democracies where, in a formal sense, governments are deemed partisan in the way that state functionaries like judges and civil servants are not. But this is not the way that state is here distinguished from government.

Indeed, judges and administrators, like civil servants and law-makers, are part of government (as defined here), in the sense that they seek to resolve conflicts of interest directly or indirectly. These roles would exist in any society. They need to be distinguished from those who use force or invoke force. This is a complex distinction to make in state-centred societies because in these societies not only do governmental figures act in a statist way – judges may embrace a culture that is statist and divisive – but state functionaries, like the police, may act in a governmental way where they seek to empower communities through advice, persuasion and moral pressure.

In cases such as the above, the distinction between state and government becomes logical rather than empirical. In other words, it is impossible to identify any institution as being 'purely' governmental or 'purely' statist in character. But the distinction is still worth making. The notion of a citizenship beyond the state does not assume that people can act without rules and sanctions. On the contrary, we already see in state-centred societies how people regulate their lives in a non-statist way – in voluntary societies, in families, in inter-personal relationships – indeed so much so that one writer has spoken of the 'anarchy of everyday life' (Laver, 1985: 47–66). It is also clear that although states are key actors in international politics, there is no world state regulating their activity. Yet there is order and government!

The distinction between state and government only becomes empirical in domestic stateless societies of the kind that existed in the past. Mair rightly refers to 'government without the state' (1962: 14–15) in societies that clearly had order and government, but no institution claiming a monopoly of legitimate force. The distinction between state and government is not only an empirical one for most of human history, but it challenges the Hobbesian argument – deeply rooted in conventional political culture – that without the state, there can be no order. Exactly the opposite is true. The state acts in a way that disables some people through force, and therefore, it cannot provide the recognition of agency of disputants which is necessary for conflict resolution. One party emerges as victor: the other is suppressed.

Van Creveld has argued that we need to differentiate state and government, but he defines government as the person or group who makes peace, wages war, raises revenue, determines the currency and looks after internal security for society as a whole. The problem with this kind of distinction is that it ignores the fact that the state as a modern institution explicitly and abstractly exercises sovereignty on behalf of a particular and territorially based nation (1999: 415–16). It assumes that the exercise of force is governmental (and natural) in character. It may appear to look beyond the state, but in fact it does not look beyond the use of force as a mechanism for tackling conflicts of interest. It, therefore, leaves intact an exclusive notion of citizenship.

Dryzek notes a distinction between 'government' and 'governance'. The former refers to formal institutions, the latter is more informal with an emphasis upon conflict resolution and the facilitation of cooperation. The notion of governance, he argues, is crucial for the development of a transnational democracy (1999: 33). The problem with this kind of distinction is that it fails to highlight the contradictory nature of the state as an institution claiming a monopoly of legitimate force. States act governmentally in order to secure and consolidate legitimacy and this self-transcending aspect of the liberal state is lost if we differentiate between government and governance. The point is that the logical problem of the state comes from within, so that it is here that the tension between the state and democracy (which is a governmental concept) arises.

More meaningful than the distinction between government and governance is that between state and government. This distinction is vital for an emancipatory notion of citizenship since it sees questions of participation and responsibility, democracy and rights as ultimately governmental in character. Voet argues that autonomous citizens are only possible if people are free from poverty and protected 'by and against the state' (1998: 138). But the task of giving people the material and psychological security to participate in decision-making is ultimately the task of government. Only by differentiating between the state and government can we chart a path beyond the state that is both realistic and 'utopian'.

When Miller gives examples as to why states need to protect national cultures (1995: 88), he instances states acting in what could be called a governmental fashion. Citizenship is certainly a political term, but it is because the transcendence of the state is seen as impossible, that no attempt is made to chart the kind of concepts which are necessary if we are to view the transcendence of the state in a realistic way.

The word 'transcendence' is intended to capture the need for a stateless society to build upon, and yet move beyond, the premises of the state. The state disappears, not in a puff of smoke after some kind of cataclysm like a revolution, but only through a gradual process in which statist activities are converted into governmental ones. Indeed, many of the things states already do, are (strictly speaking) governmental rather than statist in character, since they empower people by providing them with resources rather than imposing force upon them.

Force as a Self-Dissolving Reality

It is important to accept that as long as people cannot resolve conflicts of interest through negotiation and arbitration i.e., with social rather than specifically statist sanctions, states will be in business. It is true that force is inherently illegitimate since it prevents the recipient of this force from being a subject or agent who exercises choice. But it does not follow that force can immediately be dispensed with. Force arises where conflicts of interest are such that the parties to the dispute cannot, as it were, 'change places'.

The argument is not being made, therefore, that the use of force by states or individuals acting in self-defence (in ways often authorized by states) will cease tomorrow. As long as rogue states and brutalized individuals who attack others exist, the use of force is inevitable. But despite this, it is still (a) never legitimate and (b) acts against an emancipatory and inclusive notion of citizenship. In other words, a pacifist view that holds that force must be ceased forthwith is not being defended. That view implies that people always have common interests regardless of the divisions between them. But the problem is that moral or social sanctions only work where people can change places, and if they are too divided, this is unlikely, if not impossible.

There is a distinction to be made, therefore, between being *divided* and merely being *different*. When people are divided – because someone is too rich or too poor, where some assume that they have all the power and act in an oppressive or exploitative manner – then relationships (in the sense of mutually empowering encounters) become impossible, and people cannot change places.

Oppression (whether it takes a racist, gender, religious or national form etc.) not only imbues the dominant party with arrogance and hubris, but scars the victim. The victim may seek revenge and feel only hatred. Often such a victim attempts (understandably but in a futile manner) to invert the oppression he or she has received, rather than transcend it. It is the tragedy of division, in other words, that it can perpetuate the need for the state not merely because the dominant party dehumanizes his or her opponent, but because the opponent is tempted then to dehumanize the oppressor. Where this hapless dialectic is at work, violence remains inevitable and non-statist sanctions cannot function. Conflict is not resolved but only suppressed.

Opposition to violence as a norm in liberal societies is a major conceptual resource for our argument. Politics is identified (even by statist writers like Bernard Crick) with conciliation and compromise. Hypocrisy, arguably, is the homage that vice pays to virtue: in other words, liberal states create hostages to fortune by arguing that violence should be avoided. People should negotiate over conflict – naturally! But this means that if states really want the legitimacy that is a contradictory part of their definition, then they must act (suicidally) in a 'governmental' way by seeking, where possible, to negotiate and arbitrate.

Even where force is employed, it must be used transitionally, in ways that create a breathing space for policies which *can* cement common interests. Obviously, where liberal states are confronted by states that woefully abuse human rights, then forceful intervention may be necessary (although NATO's intervention in Kosovo, like the war against Iraq, demonstrates the perilous character of this activity). It is hard to oppose counter-violence against terrorism in the wake of atrocities like the one committed in the USA on 11 September 2001. But counter-violence has to be linked with the need to change the world so that terrorism becomes redundant. Only then can it be provisionally justified.

In the same way, we can argue that policies that seek to strengthen community on strife-torn housing estates in, for instance, Britain are unlikely to succeed unless force is used to stop thuggery and gang violence. But whether the examples are domestic or international, the use of force can be counter-productive unless it is seen as simply providing a breathing space for policies of a governmental kind, i.e., policies that actually cement common interests through resource provision, democratic reform, a politics of recognition, etc.

To develop citizenship, individuals and groups need protection. Where this protection requires force, the position remains one of being locked in a statist situation that includes some by excluding others. My argument is not that force should be avoided regardless of circumstance. It is rather that the objective of policies must be to make the use of force redundant, which is only possible when people become reasonably secure, can identify themselves in others and are able, as we have said already, to 'change places'.

A Relational Versus an Atomistic View of Citizenship

Relational arguments can be paternalist and authoritarian (Offen, 1992: 75–81). The relational view of citizenship defended here is one that builds upon, rather than rejects, liberal individualism. A post-statist view of citizenship must be post-liberal in character.

Classical liberalism has rightly emphasised the importance of conceptualizing people as *individuals*. A sense of common individuality is crucial to a universal citizenship. What makes classical liberalism vulnerable to criticism is the fact that it treats individuality in abstract, divisive and elitist terms. In other words, classical liberals were not concerned with *all* individuals but only with those who owned property, were educated, male, white etc.

Force is not a problem for the atomistically conceived individual for at least three reasons. First, individuals are considered to constitute an elite. Force is deemed necessary to suppress the unruly others and, indeed, even the unruly elements within oneself (Yeatman, 1994: 90). One individual can be a 'citizen' while another is not. In the second place, each individual is locked into their own separative identity. Hence, using force does not impair the freedom of the perpetrator. It is possible to remain free while extinguishing the freedom of others. And third, the community is conceived as being no more than an aggregate of atomistic individuals. The use of force by one community against another does not affect the citizenship of those who constitute the oppressor community.

Atomism can be linked with statism. Atomism collapses the distinction between division and difference and assumes that because individuals are different, they must act in violent ways towards one another. Both atomism and statism rest upon an uncritical attitude towards force as a method of resolving conflicts of interest, and it is therefore not surprising that the classical text for the state – Hobbes' *Leviathan* – rests upon militantly atomistic premises.

Central to a relational view of citizenship is an emphasis and indeed a celebration of difference and diversity. A relationship is only possible because the parties to the relationship differ from one another. But those who (rightly) stress the importance of diversity, should also challenge the existence of an institution that claims a monopoly of legitimate force. A relational view of citizenship is opposed to force since it is precisely the difference between individuals that force seeks to extinguish. Force necessarily disrupts relationships by undermining the freedom of both parties.

It is true that pain is differentially experienced when one person or group attacks another, and violent masters should never be confused with violated slaves. But both suffer as a consequence and the use of force makes it impossible for a relationship to exist. It may be that once force has been used a relationship continues (as in a situation in which a wife who is beaten by her husband remains in the household). But at the point that force is used, a relationship is terminated.

It is only possible for parties to avoid the use of force if they respect each other's differences, and they can only do this, when both manifest a capacity to 'change places'. Each has to have some understanding of what it is like to be 'the other'. Individuals are both linked and yet different. What they have in common does not undermine, but is a precondition for, their respect for diversity. This is why citizenship has to be rooted in a relational rather than an atomistic view of freedom and autonomy. It must look beyond force and the state. But why, it might be argued, if we are willing to rework the notion of citizenship, should we not also rework the notion of the state?

Eisenstein has argued for an 'affirmative' state, which would be pluralist and post-patriarchal in character (1994: 34, 172, 219), while Connell has urged the development of a feminist state as 'an arena for a radical democratization of social action' (1990: 539). Tickner comments that genuine security for all individuals requires a 'less militarized model of citizenship' that allows men and women to participate equally in 'building the type of state institutions that are responsive to the security needs of their own people as well as to those on the outside' (1995: 194). This would be a 'reformulated' state that moves beyond the exclusionary boundaries associated with traditional concepts.

Why not 're-invent' the state to make it compatible with a relational view of citizenship? But this is the point. Repressive hierarchies of an exclusionary kind continue to exist (even in 'reinvented' states) and force is still widely used as a way of trying to resolve conflicts of interest. Defining the state negatively and traditionally enables us to face the challenge of how to move society towards greater freedom, self-government and in the direction of an empowering and inclusive sense of citizenship.

SUMMARY

- Citizenship has traditionally been defined in terms of the state. While pre-liberal definitions of citizenship clearly differ from contemporary liberal views, all have one thing in common: a citizen is deemed a member of the state.
- An inclusive notion of citizenship is incompatible with the state. We define the state as an institution that claims a monopoly of legitimate force – a definition taken from Max Weber.
- Although states are territorial and monopolistic institutions, force is their central feature, and it is the use of force to address conflicts of interest that accounts for the tension between the state and citizenship as an inclusive notion.
- A sharp distinction is made between force, coercion and constraint. As a result of coercion and constraint, a person acts in an unintended way. When force is used, no activity is possible, since a person cannot be said to exercise the power of will at all.
- Linked to the distinctions between force, coercion and constraint, is the distinction between state and government. Government is here defined as the settlement of conflict through arbitration and negotiation.
- For people to be citizens in the way we are using the term here, they must be able to relate to one another. Atomism undermines the mutuality that is inherent in citizenship.
- There is a case for a residual or transitional use of force, but it can only be justified as a way of bringing about a world in which force is no longer necessary as a method of tackling conflicts of interest.

2

Democracy

Just as the term citizenship has been viewed with suspicion by sections of the left, so has the concept of democracy. The extraordinarily subversive character of the concept has not been grasped. Yet once democracy is linked to the state, it becomes evident why it is a concept with far-reaching and ill-thought out implications. Democracy, it will be argued, is post-liberal in character. A democratic concept of citizenship involves attention to the subversive notion of democracy itself.

The argument that democracy involves a tyranny of the majority, that it suppresses minorities and is capable of authoritarian and totalitarian rule, rests upon the mistaken assumption that democracy is a form of the state. I shall argue that because the 'tyranny thesis' (as it will be called) rests upon a statist view of democracy, it conceives of the people in general and majorities in particular, in abstract and non-relational terms.

Held rightly sees the archaic features of state sovereignty and what he calls the 'Westphalian model'. The problem is that Held sees the state both as an institution that ultimately uses force to settle conflicts of interest and as a benevolent repository of fairness and impartiality. This equivocation undermines the coherence of his model.

Beck argues that in the new modernity – a self-critical reflexive modernity – a new logic is necessary: one that links things rather than rigidly separates them. Individuals want to determine their own lives in ways that challenge conventional politics, but although it would seem that the new polity cannot be a state, Beck's project of democratizing democracy is ultimately and disappointingly statist in character.

Like Beck, Giddens has democracy at centre stage in his argument for a 'renewal' of social democracy. People, Giddens argues, are becoming increasingly sceptical about received authority, and in arguing for a reconceptualization of the public/private divide, Giddens extends the concept of democracy into the heart of the family. But although he eloquently warns of the cost of force to settle conflicts, he identifies government with the state.

Democracy, the State and Liberalism

It is frequently commented that democracy is an extremely ambiguous concept and its ambiguities are exacerbated because it has become obligatory for politicians of every ideological hue, to claim democratic credentials, no matter how despotic and dictatorial their system is. As I have noted elsewhere (1988: 132), some have even suggested that the term itself is too contaminated to be useful. Crick seeks to defend politics *against* democracy, not because he is opposed to the reality of democracy (at least under certain circumstances), but because he favours precision over ambiguity. Democracy, he protests, is perhaps 'the most promiscuous word in the world of public affairs' (1982: 56). But just why is democracy such a tantalizing and bewitching concept?

There is, perhaps, one basic and one subsidiary reason. The basic reason being the relationship of democracy to the state and the subsidiary reason is the relationship of democracy to liberalism. As I see it, democracy stands for self-government. It is impossible for the 'demos' to exercise 'kratos', unless each individual member of the people governs themselves. Dahl has described democracy as a concept which is tied to a 'daring vision' that forever invites us to 'look beyond, and to break through' existing limits (1989: 312). Crucial to these limits is the state and the assumption that democracy is a form of the state is the source of democracy's mystification.

This mystification can be seen in the argument that democracy in ancient Athens (i.e., in the fourth and fifth centuries BC) was pure and genuine. Here at last, it is said, is a democracy in which the ideal of popular rule became a living reality. This is not to deny the remarkably participatory aspects of ancient Greek democracy but the point is that this democracy was a form of the state, therefore the Athenians were, as one writer has described them, 'an exceptionally large and diversified ruling class' (Childe, 1964: 216). The *exclusive* character of ancient Greek concepts of citizenship has already been noted – the exclusion of free women, slaves and resident aliens – but this exclusivity flows from the nature of democracy when conceptualized in statist terms.

It is true that democracy was seen as the rule of the poor, but the poor themselves benefited from slavery (even if they did not own slaves themselves), and without Athenian imperialism, it is difficult to see how the wealth could have been generated that underpinned the working of the system. Democracy in this context meant the subjugation and enslavement of the outsiders. Conservatives like Plato exploited the ambiguity of the term even though most Greek democrats took exclusion and slavery for granted. Plato commented famously that in a democracy there is no distinction between citizens and foreigners, between fathers and sons, between men and women, and even the domestic animals are infected with anarchy (1955: 336)! Yet this was an argument based upon logic, not real historical experience.

The notion of democracy was regarded with disdain and hostility until the nineteenth century in the USA, and arguably until after the First World War in Europe. The notion that Rousseau or Locke were democrats is painfully anachronistic. The American Founding Fathers viewed with 'sensations of disgust and horror' what Madison called the 'turbulent democracies of ancient Greece' (Hamilton et al., 1961: 71, 100). Democracy was not only seen as the rule of the poor, but it implied the dissolution of the state itself. Rousseau labelled democracy 'a government without government' (1968: 112).

Tocqueville's *Democracy in America* is misnamed, since what Tocqueville explores is an unusually egalitarian form of liberalism. Tocqueville's notion of America as an 'immense and complete democracy' (1966: 390) is odd when one considers that in 1840, slavery still existed, women were disenfranchised and native Americans were being mercilessly driven off their lands. Tocqueville was speaking more of the logic of American society than its social and political realities and as a result many of his judgements read very strangely. Jefferson, whom Tocqueville describes as 'the greatest democrat ever to spring from American democracy' (1966: 249), was really a liberal who feared majority rule. Heater notes that in Massachusetts, hub of the rebellion against the British government, the franchise was restricted to free males who owned property (1999: 6).

All this helped to contribute to modern American folklore, as Hofstadter notes, which assumes that 'liberty' (i.e., liberalism) is synonymous with democracy (1967: 10). It is only after the civil war that the term democracy was used to describe the American system as a whole (as opposed to the popular element within a mixed constitution) in a book revealingly entitled *Triumphant Capitalism*. However, in the twentieth century in general, and after the Second World War in particular, liberalism and democracy are increasingly seen as synonyms. Gone is J.S. Mill's concern to defend liberty *against* democracy.

The relationship between liberalism and democracy is a complex one. Crick argues that there is 'an intimacy almost extricable' between the two, but there is also 'tension as well as harmony' (1982: 59). The harmony arises from the fact that liberalism in its classical form rests upon anti-statist premises, which it then speedily contradicts. It is particularly through the lenses of the conservative critics of liberalism that this 'harmony', i.e., the potentially democratic implications of liberalism have been exposed. After all, the insistence by Hobbes that 'men' are naturally equal and would rather govern themselves implies a democratic logic that the case for an authoritarian state sovereign soon dissolves. One of Locke's conservative critics asked sarcastically whether the whole nation was to be polled as a result of his theories (Dunn, 1979: 4) and the hapless King Charles reproached the English parliamentarians for doing away with the distinction between 'subject' and 'sovereign' by 'bringing in democracy' (Dunn, 1979: 3).

The point is that these judgements were not accurate. Neither the parliamentarians during the English civil war, nor for that matter the

Levellers (who would have excluded 'paupers' and 'servants' from the franchise), can be called democrats. But the point is that liberal assumptions about freedom and equality *appear* to challenge the very existence of the state, so that, as Cromwell's son-in-law Ireton objects, if the law of nature is held to be supreme, then he 'would fain have any man shew me where it will end' (Hoffman, 1988: 155).

Liberalism in practice remains in tension with democracy, however much liberals seek to amalgate the two concepts in the notion of a liberal democracy. For Macpherson to describe the British utilitarians as 'protective democrats' because they sought to combine male universal suffrage with an argument that government is the business of the rich, is as misleading as his reference to J.S. Mill as a 'developmental democrat' because Mill was concerned with the importance of participation (Macpherson, 1977: 58). It is rather like calling supporters of the American Declaration of Independence democrats, even though this document, for all its liberal principles, was highly exclusive.

The point is that liberalism is in tension with democracy because it takes the state for granted, and with it, the identification of order with private property and class division. Hobhouse spoke, as a new liberal, of the self-governing individual within the 'self-governing state', while Green insisted that the state that punishes, imprisons and divides in the name of the community, rests upon 'will' rather than 'force'. Ruggiero is right to say that the term 'liberal' qualifies the term 'democracy' (Hoffman, 1988: 181–2). In fact, liberalism is about the rights of property, democracy about popular rule.

In much of the post-war period, liberalism and democracy have been presented as synonyms, but the tension remains. Hayek makes it clear in his writings that 'freedom' (by which he means the unfettered operation of the market) comes first (hence his admiration, shared by Lady Thatcher, for General Pinochet, the dictator of Chile). Only if democracy is compatible with 'popular capitalism' is it acceptable. John Cotton, a seventeenth-century divine in New England, pronounced democracy to be the meanest and worst of all forms of government, since if the people governed, he asked, over whom were they to rule? Democracy must transcend liberalism because it is incompatible with the state: a democratic citizenship can only exist when citizens are people who govern their own lives. An exclusive democracy, like an exclusive citizenship, is a contradiction in terms.

Exclusivity and the Problem of Majority Rule

It is often argued that minorities suffer under democracy. Democracy, it is said, far from generating anti- or post-statism, generates statism in an absolutist and totalitarian form. The problem with Stalinist communists, Crick has written, is not that they pretend to be democratic. 'They are democratic' (1982: 56).

I shall call this hostile characterization of majority rule the 'tyranny thesis' (1995: 200), and it basically argues that the will of the majority may favour arbitrary and repressive rule. Crick endorses what Popper has called the 'paradox of democracy'. The German people elect Hitler, who proceeds to unleash persecution and genocide; the Islamic world bristles with movements that would install, if elected, theocratic rule (Crick, 1982: 58–9; Goodwin, 1997: 289).

It is crucial to rebut this argument if citizenship is to be linked with democracy. For if democracy can be oppressive and divisive, then it can privilege some citizens at the expense of others, thus making the notion of a democratic inclusive citizenship a conceptual impossibility. But the point is that majorities cannot repress minorities unless their rule expresses itself in the form of the state. Crick acknowledges this when he identifies a tyrannical democracy with the notion of popular sovereignty, for he makes it clear that this sovereignty expresses itself in statist form. Robespierre's 'democratic' use of terror (Crick, 1982: 60–1) is clearly statist in character, so that the problem is not really with majority rule: it is with the state. For how can we reconcile democracy with an institution claiming a monopoly of legitimate force?

The tyranny thesis is not only empirically invalid, it is also logically problematic as well. For it assumes a non-relational view of the individual, so that it is deemed possible for one section of the population (the majority) to be free while their opponents (the minority) are oppressed. But this argument is only defensible if a sharp (and non-relational) line between the self and the other is drawn. If we embrace (as I do) a relational approach, then the freedom of each individual depends upon the freedom of the other. As the Zimbabwean greeting puts it, I have slept well, if you have slept well: we may be separate people, but we are also related. It is impossible for a majority to oppress a minority, without oppressing itself.

This can be illustrated with an empirical example. Under the influence of loyalism and demagogues like Ian Paisley, Northern Ireland was until the 1970s a 'Protestant State for the Protestant People'. The Catholic minority were oppressed, and the Protestant majority ascendant. But how free was the majority? What happened if an individual Protestant wished to marry a Catholic, or became sympathetic to their point of view? What happened to Protestants who decided to revere the anti-colonial heritage of Protestants like Wolfe Tone? How open could loyalist minded Protestants be about the partisan character of police or the electoral malpractices designed to devalue Catholic votes? The point is that in a society in which there is a 'tyranny of the majority', no-one is free and thus able to govern their own lives.

Dahl argues that when individuals are forced to comply with the law, democracy is, to that extent, compromised. Although he is pessimistic about the prospects for a stateless democracy, he is right to challenge the view (inherent in liberalism), that force is compatible with self-government

(1989: 37, 51, 90). Dahl argues that the members of an association cannot govern themselves democratically if they strip a minority of its political rights. A person's interests are wider than one's private or self-regarding interests (1989: 171, 63). This suggests that people can both be different and yet have common interests. This is in stark contrast to the 'tyranny thesis' as evinced in the Tocqueville/Crick position that people are 'nearly alike and entirely equal' (Crick, 1982: 63). For the point is that although minorities are clearly different from majorities, the two are bound together in a relationship that makes it impossible for one to be oppressed without the other being oppressed as well.

Mouffe has argued that democracy leads to the dictatorial rule of the popular will. It embodies the logic of what she calls identity or equivalence, whereas liberalism (which she prefers to democracy) respects difference, diversity and individual self-determination (1996: 25). But is this liberal polity a form of the state? On this crucial matter, Mouffe is silent, and it is not surprising that her admiration for the pre-war conservative Carl Schmidt places her argument in still more difficulty. While she praises Schmidt for identifying politics with conflict, she is embarrassed by the avowedly statist way in which he interprets conflict (Hoffman, 1998: 60).

For Schmidt, the Other is an enemy to be physically eliminated. While Mouffe identifies politics with conflict and difference, she is reluctant to see differences 'settled' in a statist manner through force. She seeks to distinguish between a social agent and the multiplicity of social positions that agents may precariously and temporarily adopt. The pluralism of multiple identities is 'constitutive of modern democracy' and 'precludes any dream of final reconcilation' (Mouffe, 1996: 25). But if democracy is a form of the state, then it will, indeed, rest upon an oppressive logic of equivalence that suppresses, rather than celebrates, difference.

The 'tyranny thesis' rests upon premises that are abstractly individualist in character. Democracy is conceived of as a Hobbesian Leviathan in majoritarian form (Hoffman, 1995: 202). Once we argue that the mechanisms of government must replace those of the state, so that whatever the coercion and constraint, individuals are free to express their own tastes, wants and needs, then the problem of the tyranny thesis dissolves. Democracy becomes a way of respecting difference and resolving conflict in a way that acknowledges the identity of the parties to a dispute.

The Statist Problems of David Held

Held is surely right to acknowledge that the concept of democracy has changed its geographical and institutional focus over time. Like Dahl (1989: 194), he accepts that the notion of democracy was once confined to the city state, then to the nation state, and now has become a concept that stands or falls through an acknowledgement of its global character. Since local, national, regional and global structures and processes all overlap, democracy must take a cosmopolitan form (1995: 21). As Heater puts it crisply, 'if democratic national citizenship, why not democratic world citizenship?' (1999: 147).

Held argues (as, indeed, Dahl does) that people in states are threatened by activities occuring outside their borders. Whether it is the movement of interest rates, the profits that accrue to stocks and shares, the spread of AIDS, the movements of refugees and asylum seekers, or the damage to the environment, government is clearly stretching beyond the state. What obstructs the notion of international democracy is the assumption that states are sovereign and that international institutions detract from this sovereignty. The position of the USA under George W. Bush's leadership (alarmingly reinforced rather than undermined by the reaction to the appalling events of 11 September, 2001) is rooted in the archaic belief that institutions that look beyond the nation state, are a threat to, rather than a necessity for, democratic realities.

The post-war period has seen the development of what Held calls the UN Charter Model (1995: 86). However, although this has made inroads into the concept of state sovereignty (hence US hostility to the UN), it co-exists uneasily with what Held calls the 'the model of Westphalia' – the notion that states recognize no superior authority and tackle conflicts by force (1995: 78). A first step forward would involve enhancing the UN model by making a consensus vote in the General Assembly a source of international law, and providing a means of redress of human rights violations in an international court. The Security Council would be more representative if the veto arrangement was modified, and the problem of double standards addressed – a problem that undermines the UN's prestige in the south (1995: 269). But welcome as these measures would be, they still represent, Held contends, a very thin and partial move towards an international democracy.

Held's full-blown model of cosmopolitan democracy would involve the formation of regional parliaments whose decisions would become part of international law. There would be referenda cutting across nations and nation states and the establishment of an independent assembly of democratic nations (1995: 279). The logic of this argument implies the explicit erosion of state sovereignty and the use of international legal principles as a way of delimiting the scope and action of private and public organizations. These principles are egalitarian in character and would apply to all civic and political associations.

How would they be enforced? It is here that Held's commitment to the state as a *permanent* actor on the international scene bedevils his argument. The idea of the state remains but it must, Held contends, be adapted to 'stretch across borders' (1995: 233). While he argues that the principle of 'non-coercive relations' (I prefer the term non-violent relations) should prevail in the settlement of disputes, the use of force as a weapon of last resort should be employed in the face of attacks to eradicate cosmopolitan law.

Held's assumption is that the existence of this force would be *permanent*. Yet these statist assumptions are in conflict with the aim of this second-ment, which is 'the demilitarization and transcendence of the war system' (1995: 279). However, this is only possible if institutions claiming a monopoly of legitimate force give way to governments and the logic of government is, as I have argued above, profoundly different from that of the state. Quite rightly, Held argues that we must overcome the dualisms between (for example) globalism and cultural diversity; global gover-nance from above and the extension of grass roots organizations from below, constitutionalism and politics. These polarities make it impossible to embed utopia in what Held calls 'the existing pattern of political rela-tions and processes' (1995: 286).

But as challenging as this model is, its incoherence is manifest in Held's continuing belief in the permanence of the state. In an analysis of democracy and autonomy, he argues that the *demos* must include all adults with the exception of those temporarily visiting a political com-munity and those who 'beyond a shadow of a doubt' are legitimately dis-qualified from participation 'due to severe mental incapacity and/or serious records of crime' (1995: 208). The exclusions he refers to are 'natu-ralized', because they are taken as self-evident and do not appear to have any adverse consequences for the citizenship of others. Temporary visi-tors would, it is true, be citizens of other communities. But the fact that in many societies today, people can be resident, wish to stay where they live and work and yet still be deemed aliens, simply indicates how far we have to travel before a universal citizenship – citizenship as a universal human right – has been achieved. Excluding the mentally incapacitated from citizenship is far from self-evident and while there may be a tactical argument for excluding serious criminals from citizenship, the very exis-tence of such a category of intransigent outsiders indicates that we are indeed a long way from an inclusive (and emancipated) citizenry.

The relational argument remains. The exclusion of some cannot but undermine the freedom and thus the citizenship of all. Held rightly notes that in his cosmopolitan model, people would enjoy a 'multiple' citizen-ship since they would be members of diverse political communities – local, regional, national and global (1995: 233; Carter, 2001: 193–4). But where does the idea of a multiple and multi-layered concept of citizenship leave the state? Held argues that the nation state would 'wither away' but by this he does *not* mean that the nation state would disappear. What he suggests is that states would no longer be regarded as the 'sole centres of legitimate power' within their own borders but would be 'relocated' to, and articulated within, an overarching global democratic law (1995: 233).

Citizenship would, it seems, be simultaneously statist, supra-statist and sub-statist, but although this is an attractive argument, there remains a problem. States, after all, are institutions that claim a monopoly of legit-imate force in 'their' particular territory. They are jealous of this asserted monopoly (which lies at the heart of the notion of state sovereignty) and, therefore, cannot co-exist equally with other bodies that do not and cannot even claim to exercise a monopoly of legitimate force.

In a revealing footnote, Held accepts that he uses the term 'politics' in two conflicting ways. On the one hand, politics is defined in terms of the state; on the other hand, politics relates to the capacity of social agents to transform their environment (1995: 191). Here we see in a nutshell the problem with Held's notion of democracy. It seeks to transform the world environment in the interests of self-government and emancipation, but it remains prisoner of the liberal view that the state is permanent. As far as Held is concerned, the state merely remains one among many organizations. Yet the state is incompatible with democracy, and as it gives up its claim to a monopoly of legitimate force, it ceases to be a state.

Beck's Democratic Reflexive Modernization

Beck's *Democracy Without Enemies* contains a brilliant and witty critique of conventional notions of the state, modernity and the market. His argument for 'democratizing' democracy will be examined closely here.

We have inherited from modernity, he argues, a linkage between 'political freedom, citizenship and civil society' (1998: 2). The very language that is conventionally used sounds appealing until it is critically examined. We speak enthusiastically about 'self-determination and democracy', provided, as Beck notes sarcastically, these ends do not conflict with the imperialism of technology, science and industry (1998: 30). Undermining job security is hugely damaging: unemployment, he argues, no longer only afflicts those on the margin of society – it has the potential to strike at all of us – and put democracy as a way of life at risk (1998: 55).

Beck is particularly critical of those who identify democracy with the neo-liberalism of the New Right, since he argues trenchantly that the market fundamentalism which pseudo-democrats idolize, is a form of democratic illiteracy (1998: 58). He is particularly concerned about reckless ecological exploitation, arguing that capitalism remains dependent upon the destruction of the environment (1998: 107). This is an issue affecting everyone, as he puts it, 'pollutants do not spare the drinking water of director generals' (1998: 25). The conventional sites of politics – parties, administrations, legislatures – are becoming less attractive particularly to the youth who increasingly question the monopoly of the custodians of the public interest on defining the public interest (1998: 5).

We are confronted, Beck argues, with a new kind of modernity (he prefers to call it a second, rather than a post, modernity), and central to this reflexive modernity (a modernity that looks critically upon itself), is a new logic. The old logic was exclusive and exclusionary; it rested upon an either/or scheme (1998: 65). It assumed that we have clear-cut identities as men or women; nationals or foreigners. We are either insiders or outsiders, with what he calls, 'an ultimately essentialistically based architecture of unambiguous identity' (1998: 74). The old modernity rests upon an ontology of difference. The new logic revolves around the concept of 'individualization', which does not mean that individuals turn their back on society: it means that they are flexible, live in many places and do not see any antagonism between attending to their self-interest and working for others.

Beck devotes a whole chapter to the concept of the 'stranger', arguing that the concept of the stranger neither ignores difference nor supports a repressively hierarchical ordering. Strangers, he argues, are proof that the 'naturalness' of the local order is artificial and conventional. Strangers are neither enemies nor friends, natives nor foreigners, for as people are being released from the industrial society of the nation state into the turbulence of global risk society, we are all strangers. There is, as he puts it, universal estrangement (1998: 130-3).

The crises building up – in the environment, the economy, in the transport system (just to take three examples) – all point to the need to move beyond the primary, industrial modernity to a second, enlightened, reflexive modernity (1998: 166). Congestion has become, Beck argues, a metaphor for the involuntary politicization of modernity. It plunges us into a kind of Hobbesian war of all against all, for congestion means the involuntary sit-down strike of everyone against everyone else (1998: 163).

He is particularly intriguing in the implications he sees for his argument concerning the institution of the state. Beck argues that the contradictory unity of bourgeois and citoyen, as assumed in the scenario of the nation state, is shattering (1998: 75). Indeed, he even goes so far as to suggest that the state is losing its specific characteristic, the 'intimate relationship to force' (Weber) and is being 'de-statized'. Politics is being reopened outside of the political system (1998: 152).

All this has crucial implications for democracy. For if democracy is a concept of a polity 'without enemies' (as Beck puts it), then this must have an effect on the question of the state. With advancing individualization, Beck argues, it is becoming true for the first time in history that 'states that bark don't bite' (1998: 147). But if states are losing their bite – the intimate relationship to force that is their 'specific characteristic' – can we still call them *states*?

I agree with Beck's point that people are demanding the right to determine their own lives in ways that are startling and subversive for conventional politicians, and Beck argues that individualization should not be confused with 'individuation, emancipation or autonomy: the revival of the defunct bourgeois individual' (1998: 33). But caution is required. Notions of the individual, emancipation and autonomy have to be reconstructed in the light of the new modernity, and Beck himself speaks of individualization as 'self-organization' and refers approvingly of the need for actors to become more autonomous in their decisions and responsibilities (1998: 36, 166).

There is a secret elective affinity, he argues, between democratization and deceleration (1998: 167). The democratic process must allow individuals time and space to organize their own lives – there are no short cuts to emancipation, as the Communist Party states of Eastern Europe painfully demonstrated. But this raises the question: should we not link the process of democratizing democracy with the overcoming of the state?

It is on this crucial question that Beck equivocates. He implies that the new polity is no longer a state, but he still continues to use the term as though it is inconceivable that democracy could be anything other than a state. A Germany 'encircled' by friends is a state without enemies (1998: 141). He urges that the state without enemies should become an ecological state (1998: 151). Is it not inappropriate to talk of the 'ecological state' if, as Beck clearly envisages, social rather than statist sanctions are increasingly being applied? Of course, we are talking about a process still at a very early stage of its development and Beck is right to warn that lack of an enemy does not mean lack of what he calls an enemy stereotype (1998: 150). Those who subscribe to notions of state sovereignty will argue for the creation of such stereotypes (1998: 144).

Beck's analytical equivocation over the status of democracy is sharply portrayed in his treatment of youth. On the one hand, he sees in youth, an impatience with conventional politics and the old either/or logic: on the other hand, he comments that individualized young people may show not a friendly face but a violent one – a face in which violence for its own sake becomes the ultimate proof that something still exists (1998: 79). But surely violence works against the whole notion of individualization, since self-organization, respect for difference and a desire to govern one's own life is undermined by violent acts that enable some individuals to repress others. Where young people resort to violence, they are acting in a statist manner, and in a contrary way to the democratic individualization that Beck urges.

Although his argument for democracy is attractive, he lacks the conceptual resources to distinguish between statist actions (strictly speaking) and governmental ones (i.e., policies that seek to empower people and cement common interests). He argues, for example, that in Sweden the right of the child to a self-determined life can be enforced against parents if necessary (1998: 77). But is the Swedish polity acting governmentally here or in a classical statist fashion? In so far as rights have to be implemented with state force, then the latter holds. The point is that there is an important logical tension involved in using the state to enforce policies that ultimately seek to strengthen democratic capacity.

Beck is still victim to what Bull colourfully calls the 'tyranny of existing concepts' (1997: 267). Beck assumes that despite the dramatic changes that have occurred, the state remains, although the question could be asked: how do you define a democratic polity that no longer has enemies and lacks an intimate relationship to force which is the state's 'specific characteristic'? Beck would strengthen his case for a reflexive modernization if he freed himself from all conventional political notions – central of which is the notion that a polity has to be a state.

He *implies* that a democratic state is a contradiction in terms, but he fails to spell this out.

Giddens: Democracy and the 'Third Way'

The problem of globalization, a subject about which Giddens has much to say, will be examined later. What I will consider here is Giddens' view of democracy as expressed in his concern to 'renew' social democracy as a distinct political philosophy (1998: vii).

Giddens acknowledges that the context of his argument is one in which there is an increasingly sceptical attitude to authority. This attitude, he warns, 'can be depoliticizing, but on the whole pushes towards greater democracy and involvement than is currently available in conventional politics' (1998: 21). Indeed, elsewhere he argues that what he calls the 'paradox of democracy' arises because at a time when more and more countries in the world are adopting democratic forms, more and more people, particularly among the young, appear to be disillusioned with democracy (1999: 53). Although Giddens appears critical of the left–right distinction, this distinction is, in fact, crucial to his case for renewal. A renewed social democracy has to be left-of-centre since social justice and emancipatory politics remain at its core (1998: 33).

Like Beck, Giddens stresses the importance of 'sub-politics': the politics of families, voluntary organizations, single-issue groups etc. Trust in conventional authority figures – police, lawyers, doctors and not just in politicians (1998: 51) – is declining, and it is increasing in terms of 'sub-political' groups that associations of citizens will play a part in politics on a continuing basis (1998: 53). He is eloquent, indeed, on the case for 'democratizing democracy'. This case arises from a growing demand for autonomy and the emergence of a more reflexive citizenry, and it appears that democracy involves a new kind of polity.

Certainly, he argues that in the case of the European Union (EU), a political order needs to be constructed that is neither a superstate nor a free trade area (1998: 73). It would seem that logically, democracy for Giddens (as for Beck) cannot take the form of a state. Indeed, he uses the term 'governance' where I would use the term 'government', i.e., as a way of settling conflicts of interest that is post-statal in character. Thus, Giddens refers to the fact that the EU is pioneering forms of governance that do not fit any traditional mould (1998: 143; 1999: 56). Modern government is a matter of 'multi-layered governance'. Governance has to stretch above the level of the nation as well as below, since many of our problems cannot be dealt with only at the national level (2001: 79). Democracy, he stresses, must become transnational (1999: 54).

So what exactly is democracy? Giddens argues for a notion of politics that is inclusive, participatory and comprehensive. There need to be experiments with democracy – local direct democracy, electronic referenda, citizen's juries, etc. (1998: 75; 1999: 5). There should be no authority without democracy, he argues, since the new individualism demands that authority should be cast on an active and participatory basis (1998: 66). He speaks of a 'cosmopolitan nation' that helps to promote social inclusion and has a key role in fostering transnational systems of governance (1998: 69).

The division between public and private needs to be a fluid distinction, since, as he puts it, the new mixed economy involves a synergy between public and private sectors (1998: 100; 2002: 36). He warns that a meritocratic society destroys social cohesion because it leads to widening inequalities. Equality should be defined as inclusion (1998: 102).

The welfare state is an issue for democracy and it is Giddens' view that some of the criticisms of the welfare state should be accepted. The welfare state depends upon top-down distribution of benefits and, to the extent that it does not give enough space to personal liberty, it is essentially undemocratic (1998: 112–13). Science and technology cannot stay outside democratic processes. Experts cannot be automatically relied upon to know what is good for us (1998: 59). Freedom for social democrats should mean autonomy of action, which in turn demands the involvement of the wider community.

All this points to a view of democracy that is incompatible with an institution claiming a monopoly of legitimate force i.e., the state. Giddens stresses the importance of fostering social peace through control of the means of violence (1998: 47). The police, he says, need to work with citizens to improve local community standards and civic behaviour, using education, persuasion and counselling. A renewed emphasis on crime prevention rather than law enforcement can go hand in hand with the reintegration of the police with the community (1998: 87–8).

Giddens identifies democracy with the private as well as the public spheres. Democracy is crucial in the family, and in the public sphere involves formal equality, individual rights, public discussion of issues free from violence and authority, which is negotiated. Democratization requires mutual respect, equality, autonomy, decision-making through communication and freedom from violence (1998: 93). The point is that democracy is undermined by violence. In an older work, he argues the case for a dialogic democracy – a democracy based on dialogue – and contends that this rests upon a relationship based on respect for the other. Not surprisingly, he finds that there is likely to be a stark trade off between dialogic democracy and violence (1994: 124).

If this is democracy, what is the state? Curiously (and in my view inconsistently) he assumes that overcoming the state is a position of the right (the naive view that the state can be replaced by free markets). Disappointingly, Giddens argues merely that the shape of the state is being altered (1998: 31). He adopts the conventional equation of state and government, arguing that governance becomes a relevant concept which extends to agencies that are not part of any government (1998: 33). Government (i.e., the state) must be reconstructed to meet the needs of the age (1998: 53, 70). The nation state and the national government retain a decisive importance in the present-day world.

Although Giddens shares with Beck the formula of a democracy without enemies, he contends that state legitimacy must be renewed on an active basis. But if the nation state is an institution claiming a monopoly of legitimate violence, then surely the renewal of its legitimacy works against its use of violence (Hoffman, 1995: Chapter 6) and its authority is strengthened as its statist qualities decline. The only way of reconstructing or democratizing the state is to move beyond it!

Giddens argues that the public sphere needs to be expanded by the state so that there is constitutional reform directed towards greater transparency and openness and there are new safeguards against corruption. But when this entirely laudable process occurs, surely the state is acting against itself? It is contributing unwittingly to its own dissolution. In Britain, Giddens points out, the executive has too much power and existing forms of accountability are too weak (e.g. parliamentary committees in the Commons) (1998: 74). This is true, but it is the state that stands in the way. To argue that to retain or regain legitimacy, states have to elevate their administrative efficiency, inevitably raises the question: what has happened to the state's close association with violence?

We agree that the legitimacy is strengthened when public and private bodies help people with the capacity to manage risks (1998: 76), but to argue that this contributes to the new democratic state is to adopt a naive and uncritical view of the state itself. When Giddens argues that the concept of a democratic state is 'an ideal' (1998: 77), this unwittingly points to an otherworldly ideal that can never be progressively realized. The high levels of self-organization for which Giddens rightly argues (1998: 79–80), cannot be reconciled with the use of violence to settle conflicts of interests. We agree that conflicts of interest are inherent in society, but these conflicts of interest cannot be meaningfully resolved by the state (as Giddens suggests, 1998: 85–6), since the state *qua* state, can only undermine the positive forms of encouragement, which Giddens argues, should go along with other sanctions (1998: 94).

Giddens recognizes, with his concept of the cosmopolitan nation, that national identities are fluid and multiple in character. To speak of national identity as benign only if it is of multiple identification (1998: 130), on the one hand, and yet identify this national identity with the nation state, on the other, is to move from the critical to the conventional in one breath.

If Giddens is right – as I believe he is – that where violence begins, dialogue stops, then there cannot be a democratic state. Dialogic democracy is a prime means for the containment or dissolution of violence (1994: 244), since such a democracy involves autonomy, communication and mutual tolerance. How can pacific rather than war-like values be nurtured in a democratized polity as a way of developing the active side of citizenship responsibilities (1998: 234), unless such a polity is ceasing to be a state?

SUMMARY

■ Citizenship is closely linked to democracy, but what prevents the latter from being rigorously and coherently conceptualized is the notion that democracy is a form of the state.

■ Horrendous authoritarian policies have been justified in the name of democracy but the problem of this tyranny lies not with democracy but with the state. It is the state that seeks an abstract sameness and is threatened by difference, not democracy.

■ Held's cosmopolitan democracy, like Beck's democracy without enemies and Giddens' renewal of social democracy, all raise exciting and valuable arguments for advancing the capacity of people – of all people – to govern their own lives. The problem with each of these arguments is that democracy is still seen as a form of the state and this makes it impossible to argue in a coherent and consistent way for an inclusive citizenship.

Part Two
Barriers to
Democratic Citizenship

3

State and Nationalism

This chapter will explain the link between nationalism and the state, arguing that both are barriers to democratic citizenship. A distinction will be defended between nationality – or national identity – and nationalism, defined here as the view that a person's ultimate loyalty is to the nation. The latter is tied to the state, either as a reality to be defended, or as a dream to be realized. In either case, the monopolistic exclusivity of the state translates itself into the exclusivity of nationalism and it will be argued that although national identity is part of a democratic citizenship, nationalism is not.

This proposition holds whether we think of either ethnic or so-called civic nationalism, since the problem here is not simply one of overt xenophobia: it is linked to the state itself.

State and Nation: The Problem of Exclusivity

We have defined the state, following the argument of Max Weber, as an institution claiming a monopoly of legitimate force for a particular territory. Citizenship defined in statist terms necessarily privileges a particular national identity and marginalizes all others. Oommen refers to the 'terminal loyalty' of the citizen to the state, but this is inherently problematic. To say, as Oommen does, that we need to conceptualize 'the co-existence of a series of terminal loyalties, each of which has a different context or content' (1997: 25) is to continue with a statist notion as though 'terminal loyalties' can co-exist with one another. But this is merely naive. For the truth is that statist citizenship is inherently exclusive. It places one 'terminal loyalty' above all others.

The concept of a nation develops hand in hand with a notion of territory. What gives this territorial identity its overarching and 'quasi-ontological significance' (Parekh, 1990: 249) is the link between state and nation. Of course, we accept that in pre-modern states, national identities are incoherent and inchoate. But it is worth noting that ancient city states like Athens or Sparta justified slavery as something that was fitting for non-Greeks, indeed, empires viewed those beyond their borders as 'barbarians' i.e., peoples bereft of civilization and incapable of enjoying what we concede was an embryonic notion of citizenship. Smith speaks of the ethnocentric nationalisms of the ancient world, while not denying the qualitative differences between pre-modern and modern nationalism (1998: 188).

Anderson is right to say that the concept of the nation comes 'to maturity' in the age of the Enlightenment, for this implies that a national consciousness, in immature form, exists much earlier (1991: 7). In his fascinating quotation from Marco Polo in the thirteenth century, he detects the seeds of a territorialization of faiths 'which foreshadows the language of many nationalists' (1991: 17). In the eighth century, the people who lived in what is Wales today, were hemmed into the territory by a people who called them *weallas* (i.e., Welsh) (Guibernau: 1996: 50). Gellner speaks of a 'dormant' nationalism during the pre-industrial age, capturing well the potential for nationalism that developed in earlier periods (1983: 43), while Guibernau comments that nationalism has its 'basis in kinship and pre-modern ties' (1996: 145). There are a considerable number of specialists on nationalism who argue that nations exist before nationalist modernity (O'Leary, 1998: 54; Smith, 1998: 170–81).

Smith is right to stress that ethnic identities are separate and separable from nationalist exploitation (1998: 130) and he finds Armstrong's argument persuasive that modern national identities are tied to ethnic persistence (Smith, 1998: 185). This argument has a crucial bearing on the distinction advanced below between nationalism, on the one hand, and nationality, on the other. Historically, a national identity could not become explicit without the divisive institutions of the state. With the development of state sovereignty in its modern form as a power that is impersonal and abstract, the territorial 'container' for this power assumes an explicitly national form. Nationalist symbols provide the moral component of state sovereignty (Giddens, 1985: 220–1). If the state is to plausibly assert a monopoly of legitimacy for its acts of violence, it must give this claim to legitimacy cultural content and linguistic focus. In territorializing its subjects, it must also 'nationalize' them. State sovereignty in its modern form allows no competitors. The exclusivity of the state is counterpointed by the exclusivity of the nation (Hoffman, 1995: 67). To say that nationalism is at odds with statism, as O'Leary does (1998: 70), is not to understand the state itself.

It has been frequently pointed out that the notion of the nation state is problematic since states contain many nations, not just one. It is true that national consciousness is notoriously fluent and difficult to pin down, but so too is the state. It is just as easy to give a legal content to nationality as it is to the state, and indeed in British law, nationality is defined (rather confusingly) as membership of the state. Nations are as material as the state. They certainly exist! As Hugh Trevor-Roper has put it, 'Thus I am *driven* to the conclusion that no "scientific definition" of the nation can be devised; yet the phenomenon has existed, and exists' (cited in Anderson, 1991: 3).

This seems the correct response to Breuilly's argument that nationalism has no objective reality because it arises from 'shared views' (1993: 6). In rejecting the naturalism of the nationalists, we should not conclude that nations and nationalism are bereft of objective features. Smith is persuasive in his argument that 'modernists' simply invert the 'primordialism' of the nationalists: the latter sees nations as purely concrete and 'natural', the former see nations as mere abstractions and artificial (1998). Neither is correct. Moreover, in contending that nationalism is inherently statist in character, we are not defining nationalism as 'state-seeking' since clearly nationalism may arise in established states (Brubaker, 1998: 278). But what makes nationalism statist is not that nationalist movements necessarily seek to create *new* states, but that the privileging of one national identity over others requires the claim to exercise a monopoly of violence, i.e., the existence of the state.

The point is that it is impossible to assert this monopoly of legitimate force without giving such a monopoly some kind of national form. If nationalism is an emotional artifice, its incoherence arises as part and parcel of the incoherence of the state itself. Force is required not only to justify state adventures abroad, but to impose a dominant national identity at home, and the single national language that generally characterizes the nation state has usually been imposed with a good deal of violence upon those who would rather speak a different tongue, or who prefer local dialects eradicated by public education policies (Poggi, 1978: 93).

Anderson notes that English elbowed Gaelic out of most of Ireland, French pushed Breton to the wall, and Castilian reduced Catalan to marginality (1991: 78). Only one language counts! In 1887 Russian was made compulsory as the language of instruction in all state schools in the Baltic provinces as a way of trying to crush rival national identities (Anderson, 1991: 87). It is not difficult to see that national unity, in terms by which states assert their identity, is of a contradictory kind.

The assertion of a national identity through the state signals both internal and external challenge and division. As nation states find themselves beset with dissenters and rebels, emphasis has to be placed upon the 'national' character of their exclusivity. Attempts to deny citizenship to 'others' – witness the extraordinary hysteria in Britain about 'bogus' asylum seekers – is integral to the monopolistic institutions of the state. Oommen sees the nation state as an 'unfortunate aspiration' that was never realized even in Western Europe (1997: 136) but the mystification of nationality that this unfortunate aspiration involves, is inherent in the notion of the state itself. Multi-national states (despite their claims to liberalism and tolerance) inevitably privilege one of their constituent nations insofar as they remain states as such. Britain, arguably, will only cease to privilege the English over the other nations in the UK as it ceases to be a state.

Homogeneity and Nationalism

Despite this critique, it has to be said that there are features in nationalism which, historically speaking, are positive and potentially emancipatory. Smith argues that at its outset nationalism was 'an inclusive and liberating force' (1998: 1). Nationalism in its modern form requires a notion of 'sameness' and individuality, a common identity allowing people to be welded together, in their imagination at least, as *ein volk*. A system of universal education is clearly crucial if people are to be able to identify with one another even if they are not known to their fellows personally. A common culture provides the common concepts that enable people to relate to each other. It is not simply that people can be categorized as individuals with the 'same' rights, but in the international arena, each 'nation state' is deemed formally equal to every other.

Gellner identifies the development of nationalism in its modern form with the concept of homogeneity. In the agrarian order – by which Gellner means traditional or pre-modern society – no homogenized culture can be imposed upon society at large. Hence it is not possible for people en masse to think of themselves as citizens with a national identity, although we have argued that both citizenship and nationalism are embryonic (and explicitly selective) in pre-modern society. It is only with the rise of capitalism or industrial society (as Gellner calls it) that we have a 'universal conceptual currency', a notion, crucial to modern nationalism, of common identity. Notions of the unified and the standardized find their analogue in the 'anonymous and equal collectivities' of a 'mass society' (Gellner, 1983: 17, 21–2). He puts the matter pithily when he says that homogeneity, literacy and anonymity are the 'key traits' of nationalism (1983: 138). The modern notion of citizenship is premised upon the idea that 'everyone' in society is entitled to the same rights and responsibilities.

Yet, as Gellner also notes, homogeneity goes hand in hand with division (1983: 52). The egalitarianism of a mobile and culturally homogenous society also engenders very sharp and painful inequalities (1983: 73) – inequalities, we might add, that are all the more painfully felt because equality is the official norm of a modern society. Division may express itself in national form, even where (as with Disraeli's 'two nations') rich and poor speak the same language (though not in the same way!), and national differentiation is a way of indicating significant cleavages. The notion that those who supported the king during the English civil war were descendants of the Normans and not true 'Anglo-Saxons', demonstrates just how potent (and of course mythical) national beliefs can be.

Once we link the notion of sameness with the liberal *state*, then the coexistence of (abstract) equality and (concrete) inequality becomes perfectly intelligible. In order to claim a monopoly of legitimate force, people must be both united in an abstract assimilationist manner, and divided in a starkly 'otherized' fashion. Statism rests upon an abstract sameness for the (exclusive) citizen and an abstract difference for the outsider. An inclusive notion of citizenship must break with both, since national identity/identities need to enshrine both sameness and difference. Oommen argues saliently that individuals and collectivities have multiple identities and no-one can acquire primacy in all contexts (1997: 10). Yet his warning about the pernicious effects of the ideology of homogenization applies not merely to nation states, but to states in general (1997: 145). Gellner's contention that sharp cleavages are only associated with an early stage of nationalism is too complacent, particularly as he himself concedes that even in 'late industrialism' as he calls it, 'great power inequality persists' (1983: 90). The point is that divisions are inherent in the state.

Gellner's scathing indictment of nationalism is well taken. Among other things, he argues that nationalism 'preaches and defends cultural diversity, when in fact it imposes homogeneity both inside and, to a lesser degree, between political units'. Its self-image and its true nature are inversely related (1983: 125). But this stricture applies equally to the state, of which nationalism is an inherent part. It is crucial to see that since the homogenizing tendency of nationalism is oppressive and (in our view) ultimately self-destructive (however positive it may have been historically), strategies need to be developed that integrate politically (i.e., incorporate while respecting) diversity and difference (O'Leary, 1998: 64).

Of course, it is 'functional' for the modern state to homogenize its population, but it is also dysfunctional since it involves imposing a dominant identity upon the population at large, with all the violent conflict this can engender. The more explicitly nationalist the drive to homogeneity, the more diverse we can expect the population to be. Nationalist homogeneity, like the state's assertion of a monopoly, presupposes the very differences that threaten a statist sense of identity. To link homogenization with the demise of the state, as Smith does (1998: 214), is to use a statist tool against the state: it can't be done.

To blame globalization for homogenization (as is often argued), is to mistake propaganda for reality. It is true that the USA in particular, and the Western capitalist countries in general, present themselves as globalizing powers, but this simply expresses the arrogance of the state, which in one form or another, has characterized the 'mortal god' since its inception!

Nationalism Versus Nationality

Löwy argues that whereas nationalism embraces the feeling of national identity, it also embraces something else – its 'decisive ingredient' – 'the choice of the nation as *the* primary, fundamental and most important social and political value, to which all others are – in one way or another – subordinated' (1998: 57, 52). Hence we disagree with Miller's use of the term 'nationality' as a synonym for nationalism (e.g., 1995: 155), and Miller takes it for granted that national identities can only express themselves in statist terms (Miller, 1999: 60; Bankowski and Christodoulidis, 1999: 89).

Nationalism, we insist, is inherently statist in character, and the problem with the state is two-fold. The first is that it requires allegiance to a dominant nation as part of its claim to have a monopoly of legitimate force. Miller refers repeatedly to British national identity (e.g., 1995: 99) as though being a Briton is an unproblematic way of identifying oneself. The second problem with the statist concept of the nation is that it is singular rather than plural in character. Individuals may only have one national identity. Yet it is becoming clearer that many people in Britain do not see themselves as uni-national, but feel quite comfortable if they are described as British *and* English *and* Indian or Pakistani, etc.

Brubaker comments that while the old USSR was hostile to nationalism, it institutionalized nationality to an extraordinary degree. Nationality was registered in personal identity documents and recorded in almost all bureaucratic encounters and official transactions (1998: 286–7). What made this nationality 'statist' in character, was that it was an obligatory, ascribed status of a monolithic kind. No wonder it laid the seeds of the very nationalism that it sought to undermine. Although his terminology is problematic, Sorensen argues that in the postmodern state (as he calls it), a number of different identities coexist (2001: 139).

Gellner is right to identify nationalism with the state, but speaks of the essence of nationalism as the fusion of culture and polity as though the concept of polity is identical to that of the state (1983: 13). The same problem is evident in Breuilly's magisterial account. Politics and power are defined in terms of the state (1993: 1). Guibernau makes the same assumption (1996: 141). In fact, as we have argued, there is a necessary tension between both state and politics, and nationality and nationalism. O'Leary is right to argue that consciousness of a shared cultural, religious or territorial identity is not of the essence of nationalism (1998: 55). Nationality has to be cast in a statist mould before it is necessarily *nationalist*, and it is interesting that Anderson stresses that nationality or nationness can be separate from nationalism (1991: 4). He weakens this insight when he suggests that national identity is tied to state sovereignty (1991: 7), because, it will be argued, it is possible to have one or possibly many national identities while being critical of both nationalism and the state. Nationalism, as Calhoun puts it, promotes categorical rather than relational identities (1997: 46), and a categorical identity is one premised upon dualism. Either you are with us or against us; if you are not an insider, you must be an outsider, etc.

It is true that what is called civic (or liberal) nationalism is different from ethnic (or authoritarian) nationalism, but Brubaker rightly warns against constructing a 'Manichean' distinction between the two (1998: 298). All nationalism, however liberal, is statist (and therefore) exclusive in character. It is because Gellner is uncritical of the state itself that he can argue for a tolerant, pluralistic and rational nationalism (1983: 2). Conversely, he is certainly correct when he argues that a definition of nationalism is necessarily parasitic 'on a prior and assumed definition of the state' (1983: 4).

It is sometimes suggested that logically a nationalist should recognize that *all* nations are entitled to self-determination, but to imagine that this can happen, is to misunderstand the statist implications of nationalism itself. A nationalist can no more espouse the equality of all nations in practice than a statist can argue that all are equally free of violence (and the discrimination inherent in violence), because all states claim a monopoly of legitimate force for their particular territory. Exclusivity, both domestic as well as international, is built into the very definition of nationalism and the state. To insist that nationalism must be egalitarian would, as Brueilly dryly notes, exclude Nazism from the definition of nationalism (1993: 3).

It is true that a distinction must be made between the nationalism of the oppressed and the nationalism of the oppressor. For those who have been denied statehood and national sovereignty, the acquisition of these is an important step on the road to emancipation. The removal of apartheid required the birth of a South African nation, and a nationalism that sought to eradicate racism towards, and the humiliation of, blacks. South Africans are proud to have become since 1994 statist citizens in the land of their birth. The development of a Palestinian nation state would constitute an important step forward in the struggle to resolve the crisis of the Middle East. But none of this takes away the fact that nationalism in all its forms is ultimately exclusive, and neither African nationalism in South Africa nor Palestinian nationalism in the Middle East are (alas) exceptions to this argument. The current South African state or a future Palestinian state is, or will be, enmeshed in the same contradictory processes that characterize the state in general.

Löwy is right, therefore, to stress that the distinction between the nationalism of the oppressed and the nationalism of the oppressor is not an absolute one. Yesterday's oppressed very easily become today's oppressors – 'there is no lack of historical evidence for this in our times' – and nationalist ideology may be both liberating *vis-à-vis* its oppressors, and oppressive towards its own national minorities (1998: 59). This is why exception is taken to Davis' contention that nationalism is 'morally neutral' (1978: 31) on the grounds that when it is against oppression, it is good, but when it is aggressive, it is bad. This is too superficial a view to take of the distinction noted above.

This critique of nationalism can only be sustained if we distinguish between state and government. Organization is necessary for all societies. People cannot relate to each other without language and culture and it is impossible to articulate values through language and culture without having a national identity. As Calhoun notes, all peoples on the earth today and all known to us historically, have some method of reckoning identities and connections to each other through kinship and descent (1997: 37), and some sense, it could be added, however embryonic, of nationality. The fact that national identities are historically and humanly created (and can easily be manipulated) does not mean that they can only be defined in terms of the state.

We feel comfortable with the notion that national identity is linked to language, culture and ethnicity although, as we have argued already, there is no need to assume that such an identity has to be singular, rather than plural, in form. This is why we would agree with Delanty's concern with what he calls 'post-nationalism', but not with his idea of a 'post-national citizenship' (2000: 65) since a respect for national identity or identities is in tension with the exclusivity of nationalism. The same problem is evident with Soysal's model of 'post-national' citizenship (1994: 3). Why should a move beyond nationalism require a move beyond the 'national' itself? Habermas' view of a post-national citizenship linked to a constitutional *state* demonstrates the dangers of an abstract cosmopolitanism that confuses nationalism and nationality (Delanty, 2000: 65–6, 138).

Nations are communities that, pace Weber, do not have to produce states in order to be 'adequate' nations (Smith, 1998: 14). Gellner concedes that a group identity is inherent in society, but he prefers to call this 'patriotism' (1983: 138). What Gellner calls patriotism, is often called national identity or nationality. Unlike the state, it is unavoidable. We would not, therefore, accept the notion of McKinnon and Hampsher-Monk that patriotism is a more nuanced, classical form of nationalism. (2000: 7). Taylor (1998a: 201) defines patriotism as the love of a particular country or tradition in a non-exclusive way (see also Canovan, 1996: 88). The concept of the nation is not, as Smith rightly emphasizes, just an abstraction and an invention: it is felt as a concrete community and this 'feeling' would not be held unless it was based on something more than a mere artifice (1998: 140).

National identity seems to us to be one of the ways that people differentiate themselves. National differences – like all differences – lead to disputes and conflict that require negotiation and arbitration to resolve them. Such national differences only become threatening when they are used to justify domination and exploitation. Marx is wrong in *The Communist Manifesto* to speak of 'national differences and antagonisms' increasingly vanishing, as though differences in themselves generate violent conflict (Guibernau, 1996: 17–18). Differences are 'natural' (using the term 'natural' to mean developmental), and government involves the use of sanctions to ensure that these national differences are respected and tolerated (if not celebrated). Violence and domination, however, involve the suppression or marginalization of these differences. Hence the state (which necessarily embodies violence and domination) requires nationalism, but is the ultimate foe of national identity.

Miller contends that 'a person's final identity' should have a national expression as one of its constituents (1995: 45). But identities are fluid so that talk of a 'final' identity sounds dogmatic (and statist). Nor do we see why a person should only have one national identity. Like the notion of an ultimate identity, the idea that loyalty is to 'one-ness' reflects statist prejudice. This prejudice can take an abstractly humanist form. Durkheim's argument that the national ideal must become the human ideal is useful insofar as it appears to separate the notion of nationality from exclusiveness and violence. And yet the language of ideals is invariably the language of the state with its notions of finality and ultimate realization, so that it is not surprising to see Durkheim identify the human ideal with the state (cited by Guibernau, 1996: 29).

Brubaker argues that national conflicts are in principle irresolvable (1998: 279). But this pessimism arises because we assume that contestation and conflict must take violent forms. The 'national question' is indeed insoluble if we accept the state and statist categories uncritically. But conflict and contestation do not need to express themselves through violence: in fact the kind of conflict that can be resolved is a conflict in which people present differences rather than divisions. When divisions exist – by which are meant differences that make it impossible for people to change places and imagine what it is like to be the 'other' – then indeed conflicts are insoluble. If conflicts are to be resolved, ways of converting divisions into differences are required. Of course, the resolution of a particular conflict does not mean that conflicts *per se* come to an end. The notion that conflict is 'finally' resolved, arises from a misconception of human relationships: a product of the 'idealizing' and fossilizing consequence of statist thought. To resolve a conflict merely means that a particular difference can be acknowledged and accepted so that conflict in general can continue in other ways.

The strengths and weaknesses of the Marxist approach to nationality and nationalism are instructive in developing the case for an inclusive citizenship that embraces nationality, but opposes nationalism.

The Marxist Contribution

Marx and Engels seek (at least on occasion) to distinguish between nationality and nationalism. It has been argued that 'the theory of nationalism represents Marxism's greatest historical failure' (Nairn, cited in Anderson, 1991: 3); certainly, Marxists have often failed to get to grips with the national question.

The statement by a young Marx that 'the nationality of the worker is neither French, nor English, nor German, it is *labour, free slavery, self-huckstering*' (cited by Löwy, 1998: 55) wrongly assumes that national identity can be transcended by class identity. It is an older and wiser Marx who tells Engels that 'our friend Lafargue and others, who had done away with nationalities, had spoken *"French"* to us i.e., a language which nine-tenths of the audience did not understand' (Marx and Engels, 1975d: 168). The point is that no-one escapes a national identity, even if the latter is multiple and plural in form.

The *Communist Manifesto* makes the distinction between a struggle that is national 'in form' (inevitable) and one that is national 'in substance' (to be transcended) (Marx and Engels, 1967: 92). Marx and Engels looked towards the abolition not of nations, but of national exclusiveness or what has here been defined as *nationalism* (Löwy, 1998: 20). The dictum (supported by Engels) that a nation which oppresses another, cannot itself be free, injects a relational view into the debate. A global or international identity must be premised upon the existence of national diversity. Every citizen has one or many national identities – but citizenship is incompatible with nationalism which, as we have defined it, implies the superiority of one nation over another.

Marx and Engels envisaged the withering away of the state, but not the withering away of nationality (Davis, 1967: 15). Guibernau is correct to argue that Marx's internationalism did not rest upon an attempt to eliminate national distinctions (1996: 18), even though this is not always clear in Marx's writing. It is important that Marxist theory is not caricatured, with its weaknesses presented as though they constituted its essence. This, in a word, is the problem with Nimni's exposition, which depicts Marx and Engels as economic determinists and reductionists (1989; Hoffman and Mzala, 1990–91; Löwy, 1998: 16–17). Marx and Engels sought, at their best, to see nationalism as a political phenomenon tied to the state and separate from nationality. Engels contended that southern Slavs, Gaelic speakers in Scotland, the Bretons, the Basques and Yiddish-speaking Jews of Eastern Europe (to name just some) are non-historical peoples, but this astonishing and manifestly problematic assertion has been criticized by other Marxists, from Kautsky to Bauer, and classically by Rodolsky (Löwy, 1998: 25–6). Engels' theory here represents an attempt to distinguish between nations promoting emancipation, and those whose cause is reactionary, and it involves an attempt to homogenize 'progressive' or 'reactionary' nations in a manner that is profoundly problematic (and arguably un-Marxist) in character.

This argument about non-historical nations was used by Luxemburg, particularly before 1914, to justify her argument that the Polish could not legitimately claim a right to self-determination. The end of such nationalism was seen as a short-term project requiring nothing more than heroic will power (Löwy, 1998: 36). Stalin's pamphlet *Marxism and the National Question* (1913) conveys an opposite difficulty. It seeks to define the nation in a rigid manner that underplays the fluidity and thus the change of national identity. It would be impossible, for example, in terms of Stalin's theory, to explore how Britain is sometimes seen as a single nation people by 'Britons'; at other times as a complex of nations – the Scots, the Welsh and the English – while during the funeral of Princess Diana the 'nation' seemed to embrace all who felt her loss keenly whatever their otherwise 'outsider' status! The concept of the 'nation' is necessarily fluid precisely because it is part and parcel of political discourse and when used as the basis of nationalism, it becomes subject to all the contradictions of statist language.

Löwy is, in our view, right to praise Bauer for his attempt in *The Question of Nationalities and Social Democracy* (1909) to stress this fluid character of the nation. Bauer speaks of the nation as' common historical fate', 'the never completed product of an unending process, in a continual process of becoming and disappearing' (Löwy, 1998: 46–7). The problem with Bauer seems to lie in the notion of a 'national-cultural autonomy' that may even exist as a *substitute* for the right of an oppressed nationality to form its own state. It is untenable to expect some nationalities to accept that they must express their aspirations in political institutions that fall short of independent statehood while allowing others to have states of their own (Hoffman, 1998: 98).

The state as an institution must be *generally* discredited. We cannot expect certain nationalities to forgo sovereign statehood while others declare themselves to be nation states. Indeed, the quickest way of encouraging an oppressed nationality to aspire to independent statehood (as the admittedly problematic solution to its problems) is to argue that it should accept nationhood without the state in a world in which statehood is still regarded as a badge of independence and a vehicle of self-determination.

Lenin's comment that the question of national self-determination 'belongs wholly and exclusively to the sphere of political democracy' (cited by Löwy, 1998: 41) rests upon a narrow statist definition of politics. What makes nationality political is the fact that it can only be fully expressed (often in plural and multiple forms) when states, including so-called democratic states, have become a thing of the past. The insistence by Lenin that democracy is a form of the state rests upon the insupportable view that self-government (the power of the people) is compatible with an institution claiming a monopoly of legitimate force (Hoffman, 1984: 207).

It is not only a statist view of politics that is the problem. To detach nationality from nationalism, we need to detach nationality from the *state*, and we can only do this when we have a realistic way of looking beyond the state. It is precisely this residual statism within Marxist thought that makes it possible for Guibernau to argue that both Marxism and nationalism share the myth of 'a final era of justice and freedom' (1996: 20), for this notion of 'finality' (as we have seen) is linked to a belief that the state can bring ultimate order to a world of chaos.

Guibernau raises the problem of achieving a global identity. Since there are no common memories, she argues, and no common language, the notion of a global identity stands 'as a soft alternative to the passionately felt national identities' (1996: 132). Her difficulty, however, arises out of the modernist framework through which she conducts the argument. A global identity is not an alternative to a national identity: it can only arise through national identities as people increasingly see that they have a common destiny with others while retaining their national and indeed local loyalties as well. Cosmopolitanism becomes itself a dogma, a fundamentalism, if it is counterposed to a national identity.

To dream, as Kautsky did, of a socialist future without nations – a world in which humankind will speak only one language – is to privilege (however unintentionally) one identity at the expense of others. While we would accept that the disintegration of the former USSR and the liberation of countless nations from domination represented an important historical moment in the development of emancipation, it would be naive to underestimate the terrible problems that arise when empires are replaced with fractious sovereign states. The development of independent nation states – whether in the former Yugoslavia or among previous victims of so-called 'proletarian internationalism' like Hungary and the Czech Republic – has seen the proliferation of enemies to be crushed in the name of state sovereignty. War, bloodshed and horrendous levels of violence have characterized the so-called new world order that followed the disintegration of the Soviet bloc. Anyone who thinks that the state solves national problems should look at the carnage following the developments of 1989.

Democracy and National Identity

It is surely wrong to describe nationalism as democratic in character when democracy is not a form of the state. Bankowski and Christodoulidis are right to challenge the link between democracy and the state (1999: 95). It is because O'Leary is himself uncritical of the state, that he can describe national self-determination as the right of every nation to form its own state, and to see this liberal statism as 'a recursive principle of democratic consent' (1998: 69; 79).

Critics of Gellner complain that he failed to adequately link democracy and nationalism and yet, as we see it, nationalism undermines democracy. How can one advance popular self-government by privileging one national identity above all others? If states increasingly abandon the use of violence in seeking to resolve conflicts with minorities (as Guibernau advocates, 1996: 144), then they are ceasing to act as states, and behaving (as the democratic principle, indeed, requires) *governmentally*.

Once we accept that diversity and plurality characterize all contemporary societies, the problem is to find policies that recognize and protect this diversity. In our view, we cannot move towards an inclusive citizenship unless we identify the state itself as a problem rather than as a solution.

Violence can only be justified where one national group does not respect and acts with violence against the human rights of others, whether members of another group or members of its own group. Nationalists may feel threatened either by those who espouse other national identities or by those who insist that they possess multiple and plural identities. Unfortunately, we cannot always assume that the harassment result- ing from nationalist positions, can always be tackled by non-violent sanctions.

It depends. Counter-violence may be necessary to create a framework for policies promoting the recognition and celebration of diversity. It is this recognition and celebration of diversity which must be the principle guiding a democratic attitude towards national identity. We agree with Stepan that in multinational and multicultural polities, 'nation-state building policies and democracy-building policies are conflicting political logics' (1998: 238). In areas like schools and the media, policies that make minorities feel comfortable, secure and recognized are crucial. Nothing creates cultural alienation more quickly than policies implying that minorities have nothing to offer majoritarian values. We need to avoid the dualism of either promoting assimilation, on the one hand, or neglect on the other – as though this exhausts the choice facing us. As Young puts it pithily, 'Self-annihilation is an unreasonable and unjust requirement of citizenship' (cited by Miller, 1995: 133). Recognition involves a political process that avoids both assimilation and neglect, by recognizing differ- ence in a non-divisive way.

Citizens can only enjoy their differences if they are aware that we are *all* different and yet the same. Integration is not a synonym for assimila- tion, but an attempt to bring people together in a way that does not down- play their differences. Of course this democratic ethic will not be shared by all. Nevertheless, we should have the confidence to pursue it, secure in the knowledge that it is not a 'western' or 'ethnocentric' position but one deriving from a multiplicity of historical and cultural traditions. While a democratic ethics builds upon the liberal tradition (itself far from being a 'Western' construction), it also takes account of pre-liberal emphases upon relationships and community. Those who do not agree with democracy are necessarily undermining the rights and freedoms of others (and indeed themselves) and, therefore, we should seek to handle their 'dis- sent' with negotiation and argument, in the first instance, and only with force where anti-democratic individuals and movements themselves resort to violence.

It has been argued that we cannot decide in the abstract when nations should be self-determining. Just as the boundaries of the demos presup- posed by democratic institutions cannot themselves be democratically determined, so too, it is said, the boundaries of the national self presup- posed by national self-determination cannot themselves be self-determined (Brubaker, 1998: 279). There is, however, a way out of this dilemma. It is to assert that the objective of democracy is self-determination so that the correct units of governance are those that facilitate this objective under particular circumstances. National self-determination is part and parcel of democracy and individuals cannot govern themselves if they feel uncomfortable with the national identity or identities through which they express themselves.

Yuval-Davis is right to warn against (so-called) multiculturalist policies that 'homogenize' minorities by attributing to all members the same relationship to their culture and tradition (Yuval-Davis, 1999: 131). We are unable to work towards democratic policies without (in the eyes of anti-democrats) privileging democracy. Anti-democratic practices cannot be condoned in the name of national tradition, since all national traditions contain democratic and anti-democratic features. We need to encourage the former and discourage the latter whether we are dealing with attitudes towards women, gays, atheists, blacks, etc. The role of democratic policies is to ensure that *all* (and not just some) have a right to be different.

How would we seek to develop democratic policies towards national differences? In the short-term, people must be allowed to have multiple 'citizenships', so that the position evident in Britain in which individuals are the 'citizens' of different states is clearly preferable to the notion that only one statist 'nationality' is possible. It is true that the greater tolerance of the British position doubtless reflects the security and confidence of a former imperial power – but it is a 'good practice' and should be followed elsewhere. The implication of allowing people 'dual' or indeed multiple citizenship is potentially subversive of the monopoly of legitimacy claimed traditionally by the state.

The policies of devolution followed by the UK government over the last few years have also been timely and helpful. They demonstrate to the Scots and Welsh that being different is a positive feature, while the recognition that both the unionists and the republicans in Northern Ireland have national identities that need to be understood by their opponents, has been crucial for moving forward in that troubled part of what is still Great Britain. The link between democracy and 'mutual and complementary' political identities is a potent one so that, as Stepan indicates with regard to federalist policy in Spain, a significant majority of those polled in 1982 declared that they were 'proud to be Catalan, proud to be Spanish, and in favour of a united Europe via the European Community' (1998: 231–2; Carter, 2001: 133). It is true that for many, a European identity is weaker than, say, a British identity, but why should we suppose that identities are homogenous in the sense that all must subscribe to them in the same way?

SUMMARY

■ Pre-modern concepts of national identity differ radically from modern ones and yet all nationalism is tied to the state. The universality and egalitarianism implicit in the notion of citizenship cannot express itself consistently as long as citizenship is confined to the state.

■ A national identity or (as is increasingly the case) national identities, are part of the way we express ourselves – they constitute one of the infinity of differences that have and always will exist. The drive towards homogenization, which the state promotes, crushes diversity and is incompatible with democracy and thus a democratic and inclusive notion of citizenship.

■ The Marxist contribution distinguishes between nationality and nationalism. Democratic policies involve the recognition and celebration of differences for all, and therefore the use of force (where violence is threatened) and governmental sanctions (where it is not).

■ We need to support policies that make it easier for residents to become citizens, and for citizenship to be 'dual' and 'multiple' in character. Nations have a right to their own state but short-term expedients must be coherently linked to longer-term goals. A citizenship can only be inclusive and democratic when people govern their lives, secure in the knowledge that the identities they adopt, are respected and acknowledged by their fellows. This is only possible when we look beyond both nationalism and the state.

4

Gender and Violence

Are women citizens in modern liberal states? Although women have been citizens in a formal sense in Britain, for example, since 1928 (when they received the vote without condition) there are important senses in which women have yet to obtain real citizenship in the way we want to define it here.

The question of the state is crucial to the question of women and citizenship because the state enshrines a public/private divide; a patriarchal division between men and women and a gender inequality which means that women in particular (and people in general) can never be citizens as long as states exist. A feminist view of citizenship requires a view of citizenship outside or beyond the state, so that only if we can meaningfully chart a path to a stateless society, can we speak of women as citizens.

The State as a Barrier to Citizenship

Lister comments that 'at its lowest common denominator' we are talking about the relationship 'between individuals and the state' (1997a: 3). Voet likewise takes it for granted that citizenship is tied to the state (1998: 9). Lister makes many admirable points in favour of women as citizens, and what is particularly impressive is the way in which she defends a notion of 'differentiated universalism' so that she (rightly) rejects the 'choice' between rights and responsibilities, care and justice, the individual and the community: she seeks instead to synthesize these binary divides around the notion of human agency (Lister, 1997b). Despite the excellence of much of Lister's analysis, there are serious problems with any view linking the state to citizenship.

Virginia Held argues that the notion that the state has a monopoly on the legitimate use of force is incompatible with a feminist view as to how society should be organized (1993: 221). Hutchings speaks of feminism's grasp of the complexity and plurality of political identity within states, and Jones sees the nation state 'as an out-moded political form' (1990: 789) and speaks of the need for a women-friendly polity. Dickenson is not surprised that women have appealed to alternative models of association (1997: 107). But what is the relationship between a feminist polity and the state?

It is one thing to speak of the inadequacies of the position of women in liberal states: quite another to postulate the need for a post-statal polity – a citizenship beyond the state. The question of the state needs to be addressed explicitly. Sylvester comments that 'citzensandstates' conflate into one gendered entity (2002: 249). It is not enough to speak, as Held does, of limiting drastically the influence of the state and market (1993: 224). There has to be a plausible way of looking beyond both institutions, so that an emancipated society becomes possible. Women, even in developed liberal societies like Britain, are significantly under-represented in decision-making, and this occurs because of structural and attitudinal factors. Arguably, the state and statist institutions and values constitute the major barrier, such that the exclusion of women from political processes has been justified by a naturalistically conceived public/private divide. It is not coherent to drastically limit the influence of an institution that claims a monopoly of legitimate force for a society as a whole. After all, a monopoly is a monopoly whether it is limited or not!

It is true that with Wollstonecraft's *Vindication of the Rights of Woman* (1792), the Enlightenment concepts of freedom and autonomy are extended to women. At the same time Wollstonecraft does not (explicitly at any rate) challenge the division of labour between the sexes or a male-only franchise. Women, she contends, if they are recognized as rational and autonomous beings, become better wives, mothers and domestic workers as a result: 'in a word, better citizens' (Coole, 1988: 107–10; Gatens, 1991: 117–24; Bryson, 1992: 22–7). Here the term does not imply someone with voting rights, although it does suggest that the citizen is an individual whose activity is both public and private in character.

The problem with women as citizens arises not with the concept of democracy or citizenship, but with the way in which the emancipatory potential of these concepts and institutions have, since antiquity, been compromised in practice by gender inequalities. Such inequalities are linked to the problem of violence and state patriarchy. Feminism has revolutionized political theory by extending the notion of power and politics into so-called private realms. The public/private divide requires a new formulation. It will be argued that the divide needs to become a recognition and celebration of difference, so that what has been a barrier to citizenship, becomes a concept that contributes to emancipation. Male domination undermines not only the citizenship of women, but works against a meaningful and coherent concept of citizenship for men as well.

The question of violence is crucial here. Feminist theory is right to problematize violence by extending the liberal antipathy to violence into the arena of what is sometimes called 'intimate citizenship'. Violence, it has been argued, undermines relationships and makes citizenship impossible. This is not to say that women, like society in general, may not resort to violence as a defensive measure (e.g., the apprehension and punishment of rapists). But it is to argue that violence, nevertheless, remains antirelational in character and a case will be made for suggesting that violence is not natural, but tied – in its institutional forms – to patriarchy and statism.

Violence constitutes a barrier to a democratic notion of citizenship. As has already been argued in Chapter 1, violence needs to be distinguished from coercion and constraint; concepts involving pressures (whether negative or positive) on people to do things that they otherwise would not do. Coercion and constraint, strictly defined, are part of relationships, since it is impossible to relate to others without sanctions and pressures of some kind being involved. But when violence is invoked, people cannot be said to be free or autonomous.

The Public/Private Divide and the Marginalization of Women

Bryson has noted that women find it more difficult to have their voices heard, their priorities acknowledged and their interests met (1994: 16; see also, Freedman, 2001: 26). A recent report documents in detail the underrepresentation of women in all major sectors of decision-making, from parliament, the civil service, the judiciary, the legal profession, the police, local government, health, higher education, the media, public appointments and the corporate sector. For example, the UK is the fourth lowest in terms of the representation of women in the European Parliament at 24.1 per cent in 2000; it does better in a relative sense (in 1997) in terms of representation in national parliaments where it has 18 compared to Denmark's 33 per cent. Only 4.3 per cent of life peers in the House of Lords were women in 2000, while in the most senior grades of the civil service, 17.2 per cent were women in 1999. Nine per cent of the High Court Judges in 1999 were women, although this is three times as many as women who were Lord Justices. There were 6.4 per cent of Chief Constables who were women in 2000; ten years previously there were none (Ross, 2000).

It is true, as Voet has argued, that the representation of women is complex and it does not follow that female representatives automatically and necessarily represent the interests of women in general. But there is clearly something wrong, as Voet acknowledges, with political institutions that dramatically under-represent women (1998: 106–8). Citizenship requires both the right and the capacity to participate in political decision-making, an alternation of being ruler, on the one hand, and being ruled, on the other (Oliver and Heater, 1994: 116). The real difficulty of women's citizenship is 'the low level of female participation in social and political decision-making' (Voet, 1998: 124, 132).

The public/private divide, as formulated in liberal theory, prevents women from becoming citizens. It undermines the confidence of women; prejudices men (and some women) against them; puts pressures on leisure time; trivializes and demonizes those women who enter public life, and through a host of discriminatory practices, which range from the crudely explicit to the subtly implicit, prevent women from taking leadership roles. Female members of the British Parliament still complain that their dress or physical appearance is commented upon in the media, although it would be unthinkable to do the same for men.

It is true that the public/private divide, operating as a barrier to citizenship, is only implicit in liberal societies today. Whereas ancient (by which is meant slave-owning) societies and medieval societies explicitly divided the activities between men and women, under liberalism the public/private divide focuses on the relationship between individuals and the state.

Yuval-Davis has argued that we should abandon the public/private distinction altogether – a position Voet rightly challenges (1998: 141). Not only is the boundary between the public and the private itself established through a political act, but the public can be seen as identical to the political (Yuval-Davis, 1997a: 13). The term *political* is interchangeable with the term *citizen*; therefore, Lister's argument that citizenship excludes the politics of the personal or intimate sphere can be disputed (Lister, 1997a: 28). Where the intimate sphere generates conflict, any outcome is both political and linked to citizenship. If women are dominated or humiliated by men (or their partners) in the bedroom, this surely has an effect on their capacity to participate in more conventionally defined public arenas.

What is private are situations in which conflict is so implicit as to be imperceptible, and since conflict arises through difference, that means that what is private is momentary and fairly rare! Of course it does not follow that conflicts in the political or public sphere necessarily require punishment to sort them out. As noted above, a distinction between violence, coercion and constraint alerts us to the existence of what J.S. Mill called natural penalties (Mill, 1974: 144). Only when spontaneous social pressures are insufficient, do we require something more specific and concentrated to resolve the difficulty, but even here, this may involve merely moral judgements (i.e., coercion) rather than the use of force.

It is both possible and necessary to reconstruct the concept of the public and the private so that it ceases to be patriarchal in character. Liberal theory sees freedom, in Crick's words, as 'the privacy of private men from public action' (1982: 18). As Crick's comment (and his revealing use of language) suggests, this is a freedom that extends only to males, since (as MacKinnon puts it) 'men's realm of private freedom is women's realm of collective subordination' (1989: 168). Citizenship requires participation in public arenas. Domestic arrangements are crucial that allow women to be both child-bearers (should they wish to), and workers outside the home, representatives at local, national and international level, and leaders in bodies outside of the domestic sphere. This is not to say that women (like people in general) should not cherish privacy, but the public/private concept needs to be reconstructed (as we have suggested above), so that it empowers rather than degrades and diminishes women. The idea, put forward by MacKinnon, that the interest of women lies in the elimination of the distinction itself (1989: 120–1) is problematic, since the individual can only develop if there is both private and public space, and individuals who neither harm others nor harm themselves should be spared deliberate interference.

Indeed, patriarchy has never acknowledged the privacy of women, from the titles patriarchs use, to the status of women as the property of men. It is crucial, therefore, to preserve a public/private divide, but in a post-liberal and empowering way (Faulks, 2000: 125; Sperling, 2001: 184). Women cannot be citizens unless they are treated as equal to men, and by equality I mean not sameness but an acknowledgement (indeed a celebration) of difference, not only between women and men but among women themselves.

For this reason, it is worth making a distinction between difference and division. Differences generate conflicts that can be resolved without violence – through negotiation, compromise and conciliation. It is wrong, as Isin and Wood do, to conflate conflict with division (1999: 18), for divisions (unlike differences) imply the kind of conflicts that provoke violence and therefore can only really be suppressed, not resolved. In this terminology, the public/private divide should be renamed the public/private difference, since conflicts can and increasingly should, be dealt with in a non-violent manner.

Citizenship and the Problem of Force

Citizenship, then, is in tension with the exercise of force. A citizen, who either uses or is the victim of force, should be regarded as a contradiction in terms. In today's world, citizenship is invoked in the context of support for democracy. It has become increasingly controversial to exclude native or 'naturalized' adults born in a particular country from the formal entitlement of citizenship, although in countries like Kuwait in the Middle East, women are still prevented from exercising the right to vote.

But even when all adults are deemed to be members of a democratic state, citizenship is still problematic in character. Force is gendered, not simply because it is normally inflicted by men, but because it represents a patriarchal and statist view of conflict. Whereas MacKinnon implies that force is somehow inherent in the behaviour of males *per se*, Lerner offers powerful evidence for suggesting that force as a method of settling conflicts of interest arises with the development of the state. The domination of women by men, she argues, is inherent in the repressive hierarchies that express themselves in rape, concubinage, (patriarchal) marriage, and outright slavery (Hoffman, 2001: 78).

The involvement of women in contemporary liberal societies as members of the armed and police forces is a necessary but not sufficient condition for women's citizenship. It is necessary because it helps to demystify the naturalistic argument that only men can bear arms and fight for their country. It is not sufficient, however, because the use of force (whether by women or men) acts as a barrier to the emergence of an inclusive and coherent citizenship.

Force undermines both the freedom of the recipient and of the administrator of this force so that, in Rousseau's words, 'those who think themselves the masters of others are indeed greater slaves than they' (1968: 49). Faulks is right to emphasize the mutuality involved in oppression (2000: 94), for the point here is that even perpetrators of force harm themselves. This is not simply the observation, depressingly confirmed when murder cases are examined, that today's brutalizer is yesterday's brutalized. It also involves the argument that aggressive people themselves suffer from stress and psychological turmoil, even if we should never fail to distinguish between those who inflict violence and those who are the hapless recipients. Violence is a mutual malaise in which even those who appear to be victors suffer as a consequence of their actions.

The fact that violence adversely affects both parties does not mean, however, that there is never a case for retaliatory violence. Force may be (provisionally) necessary in order to create a breathing space for policies that cement common interests of the kind which make post-statist methods of conflict resolution effective. But the conceptual point remains valid nevertheless: as long as force is used, it works against freedom, democracy and citizenship.

Gender, Coercion and Force

Force has a gendered character and it reflects the institutions of male domination. This analysis can only be sustained if, as was argued in Chapter 1, we make a distinction between force and coercion (and constraint). Otherwise the problem of domination appears non-historical and the result leads to pessimism. Indeed, the reason why MacKinnon is unable to provide an historical explanation for the rise of patriarchy, is that she identifies politics with power in a way that merges state and government, violence and coercion. The point about Dahl's definition of the political system that she uncritically cites (MacKinnon, 1989: 161), is that it equates politics with 'power, rule and authority' as though it is impossible to resolve conflict without a repressive hierarchy of some kind.

Not only does a failure to distinguish between coercion and force make a stateless society impossible to seriously consider, but a sophisticated analysis of patriarchy – a barrier to citizenship – cannot be made.

For Lerner, it is important to distinguish between force and constraint – or coercion and constraint. Constraint can take the form of a natural necessity or the form of explicit social pressures and it arises simply because we are social beings who are part of, and creatively relate to, the world of nature. Every relationship – whether it is parent and child; teacher and pupil; doctor and patient, etc. – involves coercion and constraint. Anyone who cycles on a windy day is conscious of doing things that they would not otherwise do. These constraints and coercive pressures, whether they are social or natural, need to be rigorously distinguished from force.

Lerner argues that in the earliest societies of which we have knowledge, women bore and reared children while men hunted and became warriors. 'Necessity' she argues, created this first division of (or more strictly speaking, differentiation of) labour. The survival of at least two children into adulthood for each coupling required many pregnancies for every woman. Most nubile women would devote most of their adult life to pregnancy, child bearing and rearing. This necessity created the illusion that the sexual division of labour arose from biological sex differences (Lerner, 1986: 41–2) so that the later exclusion of women from citizenship when states arose, appears natural. Connell has referred to the 'practical relevance' of biological differences between men and women, even though, as he rightly stresses, this 'practical relevance' is not the actual cause of the division of labour (Connell, 1987: 82–3, 139–40), which becomes the basis for a naturalistically conceived public/private divide.

The point is that the circumstances in which we find ourselves, are constraining or coercive because these circumstances compel people to do that which they otherwise would prefer not to do. The differentiation of labour in early societies explains why in statist societies it is (in the main) men who oppress women rather than women who oppress men. A distinction between coercion, constraint and force alerts us to the distinction between the *seeds* of patriarchy, which are undoubtedly sewn in these early societies and patriarchy itself as a system of force, which only develops with the state. The necessity arising out of our relationships with nature is clearly linked to the necessity arising out of our relationships with other humans. The link between natural necessity and social necessity explains why technological changes have important (and inevitable) social consequences.

In early societies, men and women occupy distinct 'roles' because they have to and these roles are enforced by social mores, which constrain people in particular ways. But the point is that this kind of circumstantial necessity, though crucial to the ideological justifications of later patriarchy, should not be confused with force itself. Liberalism will naturalize this necessity so that Hobbes, despite the apparently egalitarian character of his state of nature, can speak of men conquering women and making children submit to them 'by natural force' (Shanley and Pateman, 1991: 64). If we are to denaturalize force, we must denaturalize the state and patriarchy and this requires a sharp distinction between force, coercion and constraint. Patriarchy or male domination emerges as an historical development (not a natural fact) and it can only develop historically when men have the power and resources to control the lives of women. The differentiation between men and women is the product of circumstantial necessity or coercion and constraint, undoubtedly creating what might be called a 'latent' patriarchy. But the mere separation and differentiation of men and women (which reflects the particular circumstances of the time) is not itself evidence that patriarchy has arrived. Men and women can be coerced by their differences, natural and social, without having divided interests of the kind that requires force (and thus the state) to tackle them.

Van Creveld captures the development of this latent patriarchy when he comments that stateless tribal societies had no superiors 'except for men, elders and parents', but among the Nuer (of East Africa) community structures, women could count as men (1999: 2). There can be little doubt that patriarchal attitudes of this kind develop very early on, even though patriarchy as a system of male domination, requires the institutionalized force of the state.

Realism, Women and Global Citizenship

Feminist critics of realism in international relations (IR) regard realism as a 'patriarchal ideology' because it rests upon the assumption that violence between states is unavoidable. Women are seen as the 'other' which, along with a host of other 'others', are part of the chaos and 'madness' that states have to tackle if wars are to be won and a 'rational' balance of power secured (Runyan and Peterson, 1991: 69; Steans, 1998: 56).

Realism in IR roots itself in what might be described as a doubled-up public/private dualism (Youngs, 1999: 109). Not only does it accept that the state confines women to a private realm (so that they appear politically invisible as a consequence), but it reinforces this public/private divide by seeking to abstract itself from the state as a domestic actor in order to concentrate upon the state in its external role. Only in this way, realists argue, can the sovereign state retain its status as a no-nonsense, permanent, inevitable and uncontentious rational entity.

Not only is realism andocentric or male dominated, but theorists like Yuval-Davis are right to stress the gendered nature of nationalism (Yuval-Davis, 1997b). The nation is frequently projected as female and associated with virtue and sacrifice, while the state is seen as male. Raping women is regarded, as in former Yugoslavia, as a way of humiliating the nation. But we can only develop a gendered view of war, security, nationalism and of course, citizenship, when we challenge the view that violence is natural and ineradicable. For realists have an uncritical view of violence since they have an uncritical view of masculinity – admirably captured in the realist dictum that it is 'in the nature of man to enslave and dominate others' (Steans, 1998: 49).

Deeply embedded in traditionalist notions of citizenship, is the idea that only those who go to war for their country, can be citizens. Citizenship in its statist form, is tied to violence, both in the sense that the citizen has to be a practitioner of violence and in the sense that the citizen is defined by her or his membership of an institution that resorts to violence as a method of tackling conflicts of interest. But engendering war involves rather more than 'opening' up armies to women. It involves a recognition of the link between patriarchy and violence. Some writers, like French (1992), have spoken of patriarchy as a 'war against women' and there is no doubt that the 'private and localised violence' of everyday domination (Pettman, 1996: 94) underpin the rape and sexual violence that occurs in wars between states. Wars not only brutalize young children, devastate the environment and create disease, famine and the movements of refugees, but in all this they particularly affect women. It is estimated that some 75 per cent of the world's 18 million refugees are women and girls (Zalewski, 1995: 343).

War not only marginalizes women, but also highlights the contradictory attitude taken towards men. On the one hand, men are to be 'rational' individuals who suppress emotions; on the other, they are constructed as soldiers who are supposed to selflessly lay down their lives and care for their comrades. The Spartans in Ancient Greece encouraged homosexuality among men precisely for this reason. If masculinity is as natural and spontaneous as realists think, why is it necessary to create a war-like identity through protracted and intense military training (Enloe, 1993: 56; Zalewski, 1995: 352)?

It is not difficult to see that nationalism itself is premised upon a patriarchal view of the world (Hoffman, 2001: 121–2). The notion of security is being reconstructed by feminists and this reconstruction involves moving beyond the statist and violence-oriented language associated with traditional conceptualizations of the question. Tickner, who has done invaluable work on this issue, argues that a concept like security can only be feminized if we refuse to see it as a zero-sum game in which the security of one person or group can only be exercised at another's expense (1992: 54). Violence and domination devastates self-esteem, and self-esteem is crucial to security. Self-styled champions of order may in fact be the most avowed opponents of this reconstructed notion of security.

Citizenship requires security – not simply in the sense of protection against violence – but in the sense of having the confidence, the capacity and the skills to participate in decision-making. What Tickner calls a people-centred notion of security (1995: 192) identifies security as a concept that transcends state boundaries so that people feel at home in their locality, their nation and in the world at large. After all, insecurity is generated by the violence endemic in divisions between rich and poor, black and white, north and south and men and women, and these are global problems, which states aggravate rather than resolve.

Nothing is gained by inverting realism (and patriarchy) through an argument that women are naturally non-violent and inherently hostile to militarism and statist notions of citizenship. Women can be violent as well, and one way of challenging patriarchal stereotypes may be to demonstrate this in practice. Particular women in particular circumstances can favour war and the destruction of the despised 'other', and feminism can only be weakened by 'essentializing myths' (as Tickner rightly calls them, 1992: 59). These myths ascribe positively what patriarchal thought ascribes negatively to women. In fact, it is wrong to naturalize not only statist men – but also 'peace-loving' and 'nurturing' women.

The war in Afghanistan has demonstrated yet again what earlier wars have revealed – that there is a 'gender gap' of about 10–15 per cent when women and men are polled about war (see Enloe, 1993: 173). But this opposition to war arises not because women are 'naturally' peace-loving, but rather because, as the victims of violence, they are less inclined to see the use of force as a solution to social and political problems. Masculinity (or 'masculinism' if this term is clearer) is itself a cultural construct rather than a matter of hormones and this point is no less true of women who commit themselves to peace and non-violence.

Coercion, Constraint and Caring

The distinction between violence and coercion (and constraint) is particularly important in making the case for women as citizens in the inclusive sense in which we are using the term here. Because women traditionally have been confined to domestic and supposedly 'private' roles, there is a temptation to exclude them from the language of rights and a universalist discourse. We might (wrongly) wish to distinguish between obligations (that are tied to social pressures) and duties (that are linked to the state), but the point is that a concrete view of rights must link it to demands to give something in return. The idea that we have a 'choice' between rights or responsibilities misunderstands the relational character of rights themselves.

Hirshmann, for example, contrasts the 'rights model' to the 'responsibility model' (1992: 237) since she argues that the creative capacities of women develop in the context of 'non-consensual relations' (1992: 8). Granted, women are deemed by patriarchs to be incapable of rational consent, but this is because the notion of reason and consent is hopelessly abstract in liberal theory. It is true that women have traditionally experienced coercion and constraint far more directly than men, and domestic obligations underpin the coercive and constraining nature of social structures. But to argue, as Hirshmann does, that obligations are 'non-consensual' (1992: 294) because they are undoubtedly coercive, is to invert liberal theory. While Hirshmann argues (rightly) that the goal of feminist theory is not to replace 'a male-model rights orientation' with a 'female, care-centered notion of obligation' (1992: 306), this is precisely what happens if we identify obligations as non-consensual. Why should we assume that consent involves a disregard of (coercive and constraining) structures and circumstances?

It can and should be argued that the traditional caring role of many women brings an important dimension to citizenship itself. The notion that feminist conceptions of citizenship should be 'thick' (i.e., local and domestic) rather than 'thin' (i.e., public and universalist) rests upon a dichotomy that needs to be overcome. Bubeck has argued that feminists should mostly be interested in thick conceptions of citizenship (1995: 16), but 'thickness' here needs to incorporate 'thinness' if the argument is not simply to perpetuate one-sidedness.

This is why the debate between 'liberals' and 'republicans' is an unhelpful one for women (as it is for people in general), since both liberalism and republicanism presuppose that politics is a 'public' activity which rises above social life. Liberals may argue negatively toward individuals who leave public life to the politicians, while republicans stress the need to participate, but both premise their positions on a public/private divide that is patriarchal in essence. Bubeck (1995: 6) instances Conservative proposals in Britain to extend the notion of good citizenship to participation in voluntary care, protection schemes, or neighbourhood policing. These are useful ways of enriching citizen practices for both women and men. But what is problematic is a notion of political participation which ignores the social constraints which traditionally have favoured men and disadvantaged women.

The fact that the obligation to care for children and the elderly have fallen upon women as a domestic duty, does not make it non-political and private. Bubeck puts it well when she speaks of the existence of 'a general citizen's duty to care' (1995: 29) and, as she puts it later, 'the performance of this care needs to be seen as part of what it means, or it implies, to be a member of a political community' (1995: 31). When she says that such an idea 'perceives the state as having an enabling and supportive role', (1995: 32) it seems to us that Bubeck confuses the state with what we would call government. While the exercise of care is compatible with coercion and constraint, it is undermined by force – including the force of the state.

If care is to be transformed from what Bubeck calls a 'handicap' of women to a general requirement (1995: 34), then we need to reconstruct the notion of public control so that it differentiates between government and the state. Of course, the notion that people will become caring and that the provision of care is a duty of citizenship, may not be possible without a temporary use of force against those for whom such obligations are an anathema, but it is not difficult to see that forcing people to provide care is problematic.

Bubeck argues that care should seen be as much of an obligation as fighting in a war (1995: 35). But whereas fighting in a war implies a sharp and lethal division between friends and enemies, the provision of care seeks to heal such divisions, and convert division into difference. The one requires force to make it a reality: the other is undermined by the resort to violence. Care can contribute, as Bubeck rightly notes, to the correction of the worst effects of that possessive and competitive individualism, which along with atomism, have characterized modern capitalist democracies (1995: 36).

But this observation makes the tension between care and the state – care and the use of violence to tackle conflicts of interest – clear. The notion of 'conscription' into service, which could either exist alongside or be an alternative to the army, is an attractive one, but whereas military institutions stand as barriers to emancipation (however necessary they may be as temporary expedients), a caring service of some kind has an important role to play in developing a citizenship that combats patriarchy and recognizes the position of women.

Feminism and Liberalism

Eisenstein has argued that all feminism is liberal at root (1981: 4), but if feminism has a close relationship with liberalism, this relationship is also contradictory. What is sometimes called 'liberal feminism' only challenges liberalism implicitly, while other kinds of feminism, radical, standpoint, Marxist etc., challenge liberalism in a much more forthright manner.

However, strictly speaking, the notion of a 'liberal feminism' is problematic, because liberalism is itself a patriarchal doctrine that enshrines male domination within its abstractly conceived concept of the individual. Jones is right to stress the negative attitude of classical liberalism to the body. Female sexuality in particular is seen as a threat to the state – something to be cabined, cribbed and confined – whereas feminist theory underlines the importance of the citizen as an embodied subject (1990: 795). To assert the value of women – their rights as equals – we must challenge patriarchy and thus implicitly, at least, question the position of liberalism. References to Wollstonecraft and Mill as liberal feminists, overlook the fact that Wollstonecraft challenged the patriarchal dogmas of the Enlightenment associated particularly with Rousseau, and Mill questioned the subjection of women. Besides, it is worth remembering that Mill called himself a socialist (albeit a somewhat individualistic one) (Hoffman, 1988: 173).

The problem with much of the feminist writing on citizenship is that it inverts, rather than transcends, liberalism. Instead of reconstructing the public/private divide, the very notion is either overthrown – as in MacKinnon's work – or it is turned inside out. The same one-sidedness remains. Instead of moving beyond the dualistic divide between reason and emotions, some feminists emphasize the value of emotions as opposed to reason. What has historically been seen as disabling women is elevated into a source of strength.

Thus, maternalist visions of citizenship privilege the position of women as 'mothers', arguing that only in this way, can an effective challenge be mounted to the rights-based conceptions of liberal citizenship. Liberalism is identified as universalist and formal: maternalism, on the other hand, is seen as particularist and informal. As Squires points out, this is a dualistic position that presents liberal citizenship as a single, coherent entity to be accepted or rejected as a whole. She cites James' comment that there is much more continuity between liberal and feminist conceptions than is generally appreciated (2000: 40–1). It is not a question of choosing between an abstract liberal position and (a supposedly) concrete civic republican or maternalist one. The oppositional relation between liberalism and maternalism, as Squires points out, must be displaced by a focus on democratic participation in an expressly political sphere (2000: 42).

The 'maternalist' argument is an important one but it must be incorporated within a wider argument that transcends dualisms. Just as it is wrong to identify mothering as the be-all and end-all of citizenship, so it is wrong to see citizenship as too collective, inclusive and egalitarian to embrace the relation between mother (or parent) and child. Surely the way that children are reared is itself linked to citizenship, and the notion that parental relations are not political rests upon a non-developmental and abstract notion of equality and a statist view of the political process. It is true that children cannot be citizens, but an egalitarian upbringing is crucial preparation for citizenship. Here, as elsewhere, it is important that we do not simply invert liberalism.

This is why we cannot accept Pateman's argument that citizenship itself is a patriarchal category, although it is perfectly true that citizenship traditionally has been constructed in a masculinist image (Mouffe, 1992: 374). While it is correct to see the abstract individual as a patriarchal concept, individuality itself is not inherently patriarchal. Indeed, one could well object that liberalism is not 'individualistic' enough, since all kinds of individuals are either left out of consideration, or treated as though they were men.

But just as it is wrong to treat men abstractly, so it is wrong to treat women in an abstract fashion. As Mouffe points out, incorporating women as citizens requires more than arguing that women as women are different from men. Women are different not only from men; but also from one another (1992: 375; Hutchings, 1999: 126). Pateman essentializes the difference between women and men by implicitly treating each as homogenous categories. To say, however, as Mouffe does, that sexual difference is not a 'pertinent distinction' to a theory of citizenship (1992: 377) is to assume that because women are different from each other, they are not different from men. We must take care not to invert, as it were, the inversions, or we are back to liberalism!

It is not just a question of historic assumptions that have disadvantaged women and which themselves, as we have seen, are rooted in naturalistic prejudices developed in pre-statist times. It is also a question of biological differences remaining relevant to citizenship even if these biological differences cannot and should not be used as a justification for discrimination. The point is that the differences between men and women have been essentialized by patriarchs and radical feminists alike. But it does not follow that these differences cease to be 'pertinent'. We should not, in other words, throw the baby out with the bath-water. One-sided points need to be incorporated – not simply cast aside.

Abstraction, as the term is used here, involves not merely a conceptual distancing, but a denial of relevant differences – a repressive homogenizing. This is why abstraction is linked to violence, for violence arises when we either absolutize differences or insist that everybody has to be the same, i.e., like us. Mouffe argues against a gendered notion of citizenship on the grounds that a democratic citizenship embraces all individuals and not just women. Despite a claim to have moved beyond both liberalism and civic republicanism, liberal abstractions return through the back door. Mouffe claims that all forms of consensus are based on acts of exclusion – there cannot be a 'we' without a 'them' – and that it is quite impossible to create 'a fully inclusive community where antagonism, division and conflict will have disappeared' (1992: 379).

As much as a fully inclusive community cannot be realized as a static utopia beyond which no further progress is possible, a sharp distinction needs to be made between conflict, on the one hand, and antagonism and division, on the other. By running them altogether, Mouffe makes it clear that her political community is a state, thus ignoring the difference between settling conflicts of interest through negotiation and arbitration (what we have called politics or government) and tackling antagonistic or divided relationships where people cannot change places, resulting in violence. There is surely a significant difference between excluding people simply because they are not part of a particular relationship and excluding people through force from the membership of a community to which they belong.

In the first case, exclusion is part of human society and arises from difference: in the second case, exclusion is linked to statist divisions between insiders and outsiders and involves violence. We generally use the term 'exclusion' in the second sense, since the notion of an inclusive citizenship implies that everybody deserves recognition, respect and political rights. Mouffe unwittingly naturalizes violence by not distinguishing between difference and division (in our terminology), and demonstrates the link between abstract conceptions and an uncritical attitude towards force. The crucial question is whether exclusion is statist (i.e., linked to violence) or simply the kind of 'exclusion' that is inherent in a relationship (Baumeister, 2000: 51, 63).

Mouffe is certainly right to aim at constructing a feminist politics that avoids essentialism and allows for the articulation of all struggles against oppression (1992: 382). The definition of feminism as the struggle for women's effective equality is to the point. But as long as Mouffe's radical democracy is a state, then her rejection of essentialism (along with rationalism, universalism and humanism) rests upon an inversion of inversions.

Isin and Wood are right to take Mouffe to task for treating citizenship as a master political identity (1999: 12). Privileging identities – no matter how universal they seem to be – is a statist trait. To tackle liberalism, it is necessary to go beyond its abstractions, not reproduce them in a supposedly poststructuralist form.

SUMMARY

- A meaningful citizenship for women is only possible when we look beyond the state, since the state embodies male domination in its institutions.
- The public/private divide excludes women either implicitly or explicitly from involvement in politics; any case for an inclusive citizenship has to reconstruct the public/private distinction in a way that empowers women. The public/private divide is better reconstructed as a public/private difference, thus allowing space for the argument that the conflict it generates can and should be dealt with through negotiation rather than force.
- Patriarchy is best conceived as a system of force – part of the state – even though patriarchal distinctions arise in stateless societies where a division of labour naturalizes the different roles played by men and women.
- There has been a welcome upsurge of interest by feminists in international relations, and questions of war, nationalism and security have been examined through a 'gender lens'; a lens that has crucial implications for a world in which women can be citizens.
- The analysis of care needs to be handled in a way that recognizes, while seeking to transcend, the traditional position of women. Care relies upon coercion and constraint rather than force, and the more implicit this coercion and constraint, the better.
- Feminism is rooted in the liberal tradition, but at the same time necessarily challenges it. Liberalism ushers in the supremely important idea that people are all free and equal, but because it does so in an abstract fashion, liberalism leaves women out either directly or in ways that implicitly assume their subordination and invisibility. A polity in which women are citizens, cannot be a state, but must look beyond the divisions and antagonisms that have always numbered women among its victims.

Capitalism, Class and Social Rights

Capitalism, as a system, has a contradictory relationship to citizenship. On the one hand, capitalism has created a universal notion of citizenship because it legitimates and popularizes the notions of freedom and equality. On the other hand, it does so in an abstract – and therefore oppressive – way, so that an inclusive citizenship is only possible through policies and strategies that develop the process of overcoming capitalism.

Class is a barrier to a universal and inclusive citizenship. Class necessarily embodies inequality in practice, whereas citizenship must be rooted in the equal right of all to govern their own lives. Class needs to be identified in terms of an argument that ignores difference, so that class can be seen as an entity which mystifies reality. In this way, questions of gender and ethnicity, for example, are seen not as a factor outside of class, but as the concrete manifestation of class in practice.

I shall argue that Marx's critique of capitalism is much more positive than is often assumed. The notion of abstraction is crucial to Marx's whole critique of commodity production and the notion is contrasted with the concept of 'concentration'. I will argue that the centrality of the dialectic between abstraction and concentration survives the problem of a (narrowly conceived) labour theory of value, and that the process of concentration explains why a broad view of class incorporates the barriers to self-government.

The struggle for social rights must be seen as a struggle that makes inroads into the political economy of capitalism. Although the new liberals in general and Marshall in particular, conceived of social rights as an attainment compatible with capitalism, in fact there is a challenge here whose subversiveness should not be understated. Indeed, the rise of the New Right (in Britain and the USA in particular) represented a classically reactionary attempt to neutralize the social rights obtained during the period of consensus for welfarism and, although in practice, much of the welfare state remained intact in Britain during the Thatcher years, there can be no doubt that the intention was to 'roll back' inroads that had been incorporated into the logic of capitalism.

What has made the welfare state so vulnerable to the attack of the New Right is that it operates in a divisive and punitive way, diminishing the capacity of individuals to govern their own lives. A case will be made for simplifying and developing the provision of welfare through the introduction of a basic income for all citizens. There is without doubt a tension or conflict between capitalism and citizenship, but the transformation of capitalism should not be conceived as a dramatic and one-off revolution. On the contrary, under conditions of liberal democracy in which the mass of the population has obtained valuable civil, political and social rights, the process of deepening and broadening citizenship requires continuous inroads into the logic of capitalism so that the system is gradually and increasingly transformed.

The Element of Positivity in Marx's Critique

Marx appears to be bleakly negative towards the concept of citizenship. The rights of the citizen, he comments in an oft-cited passage, are simply the rights of the egoistic man, of 'men separated from other men and the community' (Marx and Engels, 1975b: 162). Not association, but separation; 'the liberty of man as an isolated monad'. Marx's language is not only sexist, but he seems to be saying that citizenship is simply the right to exploit others through the ownership of private property. Freedom and equality are seen as anti-social activities.

But the argument is not quite as negative as it sounds. Marx comments that it is not 'man as *citoyen* but man as *bourgeois* who is considered to be the *essential* and *true* man' (1975b: 164). The point about capitalism is that it apparently liberates the individual from particularity. It is true that Marx has moved away from his earlier position where he enthusiastically endorses the 'ever new philosophy of reason' and looks upon the state as the organism in which 'the individual citizen in obeying the laws of the state only obeys the natural laws of his own reason, of human reason' (Marx and Engels, 1975a: 202). But although he goes beyond this Rousseauian position, he retains his respect for the liberal argument.

In the summer of 1843, Marx became critical of what he calls the 'political state' (and which henceforth he will refer to simply as the state), arguing that in a 'true democracy', this political state will be annihilated (Marx and Engels, 1975b: 30). The 'political state' (as he still calls it) is a 'theological notion' (1975b: 119). The liberal state is 'an abstract state form' (1975b: 31). More will be said about the significance of this concept of abstraction in the next section. Politics is 'an illusory sovereignty' (Marx and Engels, 1975b: 154) – an abstract community as 'spiritual' in relation to civil society as heaven is to earth.

In *On the Jewish Question*, Marx develops his argument about the theological nature of the state, but still sees liberalism with its concept of 'political emancipation' as having made a significant contribution to political theory. It is easy to miss Marx's crucial comment that 'political emancipation is, of course, a big step forward' (1975b: 155). Political rights are important and as the 'of course' suggests, they are taken for granted. The point is, however, that they are not enough. 'Political man is abstract' and (and here Marx specifically alludes to Rousseau) 'the true man is recognised only in the shape of the *abstract citoyen*' (1975b: 157).

Marx is not rejecting classical liberal freedoms, but he points to their inadequacy and insufficiency. This point is underscored by Engels in 1845 when he comments that under capitalism, the 'principle of freedom is affirmed' and 'the oppressed will one day see that this principle is carried out' (1975b: 474). It is important to stress that for Marx, the notion of abstraction does not imply unreality, in the sense that the abstract state does not, for him, exist! On the contrary, when Marx refers to the modern state as 'spiritualistic' and as the 'appearance of the greatest freedom' (Marx and Engels, 1975c: 122, 116), this arises because the reality of the state is that it serves the interests of capital and is based upon an 'emancipated slavery'. As he and Engels put it in *The German Ideology*, the state is an an 'illusory community' because the common interests that it asserts are divorced from the real and common interests which take a class character (Marx and Engels, 1976: 46).

The *Communist Manifesto* cannot be understood unless the positive aspects Marx ascribes to capitalism are emphasized. Indeed, there is a veritable hymn of praise to a system that not only demolishes the hierarchies of feudalism, but has been the first to show what human activity can achieve. Capitalism is a dynamic system compelling humans to face with sober senses their real conditions of life and their relations with humankind (Marx and Engels, 1967: 83). Part Three of the *Manifesto* identifies a whole school of socialists whose position is seen as *reactionary* because these socialists shun bourgeois ethics and practices. The establishment of the 'modern representative State' (1967: 82) is a crucial historical achievement, since the state cannot be said (however misleading this assumption is) to be representative of the community unless liberalism and capitalism have established the notion of individuals as free and equal. The celebrated description of communism as 'an association in which free development of each is the condition for the free development of all' (1967: 105) demonstrates how indebted Marx and Engels are to the liberal tradition and the 'most revolutionary part' played by the bourgeoisie.

The Dialectic of Abstraction and Concentration in Marx's Theory

The notion of the citizen bequeathed by liberalism is, for Marx, valuable but abstract. An understanding of abstraction is crucial in *Capital* because it is here that Marx argues that the 'form of abstraction' is necessary to understand the 'commodity-form' or 'value-form' of the product of labour (1970: 8). For products to exchange and take the form of commodities, the labour that creates them has to be stripped of its specific qualities and rendered 'abstract'. This process of abstraction is essential if products as far removed from one another as boot polish and crystal palaces are to be exchanged.

The point is that this process of abstraction is perfectly real, since what makes a product a commodity is that it is the embodiment of human labour in the abstract. 'The value of commodities', Marx argues, 'is the very opposite of the coarse materiality of their substance, not an atom of matter enters into its composition' (1970: 47). The process of abstraction mystifies the whole character of commodity production, since when producers exchange, a definite social relation assumes 'the fantastic form of a relation between things' (1970: 72).

This is not just an economic question for Marx: it has profound philosophical and political implications as well. The exchange process conceals the relationships involved in the production of commodities: it appears that only 'things' exchange. Those exchanging commodities are apparently free individuals acting according to their 'wills', so that these individuals naturally view the world through the prism of liberal illusions: a world, as Marx puts it, in which 'there alone rule Freedom, Equality, Property and Bentham' (1970: 176). Commodities themselves are abstract and so are the persons who produce them. The price mechanism, as Jordan notes, acts as a cloak that smothers all the tragedies and triumphs, unlucky losses or lucky gains of those entering the market place (1985: 167). Turner makes the point that measures of national prosperity assume that all activities are equal so that it does not matter whether the services are linked to prisons or to welfare (2002: 126). This concept of abstraction makes it possible to explain why Locke and the classical liberals of the seventeenth and eighteenth centuries could imagine that individuals existed in splendid isolation from one another in a state of nature, while continuing to trade as market partners.

It seems that Marx's analysis can still be used as a critique of liberalism even though the notion of labour as the source of value is contentious. Feminists have rightly argued that reproduction as well as production (in the narrow sense) is surely crucial for the worth of communities, and there is no reason why we should not substitute the broader concept of activity for the concept of labour. It is clear that how we evaluate goods depends upon the activities of numerous people – managers, workers, supervisors, consumers, entrepreneurs etc. – and that the insistence that only the 'worker' produces value reflects a narrow view of agency, which expresses itself in Marx and Engels' analysis of revolution and class war. These are views which actually make an inclusive notion of citizenship more, rather than less, difficult.

The notion of abstraction is complemented in Marx by the concept of concentration. Concentration involves the linkages and relationships that abstraction mystifies and conceals, so that in Marx's argument, whereas abstraction suggests atomistic equality and apparent differentiation, concentration emphasizes a relationship of power and (where relevant) domination. This is why Marx argues that abstract individuals express themselves concretely as classes. These classes have radically conflicting interests, but even here it is important to stress that as far as Marx is concerned, the exploited labourer must be free in the sense that he or she can dispose of their labour power as their own commodity and they are free of having any other commodity for sale (1970: 169). Here is Marx's point about the 'emancipated slave'; unless the worker is free, in this somewhat abstract and ironic sense, he or she cannot be exploited.

For Marx, individuals concentrate their activities in the form of definite relationships. These relationships, in an exploitative society, involve membership of a class. Despite the abstraction of equality, individuals have radically conflicting interests, so that the state is necessary as 'the concentrated and organised force of society' (1970: 751). Marx's point is a good one. Because interests radically conflict force is necessary to try and resolve them. This is the link between class and the state, and both act as barriers to an inclusive citizenship. The notion of concentration suggests that individuals have definite interests, which they organize around their particular relationships. In a well-known comment, Marx argues that in class divided societies, social relations are not 'relations between individual and individual, but between worker and capitalist, between farmer and landlord, etc. Wipe out these relations and you annihilate all society' (Marx and Engels, 1975c: 77).

The problem with this comment is that it is not concrete enough. For workers also have a gender and a national identity etc., and this materially affects how they relate to others. It is not that the class identity is unimportant: it is merely that it fuses with other identities since these other identities are also a crucial part of the organizing and concentrating process. Thus we are told (*Independent*, 8 May 2003) that whereas 4.5 per cent of white British men (age 16–74) are unemployed, this figures rises to 9.1 per cent for Pakistani men, 10.2 per cent for Bangladeshis and 10.4 per cent for black men. There are not simply two sets of figures here (black men *and* unemployment): rather it is that unemployment expresses itself more severely with blacks and is integral to the discrimination from which blacks suffer.

Not only do workers differ, but nor are capitalists the same. Some, for instance, are concerned with their reputation as 'ethical' employers and attempt to make the private sector more socially responsible, injecting a particular form into the concentrating process. We must, in other words, distinguish between 'socially responsible' corporations and those committed to 'free enterprise' pure and simple.

Marx, it seems, is in danger of stressing structural formation at the expense of agency. Take the well-known assertion that the capitalist and landlord are 'the personifications of economic categories, embodiments of particular class interests and class relations' so that his or her standpoint can 'less than any other' make the individual 'responsible for relations whose creature he socially remains, however much he may subjectively raise himself above them' (1970: 10). How do we square this comment with the statement that a recognition of the existing state of things is also a recognition of the negation of that state, of its inevitable breaking up? Marx argues that every historically developed social form is 'in fluid movement' – it has a transient nature (1970: 20). In the third volume of *Capital*, Marx refers to capitalism as a 'self dissolving contradiction' (1966: 437) in which each step forward is also a step beyond.

This implies that the concentrating process is one of constant change, so that the responsibility of individuals is no less important than the structures of which they are part. If the dialectic is 'in its essence' 'critical and revolutionary', then clearly capitalists as well as workers change. It follows from this that we should not impose upon capitalism the insistence that it can only be changed through revolution that occurs as a single and spectacular event. The struggle by women to achieve respect and autonomy; the demands by blacks that they should be treated as people and not as a despised racial category, etc., is as much a blow against abstraction as traditional trade union demands for a fairer share of profits. For each time a challenge is successful, the concrete human identities of supposedly abstract individuals is affirmed, and with this challenge, the propensity of the market to deal with real people as abstractions is overcome.

Marx acknowledged the problem in two important comments. He writes to Henry Hyndman in 1880 that a revolution in Britain is not necessary but merely possible, arguing that if 'the unavoidable evolution' turns into a revolution, that would not only be the fault of the ruling classes but also of the working class. Every peaceful concession has been wrung out through pressure, and the workers must wield their power and use their liberties, 'both of which they possess legally' (Marx and Engels, 1975d: 314). The other comment, also made in the context of Britain, refers to the passage of the Ten Hours bill in 1847. This, Marx told the members of the First International, was 'the first time that in broad daylight the political economy of the middle class succumbed to the political economy of the working class'. Here is the victory of a principle – social production controlled by social foresight – the recognition of 'standards entirely foreign to commodity production' (1970: 79). The Ten Hour Act demonstrated that the market could be regulated in the interests of people and that capitalism was changing. These reforms have a revolutionary (as well as a reformist) significance, and underpin the character of capitalism as 'a self-dissolving contradiction'.

The notion, therefore, that revolution has to be a specific event because capitalists and workers are essentialist entities who never change, is, it seems, in tension with Marx's emphasis upon 'unavoidable evolution' and the fluid and dynamic character of social relationships. The problem with classical Marxism is not that it is *too* dialectical, but rather that Marx is, on occasion, *insufficiently* dialectical. His dialectic of abstraction and concentration, as I have presented it, points to a process view of capitalism and citizenship that undermines dogmatic and rigid positions.

Citizenship and Social Rights

Capitalism establishes the formal freedom and equality of all members of society itself. Those who have no independent property cannot be content with legal and political equality but must press on for social equality as well. The Chartists were fond of saying that the vote is a knife and fork question: the demand for citizenship must be a demand for resources that make individuality not simply a condition to be protected, but a reality to be attained. J.S. Mill presents a developmental view of human nature when he argues that women and workers could become 'individuals'. T.H. Green and Hobhouse argue the case for more security for workers.

It goes without saying that the intention of the new liberal reformists (like Green and Hobhouse) is conservative in the sense that they hope that by giving workers more of a stake in society, the wolves of radical socialism will be kept from the door. But the point is that common social interests can only be generated by invoking standards 'foreign to commodity production', for there is no doubt that support for the trade unions, sanitary and health acts, unemployment and accident insurance make inroads into the logic of capitalism. Theorists like Lindsay and McIver, and Dewey and Barker support the case for a welfare state, and Dewey spoke (an early version of the third way!) of introducing social responsibility into the business system (Macpherson, 1977: 74).

Marshall's much cited essay on *Citizenship and Social Class* is a classic argument that civil and political rights do not on their own create a meaningful citizenship. Social rights are also crucial. Marshall demonstrates graphically that social rights make advances into the logic of capitalism. For Marshall, as Moore comments, 'taming market forces was an essential precondition for a just society' (Marshall and Bottomore, 1992: vi). Marshall is concerned, despite the inadequacies of his argument (which has been extensively commented upon), to try and give white male workers a human rather than a purely market identity. He cites with approval Alfred Marshall's notion of a 'gentleman' in contrast to a mere 'producing machine' (1992: 5), and Marshall uses the terms civilization and citizenship to denote people who are, he argues, 'full members of society' (1992: 6). As Marshall sees things, the right to property, like the right of free speech, is undermined for the poor by a lack of social rights (1992: 21).

Faulks makes the point that nothing Marshall says subverts the structures of capitalism (1998: 45). Certainly Marshall does not see himself as a critic of capitalism. His concern is to make a case for a basic human equality not inconsistent with the inequalities that distinguish the various economic levels in a capitalist society, even arguing that citizenship has become the architect of legitimate social inequality (1992: 6–7). But the point is that he does perceive citizenship as being in tension with capitalism. In a famous passage he sees capitalism and citizenship at war, although (as Bottomore tartly comments), Marshall does not develop this argument (1992: 18, 56). It is important not to overlook the extent to which his new liberal reformism unwittingly challenges the logic of capitalism.

Of course, Marshall believes that a pragmatic compromise between capitalism and citizenship is possible, even though he can argue that the attitude of mind, which inspired reforms like legal aid, grew out of a conception of equality that oversteps the narrow limits of a competitive market economy. Underlying the concept of social welfare is the conception of equal social worth and not merely equal natural rights (1992: 24). He notes – as part of his critique – early liberal arguments against universal male suffrage. The political rights of citizenship, unlike civil rights, are full of potential danger to the capitalist system, although those cautiously extending them did not realize how great the danger was (1992: 25). Citizenship has imposed modifications upon the capitalist class system on the grounds that the obligations of contract are being brushed aside by an appeal to the rights of citizenship (1992: 40–2). In place of the incentive to personal gain is the incentive of public duty – an incentive that corresponds to social rights. Marshall believes that both incentives can be served, that capitalism can be reconciled to citizenship since these paradoxes are inherent in our contemporary social system (1992: 43).

The preservation of economic inequalities has been made more difficult, Marshall concedes, by the expansion of the status of citizenship. I have referred elsewhere to the subversive abstractions of the liberal tradition (1988: Chapter 8), and what makes capitalism a self-dissolving contradiction is that it is premised upon standards which it is forced to deny. To concede that individuals are citizens is to invite them to challenge the social despotism and repressive hierarchies of a capitalist society. The great strength of Marshall's argument is that he depicts the drive for social equality as a process that has been taking place for some 250 years (1992: 7). Like all statists (even those who are much more critical of capitalism than Marshall is), he sees citizenship as an abstract ideal, but to the extent he speaks of it as a developing institution (1992: 18), he opens up the prospect of the need to continue progress, given the fact that he later concedes that at the end of the 1970s, the welfare state is now in a precarious and battered condition (1992: 71).

It is certainly true that Marshall ignores the position of women and ethnic minorities, that he ignores the sectarianism of Northern Ireland, and that he ignores the peculiar conditions that made a new liberal compromise seem plausible in the immediate post war period – to conservatives as well to many social democrats. These conditions were, as Bottomore has noted (Marshall and Bottomore, 1992: 58), exceptionally high rates of economic growth and the deterrent example of self styled 'real socialism'. Marshall treats capitalism in terms of the income of the rich, rather than the property they owned. The point is that Marshall demonstrates that a reformed capitalism is a capitalism in which victories in the political economy of the working class have proliferated, as is clear with the attack on social rights by the New Right.

Mann has argued that the key to understanding modern citizenship is the character of a particular ruling class, which seeks both to rule in the interests of the bourgeoisie (while minimizing the disruptive impact they make upon society), and to contain working-class demands (Faulks, 1999: 128). Mann's contention is directed against the inevitability implied in Marshall's argument that obtaining civil rights leads to political rights, which in turn generate social rights. Different types of ruling class manage the problem posed to capitalism by citizenship differently, and we need to distinguish between the constitutional tradition developed, for instance, in Britain and the USA (even though there are significant differences between them) and the absolutist tradition in states like Germany, Japan and Russia. In the case of Germany in the nineteenth century, civil rights were conceded but not meaningful political rights, and social rights were granted in a flagrantly paternalistic way (Faulks, 1999: 129).

The problem with this theory is that it depicts a capitalist ruling class (a combination, Mann tells us, of the dominant economic class and the political and military rulers) as an agent exercising 'choices' in a top-down fashion. Turner complains that Mann ignores the pressures from below of associations within civil society (Faulks, 1999: 130). It is as though trade unions were simply creations from above rather than awkward organizations that have made limited inroads into the logic of capitalist production. Turner concedes that 'citizenship' can be instituted from 'above' – as in the case of Germany – where there was minimum input by activists from below. Mann's Marxist framework, we are told, prevents him from assessing the importance of struggles from below (Faulks, 1999: 130).

Both Mann and Turner, however, misconceive the Marxist view of a ruling class. For Marx makes it clear in the *Communist Manifesto* that the executive of the modern state manages the *common* affairs of the *whole* bourgeoisie (1967: 82). The ruling class is a specific political formation with the role of representing dominant class interests in general, official terms and, therefore, it has to be sensitive to pressures from below in a way that may exasperate particular members (or pressure groups) of the dominant class (Hoffman, 1984: 28–9; 1986: 356–7). The struggle for citizenship is, therefore, supremely important (a) because it challenges the imperatives of capitalism, and (b) because it weakens the cohesion and coherence of a 'ruling class' through a stream of critical interventions. As citizenship advances and becomes more inclusive, so capitalism itself is transformed.

The way that Marshall ignores the position of women in his argument about social rights arises not because he privileges class, but because he has a very limited view of what is involved in the abstractions of the market. Turner expresses a widely held view when he argues that citizenship is not only about class and capitalism, but involves debates about the social rights of women, children, the elderly and even animals (1986: 11). We can agree with Turner without straying from a concern with class. Turner argues that class analysis has normally taken a 'reductive stance' towards questions of gender, ethnicity, age etc. (1986: 88). But in my view this 'reductive stance' arises because class itself is treated in an abstract fashion. Once we argue that class can only manifest itself *concretely* in experienced inequalities, whether these link to accent, region, gender, ethnicity or whatever, we can begin to tackle the 'reductive' treatment of class as an abstraction. In other words, a class analysis is one that puts real identities into abstract individuals so that we can see oppressed people as women, Catholics, workers, immigrants, etc.

The problem of capitalism is also the problem of abstraction. I have argued that the process of concentrating or concretizing people's interests does not simply cease with the subordination of white male workers. Others are victims of the market as well: women, blacks and immigrants (to take just three examples). Nevertheless, although we should criticize the inadequacies of Marshall's arguments there is no doubt that the quest for social rights created hostages to fortune, as the reaction to social rights (evident in Britain in the 1980s) made painfully clear.

Restoring the Standards of Commodity Production

The expansion of social rights, it has been frequently noted, was checked in the mid-1970s, as the capitalist market economy became dominant over the welfare state (Marshall and Bottomore, 1992: 73). New Right or neo-liberal thought seeks to defend individualism and the capitalist system against what it sees as menacing advances created by a post war consensus around reform. The New Right project, which lasts until the 1990s, is indirectly at any rate related to the image of a citizen as a successful entrepreneur who benefits from 'free' market forces.

The argument is that society itself is a dangerous abstraction – there are only individuals – but although neo-liberals appear to return to the classical liberal position, gone is the assumption that humans are free and equal individuals. Free, yes, but equal no! Individuals radically differ according to ability, effort and incentives and, therefore, it is a myth to imagine that they are in any sense equal. Policies favouring the poor and the needy are ruled out of court. Any attempt to implement distributive or social justice can only undermine the unfettered choices of the free market. 'Nothing', Hayek argues, 'is more damaging to the demand for equal treatment than to base it on so obviously untrue an assumption as that of the factual equality of all men' (1960: 86; see also Heater, 1999: 27). Equality before the law and material equality are in conflict, and Hayek, arguably, is in the curious philosophical position of arguing for an 'ideal' or 'moral' equality while denying that any basis for this equality exists in reality.

Both Hayek and Nozick, despite their differences in many theoretical respects (Faulks, 1998: 57), agree that intervention in the market in the name of social justice is anathema. Both link citizenship to inequality. It is true, as anarchist critics have pointed out (Hoffman, 1995: 117), that to allow a state at all, is to allow an institution that necessarily operates as a market-replacing activity. New Right thinkers, in trying to 'roll back the state', seek to confine it to its so-called negative activities – the protection of contracts – and refuse to allow it a wider (in my terminology) governmental role. Not surprisingly, New Right policies under Thatcher in Britain radically increased the role of the state (in its traditional law and order functions), since weakening the trade unions, cutting welfare benefits and utilizing high unemployment as a way of punishing the poor and the protesters, involves a radical concentration of state power. Both Thatcher and Hayek share an admiration for General Pinochet who demonstrated in Chile that enhancing the power of the market may be bad for democracy!

Gray speaks of Hayek 'purifying' classical liberalism of its errors of abstract individualism and rationalism (Faulks, 1998: 61). In fact, the New Right supports the weaknesses of classical liberalism without any of its conceptual strengths. Although both Hayek and Nozick speak of individuals having inalienable or natural rights, the argument is no longer coherent, for the notion of a right is a universal one so that the right to be unequal is, it seems, a contradiction in terms. For a right is an attribute equating two people (or groups) – it emphasizes what they have in common – and therefore, the denial of factual or material equality among individuals is in practice a denial of rights.

Faulks challenges the argument that the pressure against social rights takes the form of a reassertion of civil rights, since in practice, civil rights without social rights are hollow and extremely partial. What is the point of allowing freedom of speech without the provision of education, which develops linguistic capacity, or freedom under the law in a system that denies most of the population the resources to secure legal representation? The notion of freedom as power or capacity is seen by Hayek as 'ominous' and dangerous (1960: 16–17). Hayek supports what he sees as purely negative freedom, but the truth is that negative without positive freedom is an impossible abstraction and as a distinction is alien to the classical liberal tradition. Neo-liberals, as Faulks points out, appear to be championing a notion of market rights (1998: 42–3), but the problem is that 'right' is an egalitarian term. The notion of market rights is problematic, either because the market presents a form of equality that is abstract and mystified, or, under the influence of the New Right, this 'abstract individualism' is abandoned for an explicit argument that real equality is simply a myth.

Hayek even contends that since to be free can involve freedom to be miserable, to be free may mean freedom to starve (1960: 18). No wonder traditional conservatives like Ian Gilmour see these views as doctrinaire and utopian (1977: 117), and it is revealing that in *The Downing Street Years* Thatcher discusses socialism and 'High Toryism' in the same breath (Faulks, 1998: 79). Hayek, a major figure in her own intellectual development, sees freedom as not only the absence of coercion (defined as the deliberate act of an individual) but the absence of restraint and constraint (1960: 17). The notion of freedom for Hayek and the New Right, becomes explicitly anti-relational in character.

The New Right unwittingly demonstrates the indivisibility of rights. Hayek is far from enthusiastic about the exercise of political rights since the mass of the population might be tempted to use their political rights to secure the kind of capacities and power denied them by the free market. In practice, Hayek is an elitist and, as Faulks comments, his version of liberalism is difficult to distinguish from authoritarian conservatism. Conflict of a violent kind is simply increased by the creation of vast inequalities and insofar as modern America approximates to the neo-liberal view of citizenship, it is not surprising that this is a society that marginalizes its inner city areas and is afflicted by high rates of drug abuse and organized crime (Faulks, 1998: 71–2). In the fiscal year of 1982, some 20 per cent was cut from the Food Stamps and Aid for Families with Deprived Children Budget (AFDC) (Heater, 1999: 28). A Hobbesian Leviathan state, aggravated by the hysteria following the dreadful events of 11 September 2001, reveals the free market as a Hobbesian state of nature without the equality!

Thatcher argues, as Faulks has recalled, that many people fail in society because they are unworthy: 'With such a view, Thatcherism carried to its logical conclusion the abstract and elitist logic of the individualism in neo-liberal political theory' (1998: 86). Although the co-existence of the free market and strong state seems paradoxical, in fact, as Gilmour has commented, the establishment of a free market state is a 'dictatorial venture', which demands the submission of dissenting institutions and individuals (Faulks, 1998: 89; Gray, 1999: 26).

Citizenship and the 'Welfare State'

The New Right have protested that the welfare state suffocates the individual by denying initiative and difference. As De Jasay has complained, functions once performed by the people themselves are taken over by the state, so that with the welfare state comes 'an ant hill of bureaucracies, each acting in their own selfish interest' (1985: 210).

The new liberals stressed the need for a strong and positive state, initiating the tradition that the poor require help by benevolent functionaries acting on their behalf, from 'on-high'. It is clear from any analysis of new

liberal writings that patriarchy, class divisions, politic
a point about which Hobhouse feels particularly anxio
are taken for granted in their notion of community. Ce
Tory Disraeli makes it clear that 'elevating the conditic
meant upholding the Empire (Hoffman, 1995: 203).

As much as welfarism makes inroads into the pure
production (and thereby upsets the neo-liberals), it se
excesses of capitalism through intervention of an aul
Those dependent on welfare become, in Wolin's words, 'virtueless citizens',
whose presence is both a creation of and justification for, state power. The
old liberal assumption that people who fail are morally deficient is not
really transcended: it is merely that the welfare state provides a kind of
institutionalized charity for those who need it (Hoffman, 1995: 204).
Under neo-liberal influence, the welfare state has not been dismantled
so much as made more punitive, so that the statist components of the welfare state (i.e., the emphasis upon force) have increased. Gray comments
pithily that it may not be fanciful to hear, in these developments, an echo
of the Poor Law reforms of the 1830s (1999: 29).

This is why it is hardly surprising that welfare states carry many of
the abstractions of the market within their bureaucratic breast, not least,
the view that working outside the home is basically a male activity and
that women are domestic workers dependent for their resources upon
men. Citizenship for women is construed in terms of the (unpaid) care of
the elderly, the sick, the infirm and the young and, until recently in the
UK, women were excluded by the tax system and eligibility for
allowances from the welfare state's (masculinist) construct of an
autonomous citizen (Hoffman, 1995: 204). This is why some feminists
have referred to the welfare state as an institution of public patriarchy.

But the point is that capitalism is a contradictory system, in which the
welfare state is a complex amalgam of the governmental and the statist.
On the one hand, it is patriarchal, elitist and authoritarian, and it expresses
a strong cultural prejudice against the 'lesser' citizens who cannot 'pay their
own way'. This is why the Thatcherite attack on the welfare state is not
devoid of positive consequences, since it emphasizes (albeit in a partial
and mystified way) that individuals are important and should seek to
govern their own lives. The problem with neo-liberal individualism is that
it favours the haves over the have-nots, men over women, the conventional over the dissenting, the dominant over the subordinate. It divides
individuals and as a result individualism becomes a creed for favouring
some individuals over others. The real position of each individual is
masked by market-based abstraction.

But this is the fault not of individualism, but of abstraction, exploitation, division and arrogance. The point is that we cannot go back to a
situation in which, in the name of social rights, people are treated as 'second
class' citizens who need help from those who have succeeded. It has been
argued by neo-liberals that the welfare state is a version of the feudal

e, guarded by moats and barriers, and 'offering security and shelter the loyal population which gathers round it' (Novak, 1998: 9).

This is an exaggeration and even Novak in this sharp critique of the welfare state concedes that in the USA 'in countless ways, federal and state governments have helped virtually all citizens to find better lives' (1998: 7). Although he argues that the real question is not whether to have welfare programmes, but of what kind, his basic case rests upon a hymn of praise for free market capitalism, with the insistence that people should provide for their own pensions and medical expenses, and that what he calls 'universal family capitalism' is the way forward (1998: 22).

Yet, as argued above, the welfare state is a contradictory entity. To the extent that the resources are provided to the vulnerable and the needy (as a product of democratic pressures), the state is acting (in my terminology) *governmentally* – that is, it is empowering people. As Mill said, a government (although Mill did not differentiate government from the state) cannot have 'too much of the kind of activity' that aids and stimulates (1974: 187). A government cannot have too much power of the kind that helps people to help themselves. Faulks is surely right to argue that the problem with social rights as conceived by the new liberals is that they were seen as compensation, say for unemployment, rather than an intrinsic part of citizenship (2000: 116–17). The notorious distinction between 'active' and 'passive' citizens introduced during the Thatcher era, implies that we need to separate out those who are supposedly the beneficiaries of capitalism from those who lose out. It is argued, by right-wing critics, that the welfare state has undermined morality and the family; it has increased dependency and is devastating for the economy.

In fact, as the commentators on Novak's critique have argued, it is simply not true that the more developed welfare systems of Europe in comparison with the USA, have weakened economic growth (1998: 26, 38). Moreover, as Giddens points out, there is no clear correlation between welfare expenditure and the levels of divorce and children born out of wedlock, or the argument that the welfare state undermines the family and ignores the changing role and aspirations of women (1998: 26–7). On the contrary, Gray sees a correlation between unfettered markets and the rise of divorce, the destruction of the family and the incidence of crime (1999: 37). Not only does Novak emphatically assume that the state is still necessary to police society (1998: 14), but his schemes for private medical care, for example, would only 'work' for those with resources. What about those who lack access to material and non-material goods?

A common interest – which is essential for replacing state with government – can only be developed if social rights are integrated into political and civil rights. As long as social rights are seen as special entitlements for those who have been 'failed', they will always be divisive, and reaffirm rather than undermine class differences. In her assessment of the welfare state, Pateman makes the case for a guaranteed income for everyone

(Hoffman, 1995: 205), and the value of this proposal as a citizens' or basic income is that it would be universal. All would receive it, regardless of employment status. As Faulks points out, it would decommodify social rights and break with the argument that those who lack capital, must work for others.

A guaranteed basic income would give people a real choice as to how and in what way they wanted to work, and empower citizens as a whole. It would enable people to think much more about the 'quality of life' and the ecological consequences of material production. It would enhance a sense of community and individual autonomy, and underpin the social and communal character of wealth creation (Faulks, 2000: 120). It is not difficult to see how a basic income would also dramatically improve the standing of women whose precarious economic position makes them particularly dependent upon men or patriarchal-minded partners. It is true that were this idea taken in abstraction from other policies concerned with reducing inequality (as in the development of a democratic policy for ethnic minorities and movements towards genuinely universal education), then it could be divisive, tying women to domestic duties and leaving the capitalist labour contract unreformed. But as Faulks comments, 'no-one policy can address all possible inequalities' (2000: 120).

People seek to work outside the home for social reasons (and not simply economic ones), and a guaranteed income would give people time and resources to be more involved in community-enhancing activities such as life long learning, voluntary work and political participation. The argument that universal benefits undermine personal responsibility (Saunders, 1995: 92) seems to me wrong precisely since the assumption that people will only act sensibly if they are threatened with destitution and poverty reflects an elitist disregard for how people actually think.

But what of the cost? Surely a citizens' income is not economically feasible, given the argument that the rich will not tolerate paying higher levels of taxation. The idea of a guaranteed income appears to be a nonstarter. There are a number of counter-arguments to put. The first is that a guaranteed income would markedly simplify the difficult and complex tax and benefit system: significant savings could be made here. The widespread support for, say, the British National Health Service as a provider of universal benefits shows that increasing taxation is much more palatable if people are convinced that it is linked to changes that will really improve their lives.

Adair Turner lists some of the collective goods – subsidized public transport, traffic calming measures, noise abatement baffles and tree screens to make our motorways less intrusive – which he would prefer to (for example) a bigger and more stylish car: 'I would rather pay more tax to get those benefits than have the extra, personal income available to buy more market goods' (2002: 125). A third argument, which needs to be stressed, is that a guaranteed income is in the interests of all. Just as cholera in the nineteenth century did not concentrate itself only in the poor suburbs, so a basic income would (along with many other egalitarian measures) help to reduce crime and the consumption of drugs and make society as a whole a much more secure and safer place. Would not the rich benefit from such a measure? Capitalism's beneficiaries, Adair Turner argues, should support investment in measures that promote social cohesion, out of their own self interest (2002: 244). Gray argues that British public opinion wishes to see some goods – basic medical care, schooling, protection from crime – provided to all as a mark of citizenship (1999: 34). Is it not possible that given the right leadership and explanation, this could extend to the kind of economic security provided by a citizens' income?

Of course, the political right will protest that a basic income will destroy incentives, just as they argued that a minimum wage would create unemployment, and in the nineteenth century, their ancestors contended that a ten-hour day would undermine the labour process. But a government committed to such a dramatic victory of 'the political economy of the working class', could find ways of presenting the case for a guaranteed income, which would isolate die-hard reactionaries.

It is important to stress that while a basic income would do much to increase the quality of citizenship, it would still leave open the question of including people from other countries in a global citizenship. Such an innovation would initially be limited to people of a particular community (Faulks, 2000: 123). It would only really succeed if it was part and parcel of policies that addressed the problem of inequalities across societies.

The Transformation of Capitalism

One of the problems with Marxism and the classical concept of revolution as a single event, is that it poses the problem of transformation in modernist binary terms. Either we have capitalism or we have socialism. Yet it is both central to the dialectical logic of Marx's analysis and to some of his explicit statements, that capitalism can be gradually transformed so that increasingly, a society develops in which freedom and individuality become more and more meaningful.

Avineri sees a tension between what he calls Marx's eschatology and his dialectics (1970: 251): this problem becomes clear in Marx's divided attitude towards the Paris Commune – an event that he publicly extolled but privately thought was a desperate folly. This problem is symptomatic of a wider difficulty: the notion of revolution itself – and the categories (like ruling class) that imply a modernist division between one system and another. Dialectics and the notion of capitalism as a 'self-dissolving contradiction' suggest that, on the contrary, different logics can co-exist together. This point is crucial to establishing the argument that citizenship can only develop at the expense of capitalism.

Bryan Turner is entirely persuasive on this point. He argues that while capitalism promotes early notions of citizenship, it also generates massive inequalities that prevent the achievement of citizenship. He sees a conflict between the redistributive character of citizenship rights and the profit motive of the free market (1986: 38, 24). I think that he is wrong to assume that citizenship should be defined as membership of a state, and he takes a rather abstract view of class which means that he juxtaposes class to gender, ethnicity, etc., in a somewhat mechanistic fashion. Nevertheless, he is right to reject a critique of reformism, which sees the welfare state as functional to capitalism, and he stresses over and over again the contradictory character of capitalism and its fraught relationship with citizenship.

His approach to citizenship brings him close to what, in Chapter 8 will be called a momentum concept. Citizenship, he says, develops as a series of circles or waves (1986: 93). It is radical and socially disruptive, moving through a number of expanding processes, so that social membership becomes increasingly universalistic and open-ended. Citizenship exists, he puts it pithily, despite rather than because of capitalist growth (1986: 135, 141). The argument that citizenship requires a transformation of capitalism can be posed without being saddled with the case for a dramatic one-off revolution. It is an argument for dialectics, rather than (to echo Avineri's point) eschatology.

A number of 'issues papers' put out recently by the British Department for International Development make the point that the private sector can and must change. Indeed, the argument implies that to speak of capitalist companies simply as 'private' is itself problematic: the largest of these companies can – and need to – be pressurized further along a public road so that they operate according to social and ethical criteria. The reputation and image of companies with prominent interests abroad, are tarnished by adverse publicity around issues like the pollution of the environment, the use of child labour and support for regimes with poor human rights records. Companies should join organizations like the Ethical Training Initiative (DFID, 2002: 6). It is revealing that some companies are speaking of a corporate citizenship, which shows awareness that production and sales are social processes with political implications. The link between profit and support for ethically acceptable social practices demonstrates that capitalism can be transformed by a whole series of 'victories for the political economy of the working class' – an ongoing process which, arguably, is still in its relatively early stages.

There are no short cuts to the transformation of capitalism. Where the market cannot provide universal service 'autonomously' as it were, it needs to be regulated – and it is through regulation that capitalism is transformed. Adair Turner establishes this interventionist logic when he argues that where market liberalization (i.e., making people conform to capitalist norms) conflicts with desirable social objectives, 'we should not be afraid to make exceptions' (2002: 174). If citizens desire an efficient and integrated transport service, then this is an objective that must be governmentally provided, if the market cannot deliver. Perhaps the exceptions are rather more prolific than Adair Turner – an advocate of socially responsible capitalism – imagines, but it is only through demonstrating that the market cannot deliver, that it is possible to transcend the market. Adair Turner is right to argue that the demand for a cleaner environment, safer workplaces, safe food and the right to be treated with respect in the workplace whatever one's personal characteristics, are just as much 'consumer demands' as the desire for more washing machines, Internet usage, or more restaurant meals (2002: 187).

Where the market cannot deliver these kind of consumer demands, regulation is necessary. The need for public interventions is, Turner argues, increasing as well as changing. This intervention is more explicit in the provision of services that deliver equality of citizenship (2002: 238). Who can disagree with Turner's proposition that we cannot intervene too strongly against inequality in the labour market (2002: 240)? Indeed, for Turner, the key message of September 11 2001 is the primacy of politics – the need to offset the insecurities and inequalities which capitalism undoubtedly creates (2002: 383). Here, in a nutshell, is the case for transformation.

Transcending the market means that the objectives of the market – freedom of choice, efficiency in delivery – can only be met through regulation and controls. It is not a question of suppressing or rejecting the market but seeking to realize its objectives through invoking standards foreign to commodity production. Adair Turner argues that demands for public intervention are going to rise as our markets become freer (2002: 191); this surely is a freedom that points to the radical difference between suppressing the 'pure' market and going beyond it.

'Non-market' means, which Turner decries (2002: 267), are not the same as 'post market' means, i.e., the use of intervention to achieve market objectives in a way that the market itself cannot. This is not to suggest that we reject markets in principle: I am arguing that because markets abstract from differences, at some point they will need to be transcended – but only at the point at which it is clear that they cannot deliver the objectives that a society of citizens requires. Turner takes the view that the market economy has the potential to 'serve the full range of human aspirations' (2002: 290). I am sceptical about this claim, but if Turner is right, then the case for retaining market forces would be strong. But Turner himself acknowledges market failures (as he calls them) in transport policies where there is a bias in favour of mobility and combating environmental degradation (2002: 300).

SUMMARY

- Citizenship as an inclusive concept is incompatible with capitalism, even though it was under capitalism that the notion of the self-governing individual was raised as a central attribute of the liberal tradition.
- Marx did not reject liberalism but was critical of its abstract and mystified view of the world.
- I reject the notion of revolution as a single, dramatic event and I see a tension here between Marx's own notion of dialectics and his conception of revolution.
- The notion of class needs to be broadened so that class barriers are conceptualized as practices that treat individuals abstractly. Questions of gender, nationality, ethnicity etc., are actually concrete 'concentrated' manifestations of class, rather than factors to be placed alongside class.
- The transformation of capitalism is a process through which the logic of capitalism is increasingly eroded.
- If government is necessary to ensure that capitalism has a human face, then we will find that in humanizing capitalism, it becomes unrecognizable.

6

Participation

Citizenship has historically been linked to participation. Yet a decline in conventional political participation seems to be a powerful trend in developed liberal democracies. We will note how, in the post war period, an elitist or non-participatory view of democracy has been presented in the name of realism – a celebration of what has become a major problem in the contemporary liberal world. The market model is highly imperfect: the notion that people can only elect their rulers expresses a very limited view of peoples' political capacities.

But how to make a realistic case for more participation? Many radicals run the risk of simply inverting the 'realist' argument, but Macpherson suggests linking participation to 'people as they are'. People cannot consume effectively if they are faced by a deteriorating natural and social environment, if conditions at work are alienating and employment is increasingly insecure. They are compelled to become politically involved, which in the 1970s and 1980s took the form primarily of involvement in new social movements.

The problem with participatory democrats is that while they correctly avoid the problem of revolution, they ignore the state. Moreover, the question of participation must grapple with the problem of enhancing involvement in governmental mechanisms, local, regional, national and in the case of the European Union (EU) supra-national. There is a case for compulsory voting and improved voter registration, while the introduction of community service would enhance the notion of effective and active citizenship.

Communitarianism is a promising doctrine since it stresses the importance of participation. It is presented by Etzioni as a democratic theory that emphasizes the autonomy of the individual and the importance of critical thinking within the community. But an uncritical acceptance of the state undermines the emphasis placed by communitarians on a 'moral voice' and a relational view of the question of citizenship. Republicans like Petit seek to link freedom to non-domination and some of Petit's strictures on classical liberalism are well taken. The problem is that he also dismisses the argument by classical liberals that freedom is incompatible with force and accepts the necessity and legitimacy of the state. Whether the theory is one of republicanism or, as Dagger calls it, 'republican-liberalism', the problem of forcing people to be free – so memorably presented by Rousseau – remains unresolved.

Citizenship without Participation

The new liberals not only approve of the concept of democracy, but, in the case of Mill, for example, make a strong developmental argument for participation. A rather strident moral tone tends to shut out empirical realities and the notion of 'man', introduced in the liberal tradition, excludes large numbers of people – women, the poor, and those whose life style or beliefs are considered unconventional or threatening. The other-worldliness of the new liberals leaves them particularly vulnerable to attack, since (as I have commented elsewhere, 1988: 182), references to spiritual autonomy and human personality are shrouded in a cloud of windy rhetoric that tends in practice to refer to men of middle-class status.

During and after the Second World War a much tougher view of participation emerges. Schumpeter pioneers what Macpherson describes as a 'substantially accurate' description of political behaviour in liberal democracies in his 'equilibrium model' of liberal democracy (1977: 83). Schumpeter's argument is that participation, indeed democracy, is not intrinsically desirable and it may well be – Schumpeter instances the religious settlement under the military dictatorship of Napoleon I – that the wishes of the people are more fully realized when there is no democracy at all (1947: 242).

As far as Schumpeter is concerned, democracy is simply a 'political method' – an institutional arrangement for reaching political decisions. It is not an end in itself (1947: 242). It is possible, Schumpeter argues, for witches to be burnt at the stake, or Jews persecuted in perfectly democratic ways. Those who participate in one set of circumstances, might be debarred from doing so in another. All states discriminate against some section of the population (no national government allows children to vote, for example) and therefore discrimination in itself is not undemocratic. *We* may not approve of societies that discriminate against Jews or women, blacks or workers, but that, Schumpeter argues, is not the point. Given differences in culture and circumstances, every people must be allowed to decide who is entitled to participate (1947: 245).

Schumpeter's argument is startling in its iconoclasm, but how accurate is it? Schumpeter contends that people themselves do not govern.

Nor can they. The typical citizen yields to what Schumpeter calls 'dark urges' (1947: 262), so that it is only through a definitional sleight of hand that we can refer to 'popular rule'. It is not the people who rule – it is the politicians. The people only participate insofar as they elect those who rule them. Democracy is a system of elected and competing elites. The detailed studies of the 1950s suggested that for most citizens, political participation, in the words of Dahl's celebrated study of New Haven in Connecticut, USA, is a remote, alien and unrewarding activity 'better left to a small number of professional activists' (1961: 279). Democracy works best where citizens participate least: 'where the rational citizen seems to abdicate, nevertheless angels seem to tread' (Macpherson, 1977: 92).

This picture is only accurate if we assume, as positivists do, that the facts can be abstracted from relationships. The truth is that the elitist argument is an *interpretation* of the facts – and one that is seriously misleading. Consider the view that we have a market mechanism in which the citizens are consumers, and the politicians, entrepreneurs. It can only be said that political energies and political goods are optimally distributed if we assume a model of perfect competition. This is not only methodologically implausible (it assumes atomistic rather than relational individuals), but also ignores the facts. On the 'supply' side, there are only a few sellers (i.e., competing party leaderships) who can accordingly manipulate demand, particularly with a first-past-the-post electoral system. And on the 'demand' side, competition is equally unfair, since manifestly some citizens have more political resources – money, education, status – than others.

Participation is seen as undesirable. Schumpeter even complains that the electorate is incapable of any action other than a stampede and urges that a ban be placed upon the practice of bombarding members of parliament with letters and telegrams (1947: 283, 295). This extraordinarily limited view of citizenship has arisen from the fact that post-war liberals who follow the Schumpeter analysis believe that business leadership fully deserve their confidence and that liberal democracy requires no further reform. All that is necessary is to keep 'communism' at bay.

Moreover, the cold war 'equiliberals' (as, following Macpherson, we can call them) saw no threat from the political right. For all the ritualistic denunciations of right-wing as well as left-wing 'totalitarianism', it is not difficult to detect a new sympathy and understanding for authoritarian regimes of a conservative kind. Dahl, in a work that argued that in practice minorities, not majorities, rule, followed Schumpeter's view that the politically active themselves decide who is to enjoy legitimacy as participants in the political process. A system can be deemed democratic even if women have no vote, blacks are denied political rights and communists are shut out in the cold. As far as Dahl is concerned, apartheid South Africa is only 'possibly excepted' from inclusion as a 'polyarchy' (1956: 138, 74).

This very limited view of participation lasts until the mid-1960s when under the impact of the Vietnam War and a growing critique of behavioural political science, a more robust position on participation becomes evident.

The Radical Critique

A dilemma faces many of those who react angrily to the positivism and complacency of the 'equiliberals'. How to respond in a way that does not simply turn the elitist argument inside out?

Herbert Marcuse's *One Dimensional Man*, first published in 1964, is a case in point. It denounces the equilibrium model as a demonic success, depoliticizing the public so that they become mere pawns in the hands of bureaucrats and manipulators. This is still a problem (I would argue) with Ralph Miliband's *State in Capitalist Society* which first appeared in 1969: a more conventionally Marxist critique of democratic liberalism dedicated to the memory of C. Wright Mills.

Miliband argues that in the advanced capitalist regimes of the West, an economically dominant class exercises a decisive degree of political power, so that the mass of the population do not participate meaningfully at all. A combination of state bureaucrats sympathetic to capitalism from within and structural pressures from without, is able to neutralize any elected executive mandated to introduce radical change. To Macpherson's question 'Can liberal-democratic governments be made more participatory, and if so, how?' (1977: 94), there appears no answer.

The electors, the equiliberals insist, must be allowed a choice – even though Schumpeter and Dahl equivocate as to whether universal suffrage is necessary before this choice can be exercised 'democratically'. There must, Schumpeter argues, be 'free competition for a free vote' (1947: 271–2). By being able to choose between competing parties, otherwise passive voters can at least protect themselves against tyrannical rulers. But while, as Macpherson points out, no-one should belittle the argument for 'protection against tyranny' (1977: 91), this argument endorses a minimalist notion of citizenship and is hostile to popular participation in the political process.

Miliband makes it clear that 'bourgeois democratic regimes' (as he calls them) are characterized by political competition, the right of opposition, regular elections, representative assemblies, civil guarantees, etc. (1973: 21). An equality of rights masks an inequality of power. The liberal freedom to choose sharpens awareness of the gulf between rhetoric and reality, so that workers are compelled to organize, politicians to plan, and a 'minimal state' has to increasingly intervene to stabilize the economy and diffuse social tensions. Joseph Schumpeter, it should be remembered, was a reluctant socialist (Held, 1987: 169).

Macpherson's answer to the equiliberals is the development of a model of a 'participatory democracy'. By the 1960s the 'post-war miracle' has begun to wear a bit thin. Apathy, once prized as a source of stability and an expression of social consensus, is turning to alienation. Social and 'racial' tension; student protest and peace movements; a new concern for the environment; workers' control, and women's movements all signal the fact that, in Macpherson's view, the minimally participatory system is reaching 'near-crisis proportions' (1977: 106). But how is widespread participation possible in a world in which inequalities induce apathy and apathy perpetuates inequality? Macpherson locates three loopholes within this vicious apathy–inequality circle.

Let us begin, Macpherson argues, with people as they are in the equilibrium model – infinite consumers willing to let others rule on their behalf, provided nothing interferes with their (often rather modest) material comforts in the 'good society'. What can be done to erode the vicious circle of apathy and inequality? To consume infinitely, one needs a certain quality of life – a decent environment. Pollution, holes in the ozone layer, noise and other forms of ecological interference bring the consumer face to face with problems that cannot be resolved by private entrepreneurs and are likely to be ignored by competing political elites (1977: 102). This is the first loophole.

The second relates to the social environment – the problem of urban decay; the ravages of property developers, the ill-planned housing estates. All are arguably a product of a lack of meaningful participation from below. What about the problem of the workplace environment with its mind-numbing division of labour and conveyor-belt boredom? The democratization of the workplace has been explored by a number of writers as a crucial way of enhancing participation (Faulks, 1999: 160). This is Macpherson's second loophole.

Underpinning them is a third: the challenge to the consumer posed by high inflation coupled with job insecurity and a level of unemployment not seen since the 1930s. Each of these loopholes is intended to encourage apathetic consumers to become participatory democrats. The new social movements founded in the 1960s and 1970s reflect a suspicion of established parties and a concern for participation over single issues. They mobilize around the question of greater participation for the individual, whether we think of women, gays, the environment, animal welfare or the issue of peace.

There is no doubt that greater participation in movements like these is crucial for a more meaningful notion of citizenship, but the Macpherson argument and the model he elaborates, raise sharply the relationship between political participation and the state. Macpherson's Model Four of a participatory democracy involves a pyramidal system of elected councils with a warning that such a system cannot operate in a 'post-revolutionary situation' (1977: 107). I now think, although this was not my view in the past (1988: 196), that this is a legitimate point since revolutions polarize populations and destroy the kind of consensus necessary for an inclusive view of citizenship.

But the problem is that Macpherson appears to go along with other participatory democrats who define politics in a way that ignores the state. Leftwich's *Redefining Politics* is a case in point. Anxious to avoid the traditional view of politics as a state-centred activity, Leftwich seeks to broaden the notion of politics. Politics embraces all the activities that involve cooperation and conflict within and between societies (1983: 11). But not only does this create the problem as to whether anything can be non-political, it assumes that the state is of no importance at all. The laudable goal of increasing participation must take account of how the state may be overcome, because if one defines politics as the resolution (as opposed to the suppression) of conflicts of interest, then there is a sense in which the state is anti-political because of its use of force.

Increasing participation must take account of a process of deepening citizenship so that the state itself becomes redundant.

Increasing Participation

It is true that people are increasingly involved in single-issue movements, but participating in these is no substitute for involvement in local, national and, say, European elections. Being a citizen means being responsible for policies made in your name, and although voting is not in itself a sufficient expression of participation, it is certainly necessary. How can one be concerned with damage to the environment, for example, unless one is concerned with the problem of 'balancing' resources for the environment with resources for health and education, etc.?

Non-voting is an expression of atomistic individualism. It either embraces the argument that what is happening is basically satisfactory so that there is no need to get involved, or what is more likely, governmental activities seem remote, alien and irrelevant to the daily struggle to survive; therefore non-voting seems a legitimate expression of self-interest. In both cases, the notion of self-interest is atomistically conceived and we have what Dagger rightly calls 'a market-oriented view of the individual as consumer' (1997: 134).

Those who defend apathy on democratic elitist grounds have a negative view of the capacity of people to govern their own lives. The 'satisfaction' argument probably only applies to a small number of apathetic voters. The link between participation and socio-economic status overwhelmingly suggests that non-participation (in the form of non-voting) is borne of poverty, a lack of self-esteem and low education levels. The basic case against compulsory voting rests upon atomistic grounds: humans are isolated individuals who should not be told what to do – a position that denies the status of humans as relational beings.

The argument that the citizen has a right not to vote ignores the fact that rights are indissolubly linked to responsibilities and the act of non-voting harms the interests of society at large. It is true that some may feel that voting is a farce, but the defensible part of this objection – that the voter does not feel that existing parties offer real choice – can easily be met by allowing voters to put their cross on a box which states 'none of the above'. This would signal to politicians the extent to which people were voting negatively through protest.

It goes without saying that like the arguments for a citizens' income, the case for compulsory voting would not, taken simply on its own, create a more effective citizenship. It has to be accompanied by policies which address the inequalities that underlie the problem of cynicism and apathy. A lack of jobs, housing, adequate health care, physical and material security remain critical causes of despair and low self-esteem. There is plenty of evidence that mandatory voting raises participation levels and, as Faulks point out, when the Netherlands dropped compulsory voting in 1970, voting turnout fell by 10 per cent (2001: 24). Italy, Belgium and Australia still compel their citizens to vote. Compulsory voting signals the existence of a civic responsibility that all are duty bound to adopt. It would encourage people to take an interest in political affairs – become more literate and confident – and it could reduce the time and resources parties use to try and capture the public interest in trivial and sensational ways.

The real sanctions for non-compliance would be moral. Where moral coercion was insufficiently effective and therefore state measures were still necessary, the cost incurred in enforcing these measures could be met by fines imposed on defaulters. Compulsory voting could play an invaluable role in altering our political culture in a socially responsible direction. Faulks quotes Lijphart who rightly comments that compulsory voting is an extension of universal suffrage (2001: 25). It is worth reiterating that the real sanction against those who failed to vote, would be a feeling among their peers that they had acted anti-socially, not the fine levied for non-compliance.

A simple and comprehensive system of voter registration would also assist people to take responsibility for governing their own lives, and one can think of numerous devices to facilitate voting. The greater use of postal votes, the extension of time for voting and a more proportional system, would do much to overcome the cynicism that is often expressed at election times. Additionally, we would point to the use of referenda on important issues and the employment of citizens' juries. In this latter case, a number of citizens, statistically representative of the wider population, discuss particular issues in an intense and deliberative way, and make recommendations based upon questions to relevant experts (Faulks, 1999: 155, 159).

A number of writers have argued that the use of information technology could radically enhance the possibility for direct democracy since, as a result of email, the Internet, video conferencing, the digitization of data, two-way computer and television links through cable technology, citizens could remain at home and shape policies rather than rely upon representatives to do so. Clearly such a technology has tremendous potential to empower citizens and Faulks gives the example of how a citizens' action group used the communications network to raise $150,000 in Santa Monica in the USA for the local homeless (1999: 157).

But the real problem with what Dagger calls 'instant direct democracy' based upon sophisticated computer technology is that it is premised upon (and could intensify) the atomistic individualism that undermines citizenship. It could discourage active, public spirited citizenship and weaken the sense of belonging to wider communities and making a judgement as a result of listening to, and sharing ideas with, others. The electronic referendum could contribute to a vision that is, in Dagger's words, 'narrow, cramped and ultimately self-subverting' (1997: 144).

Some societies compel young people (often men) to serve in the armed forces: why not transform this idea into a compulsory community service that could involve working with the old, the disabled, improving the environment or a country's cultural facilities? A year's community service after school would be a good way of bridging the gap between youth and adulthood, and help to reinforce a sense of sociability and an awareness of how the individual owes his or her skills to the activities of others (Faulks, 2000: 115). Spragens (1998: 33) argues that something like a universal citizen service requirement would be morally justifiable and prudentially valuable.

Communitarians argue that public life should be revitalized so that the two-thirds of the citizens in the USA who appear to be too alienated to vote, will again be engaged (Etzioni, 1998: xxxii). The role of private money in public life needs to be reduced and a reduction of the ownership of arms by private individuals – a particular problem in the USA – would help to shift an emphasis towards arbitration and negotiation and away from force. This would lead to what has been described as 'responsible participation in effective communities' (Etzioni, 1998: 3).

Communitarianism and Participation

Communitarianism has become hugely influential as a doctrine concerned to increase participation and therefore deepen the notion of citizenship. As Bellah argues (democratic) communitarianism is committed to participation both as a duty and a right (1998: 18–19).

Dagger contends (1997: 47) that a political community is a cooperative enterprise and that fair play requires obligations to match rights (and benefits). It is impossible to disagree, but why does a political community have to take the form of a nation state, indeed of a state at all? Dagger feels that unless there is a general obligation to obey the laws of the state, then what he calls the reciprocity argument – the mutuality that characterizes all communities – is bound to fail. But the problem is that by definition, the state assumes that some will not obey at all (invariably characterized as an incomprehensibly and inexplicably awkward minority), while others will obey in the knowledge that force will be used against them if they do not. It would seem that there is a tension between the state itself and the reciprocity argument (1997: 48). Dagger does concede that bodies such as the modern state should not perhaps be considered communities at all (1997: 58), but this comment does not prevent him from taking the state for granted. The state, as Dagger sees it, is compatible with both citizenship and, despite his comment above, the community.

Sandel argues in his classic critique of liberalism, *Liberalism and the Limits of Justice* (1982), that a strong view of community is constitutive. In other words, the community constitutes the very identity of the individual. But, as Dagger (who cites Sandel) points out, this argument leaves communitarianism vulnerable to the objection that unless people are able to raise themselves above their situation in society, they cannot gain a critical distance from community norms. That is to say, the community must be open to internal or external criticism or both (1997: 52). This, in a nutshell, is the standard liberal objection to communitarianism – that the community might be authoritarian and oppressive. The situated self, as Sandel describes him or her, could be cramped and crippled: in other words, free and critical thinking is crucial within a community (Dagger, 1997: 53). This surely is a legitimate point. Traditional communities might discriminate against women and be hostile to gays: they may 'constitute' the individual in a crushing and demeaning way.

If communitarianism is to contribute to the concept of an inclusive citizenship, then it must find a way around this problem. What is a community? Etzioni, who is perhaps the best known of the popularizers of communitarianism, argues that we should see community as 'a set of attributes, not a concrete place' (1996: 6). He endorses the view that people are socially constituted, but is acutely conscious of the problem of a community that suffocates the individual. He complains that Sandel comes close to suggesting that community values must take precedence over the individual (1998: 219).

The communitarian paradigm, as Etzioni advances it, recognizes the need to nourish social attachments as part of the effort to maintain social order, while ensuring that such attachments will not suppress individual autonomy (1996: 27). A relationship must be forged between order and autonomy, so that like rights and responsibilities, they go hand in hand, acting as a corollary to one another (1996: 43). Thus, Etzioni argues, the more a community accepts the notion that the person has no element of autonomy, the less room there is for a moral order (1996: 138).

In Etzioni's view, communitarian societies are necessarily democracies. People must govern their own lives and the recognition of the constitutive role of community makes this democracy all the more effective. Communitarians maintain that the concept of shared values is pivotal for social thinking (1996: 91), but the problem of the classical liberal tradition and what Etzioni calls 'libertarianism' is that it uses the language of rights as a language of no compromise. The winner takes all and the loser has to get out of town (1996: 105).

It is important that the community should not be seen as monolithic or singular in character. A community can be defined by 'a web of affect-laden relationships among a group of individuals' (Etzioni, 1996: 127) and it necessarily involves a measure of commitment to a shared set of values, norms, meanings, shared history and identity – in short to a particular culture. People can, and increasingly do, have multi-community attachments (1996: 127–8). People are members of multiple, overlapping and interlaced communities. The more individuals are monopolized by any one group, the less communitarian a society will be (1996: 205, 208). Pluralism is a permanent feature of a diverse yet united society (1996: 197).

Etzioni's argument for the existence of a moral voice is particularly interesting. The moral voice must be nurtured and cherished, for this inner moral voice is essential to forge the links of community (1996: 124), but it is here that his position loses its way. For he contends that a communitarian would recognize that the best way to minimize government coercion is to foster rather than dismiss the moral voice (1996: 131), but by government coercion, Etizioni means the force of the state. Although he quite rightly notes that a measure of psychological pressure is contained in most, if not all, social relations (1996: 131–2), he does not accept that this pressure can be conceptualized as coercive in character.

Etzioni's notion of coercion is conventional and liberal because his attitude towards the state is uncritical. He can see that reliance upon the state diminishes moral order and autonomy, but he assumes that some element of state force is here to stay. He takes it for granted that the law has to be backed by force (1996: 143), since some criminals cannot be reached by the moral voice and must be incarcerated. All societies have enforceable laws (1996: 146–8). Indeed, one of his fellow communitarians argues that the law is 'the moral voice of the state' (Galston, 1998: 146).

The same inconsistency bedevils the position of other communitarians. The logic of 'both/and' (which Bellah, as one of Etzioni's supporters, professes to endorse) implies going beyond institutions that polarize, demonize and exclude. It is, therefore, disappointing to see that Bellah construes this 'both/and' logic to be a compromise with liberalism and not a genuine transcendence. He contends that democratic communitarianism accepts the inevitability of both market and state, insisting merely that their function is to serve, not dominate (1998: 18). But if the state is an institution claiming a monopoly of legitimate force for a particular territory, how can it serve without dominating at the same time? The state, alas, is seen as 'necessary and inevitable' (1998: 19).

Etzioni raises the problem of relativism. How is it possible to judge a community's values if the community is deemed the yardstick of value? His answer would seem promising. Communities need to recognize that they are part of a more encompassing whole. What enables one to judge a particular community is that it is part of a community of communities. The notion of a community of communities captures the image of a mosaic held within a solid frame. It is true that communities cannot serve as the ultimate arbiters of their values, but a community's values can take precedence provided they do not violate another set of normative judgements to which communities are also accountable (1998: 224). These normative judgements must be rooted in the notion of the world itself as a global community.

Etzioni argues that before we can expect to see global mores have the compelling power of those of various societies, citizens of one particular country will have to engage in world wide moral dialogues (1998: 240). Etzioni rightly sees that it is not only possible but necessary to combine universal principles with particularistic ones to form a full communitarian normative account. But Etzioni's argument falters because a statist logic becomes evident. He can see the dangers of the state to the community – his paradigm has a predisposition to build a moral rather than a statist order – and he looks towards community-based rather than statist mechanisms, for example, to tackle offensive statements (1998: 29). Membership of the community must be voluntary, or largely voluntary, and it is in this qualification that we find the problem.

While it is true that states will be involved in tackling disputes where members of communities do not have sufficient common interests to negotiate their differences, the fact remains that the use of force is inimical to community and, to the extent that force is necessary, the existence of community is absent.

Like his supporters, Etzioni is the prisoner of liberal principles. His notion of the new golden rule rests upon a *balance* between order and autonomy. Too much of the one and we veer towards authoritarianism, too much of the other and we have anarchy. Communitarianism requires a bit of both if it is to express the golden mean! His notion of an inverting symbiosis (1996: 37) between autonomy and order again assumes a mechanistic notion of balance. What is actually required is a reconceptualization of both. If order without autonomy becomes a monolithic repression that generates and presupposes chaos, then surely it is not order at all, while it has to be said that autonomy without order contradicts itself since it invites and permits the invasion of people's liberties and is therefore the negation of autonomy.

Dualistic thinking of the kind that suggests a 'balance' between order and autonomy is rooted in an uncritical (and ultimately pessimistic) attitude towards the state. Taylor rightly complains that the penchant to settle things judicially is aggravated by special interest campaigns, and this effectively cuts down the possibilities of compromise (1998b: 53). But, like Etzioni, he fails to see that this is precisely the problem with the state. An institution that claims a monopoly of legitimate force cannot but 'cut down' the possibilities for compromise with those whom it deems enemies of its laws and practitioners of rival sources of force and legitimacy.

Critique has to be immanent if it is to be coherent. This is the problem with many Etzionians who grumble that views which they approve of in 'moderation', have gone too far. Thus Selznick argues that in contemporary popular liberalism, equality as difference threatens to swallow equality as humanity; moral equality becomes 'a celebration of difference and a source of misunderstanding and distrust' (1998: 5). But surely difference can only be celebrated if it is not subject to misunderstanding and distrust. Difference without equality is in fact *division*. It is divisions (of class, ethnicity, national identity, etc.) that generate attempts to obliterate difference in the name of sameness. Selznick rejects what he calls the extremes of radical multiculturalism and cultural imperialism (1998: 70), but multi-culturalism implies respect for different cultures and a willingness to learn from them. It may be that some cultural imperialists call themselves 'multi-culturalists', but surely no critical communitarian should accept them at their word.

Communitarianism aspires to be relational. A good example of this relationalism is found in Dahrendorf's comment that as long as some people have no rights of social and political participation, the rights of the few cannot be described as legitimate (1998: 76). Well said! If some are denied participation, then all suffer. The fact that most OECD countries have would-be citizens who are non-citizens is, Dahrendorf argues, an indictment of the rest of us (1998: 82). If all are not citizens, then no-one is a citizen. But this requires conceptualizing citizenship in a new way, of divorcing it from the institution that is a negation of community and participation – the state itself.

The Problem with Republicanism

Petit has written a full and extremely interesting defence of republicanism. Republicanism draws upon ancient Greek and particularly ancient Roman argument and emphasizes, as Petit puts it, that people are 'essentially social creatures' (1997: vii).

Republicanism is close to communitarianism – indeed Petit argues that republican freedom is a communitarian ideal. The value of freedom as non-domination has, he says, a strikingly communitarian character and to the extent that others are dominated, you are dominated (1997: 122). It is true that republicans like Cicero, Machiavelli and Harrington (to name just three of the classical proponents) had an exclusive view of the people, seeing citizenship as pertaining to males, the propertied, etc. Republicanism, as Petit defines it, is democratic and inclusive and it shares with liberalism the assumption that all humans are equal and that any plausible political ideal must be an ideal for all (1997: 96).

Petit finds the distinction – popularized by Berlin – between negative and positive liberty inadequate and argues for a 'third' concept: that of republican liberty. The essence of republican liberty is non-domination. Petit argues that domination is not simply a question of *intention*. A dominant person may be, as Algernon Sidney put it in the late 1660s, the best and gentlest man in the world, but he is a master if he has the capacity to act despotically towards his victim (Petit, 1997: 34).

Petit's target is classical liberalism, which defines freedom as non-interference. Liberty as non-interference is a modernist ideal and Petit is accordingly critical of Rawls' view that liberty can only be restricted for the sake of liberty (1997: 50). What works against republican freedom is not interference *per se*, but *arbitrary* interference: arbitrariness creates domination.

In place of consent, Petit prefers the idea of a permanent possibility of effective contestation (1997: 63). People must be able to contest the assumption that the state is acting in their interests and according to their ideas. Reducing arbitrariness involves forcing a powerful agent like the state to track certain interests and ideas (1997: 58). The great strength of Petit's view that humans are essentially social creatures is that he sees interference as inherent in social relations in general, and argues, for example, that you cannot enjoy non-interference in the presence of natural obstacles (1997: 83). Interference with another is not in itself a violation of freedom.

Non-domination is a form of power – the power of the agent who can prevent various ills happening to them (1997: 69), so that my freedom is not compromised by a limit in my ability to exercise it – this limitation conditions the freedom I enjoy (1997: 76). This argument creates the space for the view that one can be pressured and constrained, whether socially and naturally, and still be free. Indeed, it is difficult to see how things can be otherwise, once we accept the social character of humans.

Republicanism is very attractive in terms of the argument being made here. Although Petit does not speak of republicanism as a momentum concept (a notion elaborated on in Chapter 8), he argues that republicanism is dynamic because there is never a final account of what someone's interests are. Both the notion of arbitrary power and the notion of freedom as non-domination are developmental (1997: 146). The concept is relational and cosmopolitan, since a powerful republican case is to be made for the strategy of constitutional provision whether this operates domestically or internationally (1997: 151).

Petit argues passionately for what he calls an empire of law – a notion of law that need not commit us to an extreme and self-defeating proceduralism (1997: 176). Procedures should be tied to strengthening non-domination – they are not ends in themselves. Public matters should be decided by deliberation rather than 'bargain-based' negotiation, by which Petit means a kind of market reliance upon spontaneous and impulsive expressions of opinion. All citizens should have equal claims and powers, and there should be no bias in favour of any particular group (1997: 189). To be an independent citizen would require a substantial reduction in material inequality (1997: 161).

People in power, Petit argues, are corruptible rather than corrupt. Instead of Adam Smith's invisible hand, there should be an 'intangible' hand based on a person's honour (1997: 225). Laws must work in synergy with norms, since habits of civic virtue or good citizenship are crucial if the republic is to be established (1997: 245). What is disastrous is to impose a dichotomous view of either an invisible hand, or an iron hand upon the republican polity, since civility testifies to the 'irrepressibly social nature of our species' (1997: 260).

The problem, however, with republicanism as Petit defines it, is that it throws the liberal baby out with the abstract bath-water. He is so concerned to overcome the abstractness of the liberal tradition that he rejects its subversiveness as well. For the classical liberals were right to challenge the 'naturalness' of force and therefore to regard the state as compromising freedom. Petit avoids the Rousseauian paradox that obeying a law (based upon force) is a form of self-emancipation, by arguing that it is only when force is used in an arbitrary way that freedom is compromised. He equates the law with the force of the state. (1997: 302) and contends that the use of force only makes you unfree when this force is arbitrary. A non-arbitrary use of force, i.e., the operation of a constitutional state, does not make you unfree, although Petit does argue that such force conditions freedom. If you are imprisoned or taxed against your will, you are non-free, but not unfree (1997: 76). The force, or as Petit calls it, the 'coercion' of the state, is akin to a natural obstacle when that force is non-arbitrary, and therefore like the liberals, Petit bundles up constraint with force, arguing that all are consonant with republicanism, provided the interference is of a non-arbitrary character.

But how can force be non-arbitrary? The use of force even when it is regulated and checked, has, arguably, an irreducibly arbitrary element since you cannot treat a person as a thing (which is what force involves) without an element of arbitrariness. How do you know the way in which the person upon whom the force is inflicted will respond? The perpetrator of force must be ready to act suddenly and unpredictably, so that the notion of arbitrary force is a 'pleonasm' i.e., force cannot be other than arbitrary. Petit acknowledges the problem when he concedes that criminal law processes often terrorize the innocent as well as the guilty and in practice, if not ideally, fines and prison sentences can be exposed as domination (1997: 154). It is true that non-arbitrary force is an 'ideal' but it is the kind of ideal that the state can only undermine as an institution claiming a monopoly of force.

Petit argues that many people responsive to ordinary norms may not be so responsive if they knew that there was no great sanction attendant on breaking the norms (1997: 154). But while all norms have sanctions – and in the case of laws these sanctions are necessarily explicit and public in character – sanctions do not have to involve force. Indeed, the use of force undermines the efficacy of sanctions, since sanctions draw their strength from social recognition and force by definition disrupts social relationships. Force, while transitionally necessary in a world where negotiation cannot work, weakens norms, creates resentment and, in my view, undermines rather than consolidates responsiveness to norms. Petit argues that arbitrary interference involves a high level of uncertainty – there is no predicting when it will strike (1997: 85). This is surely a problem inherent in force.

To argue that the goal of the state is the promotion of freedom as non-domination (1997: ix), can only be naive, given the fact that the state as an institution involves arbitrariness and thus domination. Locke's argument that the law preserves and enlarges freedom (1927: 40) rests upon a theology that naturalizes force, hence Locke's extraordinary view that some can be legitimately enslaved. Petit contends that if the welfare and the world-view of the public is taken into account, then the act of law or state is not arbitrary (1997: 57). It is certainly true that a 'democratic' state is less arbitrary than an explicitly authoritarian one, but what makes the state inherently arbitrary is the use of force.

The republican case, as interesting and impressive as it is, is weakened by statism and abstraction, so that the question of citizenship in a republican state is still undermined by the arbitrariness and domination inherent in force. It is revealing that Dagger speaks of 'republican liberalism' in his attempt to combine what he calls the republican emphasis on civic devotion with a concern, subsequently associated with liberalism, for tolerance and freedom of thought (1997: 94). However, as Dagger refuses to recognize, forcing a person to be free is not simply a Rousseauian paradox: it is inherent within the problem of the state.

Dagger, like Petit, sees dangers in the criminal law for citizenship but argues that punishment may be a necessary evil, while civic virtue is a positive good (1997: 79). The state is here to stay. Although he sees citizenship in social and communal terms – we need to think of ourselves as something more than the sum of the roles we play – he argues that people must see themselves as citizens in Rousseau's abstract sense of the word (1997: 101). This surely is the nub of the problem. Whether liberalism is accepted (as it is by Dagger) or rejected (by Petit), the problem remains of trying to link citizenship to an institution claiming a monopoly of legitimate force.

Republicanism has much to say that is helpful and valid for developing an inclusive notion of citizenship. It is egalitarian and communitarian and it seeks to build upon the best of the liberal tradition in seeking security through laws and socially responsible norms. But these insights are undermined by an uncritical view of the state.

SUMMARY

- In the post-war period, participation was seen as potentially dangerous for democracy and an elitist notion of democracy celebrated apathy. Yet it is clear that apathy is a major barrier to citizenship since those who do not vote lack the self-esteem and confidence necessary for civil virtue. Ways need also to be found of revitalizing the formal political process so that people see the link between direct involvement and effective control over representatives.
- Compulsory voting, improved voter registration and the development of new computer technology, could make elections more meaningful and exciting, while the development of a system of community service could help to develop a notion of active citizenship.

- Communitarians stress the importance of participation and some of its proponents have convincingly avoided formulations that place the community in a monolithic and authoritarian position over the individual. But to reject a monopolistic role for the community while accepting the necessity of the state, is to give with one hand and take away with the other.
- The same difficulty arises with republicanism. The idea of freedom as non-domination – though hugely attractive – cannot be sustained if force is naturalized and it is assumed that an institution claiming a monopoly of legitimate force can and should act in a non-arbitrary manner. The case against domination is eloquent indeed. But its post-statist logic is suppressed if it is argued that laws can only be enforced by sanctions of force.

7

Globalization

The debate concerning globalization has crucial implications for the question of citizenship. Some reject the very concept, so the case will first be made for globalization as a process that builds upon the past, but is nevertheless new. Globalization is often construed negatively as a purely capitalist phenomenon, which increasingly divides the world into rich and poor, but if construed in this fashion, it would clearly be inimical to citizenship.

However, globalization also has positive consequences and a distinction will be made between globalization as a negative phenomenon (which can be regarded as pseudo-globalization) and the kind of globalization that has the potential for creating a world community and global governance. Once globalization is detached from what has rightly been called 'market fundamentalism', then it becomes clear that it is crucial to an emancipatory citizenship, since it is impossible to be a citizen without taking responsibilities for the freedom and development of people throughout the world. This is only possible if practical mechanisms for global governance are established and these mechanisms are post-statist in character.

What is it?

We need to begin by tackling the case made by those who contend that globalization is a rather pretentious term for what has existed since the nineteenth century.

It is certainly true that even in 1848, Marx and Engels stress the 'cosmopolitan' character of capitalism, arguing that it impacts upon 'every corner of the globe' and cements the 'universal interdependence of nations' (1967: 83–4). Adair Turner makes the point that trade as a percentage of gross domestic product (GDP) is no higher in Britain now than it was in the nineteenth century (2002: 317). There is a good deal of scepticism about globalization as something which is new. Hutton has argued that the great bulk of trade is still between the leading industrialized countries; investment in the developing world only accounts for a tiny fraction of world output. If the economy was truly globalized, it is argued, then we would expect states to be subordinate to the imperatives of multi-national companies (MNCs) and the market. MNCs would no longer be based in a particular country, and international relations would involve corporations rather than states as central players (Faulks, 1998: 181).

A similar argument is advanced by Hirst and Thompson who contend that national economies are still primary actors within the wide international economy (1996). Globalization, however, is a process and those who conceive it as 'total integration' are setting up a straw 'man' to help their critical case. Thus Barry Jones argues that 'even the most enthusiastic heralds of a brave new globalized world' admit that 'financial integration remains far from perfect' (2000: 38). But this absolutist notion of 'perfection' hinders serious debate.

It is not a question of arguing that states have become redundant or that the economy has become international as opposed to national. It is rather that there is an interconnectedness between the people of the world and this interconnectedness has been such that something new has emerged. A distinction is sometimes drawn between a 'strong' and a 'weak' globalization view (Barry Jones, 2000: 11), with the strong thesis defending the phenomenon as something new and the weak version contending that despite a significant increase in internationalization a new term isn't warranted. Barry Jones examines in detail the similarities and differences between the global situation at the end of the nineteenth and twentieth centuries and notes some differences of substance. The micro-computer revolution has dramatically transformed information gathering and the world of the twentieth (and twenty-first) century is enmeshed in a network of international organizations and transnational associations that is of far greater 'density and scope' than could have been imagined or sustained at the end of the nineteenth century (2000: 31).

Although the question of globalization is normally discussed in economic terms, it is of course a cultural and political phenomenon as well. The extraordinary and accelerating innovation in information and communications technology has shrunk the constraints of geography in a dramatic fashion. This 'shrinkage' has important implications for the development of people with global (as well as national and local) identities. Although Ohmae argues for a market fundamentalist view of globalization, it is common ground for all commentators that globalization has furthered the development of a global culture – a culture that undermines what Marx and Engels call 'national one-sidedness and narrow mindedness' (Ohmae, 1995; Marx and Engels, 1967: 84).

The real question – it seems to me – is not whether globalization exists, but whether it is a force for moving beyond the state. Will globalization increase inequalities between peoples or does it provide instruments that could reduce them? If it aggravates inequalities, this will make the state even more prominent. Many of those who oppose the concept of globalization suspect that the concept is used as a pretext for cutting back welfare state expenditure, but that assumes that the free market version of globalization is the only one which should be considered. Indeed, it will be argued that the latter is a pseudo-globalization since it advances, in practice, the interests of the 'haves' at the expense of the 'have-nots' (who are the vast majority of the world's peoples), and the interests of a particular region and system at the expense of global interests as a whole.

Globalization and the 'Free Market'

Ohmae wishes to challenge what he calls 'the fundamental integrity and coherence of the nation state' (1995: viii). The world is now borderless. Investment is no longer geographically constrained or authorized by states; industry is concerned with market opportunities rather than 'government' incentives; information technology facilitates the global reach of business and individuals are increasingly concerned with consuming products, wherever they come from (1995: 2–4). The 'middleman' or intermediary role of the nation state has become obsolete. We now relate to a 'true global marketplace' (1995: 9).

Ohmae calls the nation state 'a nostalgic fiction' (1995: 12). The nation state has become unnatural and dysfunctional as 'economic nationalism', as Ohmae calls it, exercises less and less influence on decision-making (1995: 28). He assumes what he calls the 'Californization' of taste and preference. There is a ladder of economic development, he argues, upon which more and more societies climb, reaching the US $5000 threshold of per capita development. The spread of information-related technology is infectious (1995: 38) and Adam Smith's invisible hand now works in a global context.

Although this New Right version of globalization is sometimes referred to as optimistic (Barry Jones, 2000: 26), its political implications are quite startling (and pessimistic). It is not only (as we shall see shortly) starkly inegalitarian, but also hostile to democracy. Ohmae argues, for example, that the rules of electoral logic and popular expectation lead to general, indirect, long-term benefits being sacrificed in favour of immediate, tangible and focused payoffs (1995: 42). The tyranny of modern democracy, as he calls it, seeks an equality of results, not of contributions (1995: 53). What he refers to as the 'civil minimum' is like a drug and takes the form of broad-based social programmes, welfare, unemployment compensation, public education, old-age pensions and health insurance. Established political systems have become the creature of special interests and the poorer districts. Whereas the nation state solution assumes a zero-sum game for limited resources, the region state model, he argues, open to the global economy, is a 'plus sum' as prosperity is brought in from without (1995: 55, 57, 62).

Yet Ohmae notes that huge disparities have opened up – disparities measured by a factor of 20 or more – between inland and coastal regions in countries like China. He concedes that the actual gap between the developed and developing world has substantially widened. He tries to put a brave face on this argument with his own version of the 'trickle-down' effect. When a region prospers, he contends, its good fortune spills over into the adjacent territories inside and outside the political federation of which it is part. However, disparities are also vast from city to city (1995: 74, 87, 102).

Ohmae refers scathingly to a democratic government allowing a sub-sidized and civil-minimum-ed majority to reach a point of no return. He does concede that chaos can result from 'a rush to liberalize' politics and economics simultaneously and it is crucial to focus on what works (1995: 124, 128). The assumption throughout his book, however, is basically real-ist (in the international relations sense of the term) in character. States are seen as having an unproblematic sovereignty: the problem is that they should simply yield to the market. Brussels is creating a 'supernation state'. Those constituencies desperately worried about the most economi-cally backward areas of the world, are 'vested interests', which get in the way of global logic. Wealth, he argues, grows in spots and spreads out from there (1995: 138, 144). Not only does he see sovereignty as a quality that inheres in nation states, but the state-centric character of his analysis is demonstrated by his argument for 'regional states' – states that consti-tute 'natural economic zones' (1995: 80).

The notion of globalization as an expression of free market policies sounds radical since it appears to be challenging the need for the state. In fact, it accepts the traditional tools of state-centric analysis, and it is dis-tinguished merely by its naive and extremely partial view of the market.

Stiglitz and the Case Against the International Monetary Fund (IMF)

Stiglitz's recent book, *Globalization and its Discontents*, makes an attempt to present a positive critique of globalization. Stiglitz has been chair of President Clinton's Council of Economic Advisers and Chief Economist at the World Bank.

He makes the point that if globalization is to enrich the poor, it has to be radically rethought. Despite the contentions of free marketeers, asym-metries of information are pervasive in all economies. The notion of a self-regulating market is naive and dogmatic and, as far as he is concerned, the basic lessons of Keynes' analysis remain valid (2002: 10). The events of September 11 have brought home the need for policies based upon social justice and decency so that we can live together, and far from rejecting globalization, we should stress its potential to make the world a much fairer place. After all, the international landmines treaty was brought about through the interconnectedness that has been created by globalization (2002: 5).

Stiglitz is critical of both the International Monetary Fund (IMF) and the World Bank, noting that while almost all the activities of both institutions are directed to the developing world, the heads are always chosen from the developed world (a European and an American). The representatives with which the two institutions deal, are finance or trade ministers, so that in many cases, commercial interests supersede concern for the environment, democracy, human rights and social justice (2002: 19–20). Monbiot points out that to change the constitution of the World Bank and the IMF requires an 85 per cent vote, and the US alone possesses 17 per cent of the votes (2002: 15). But Stiglitz's most scathing analysis is reserved for the IMF.

Set up by Keynes after the Second World War to assist in the reconstruction of Europe, the IMF under the influence of Thatcher and Reagan began in the 1980s to adopt a rigid and blinkered view of the market – a market fundamentalism. Its functionaries took, and still take, the view that market outcomes by themselves lead to efficient outcomes. The Keynesian notion that markets may work badly has been replaced by an ideological fervour which ignores the social consequences of policies that are imposed predominantly on relatively helpless developing countries.

Failure to be sensitive to the broader social context is the IMF's basic problem. The truth is that Smith's invisible hand works most imperfectly, particularly in developing countries (Stiglitz, 2002: 73). Social costs linked to unemployment are simply not taken into account (2002: 56). The IMF is oblivious to the effect that its policies have on inequality. Structural adjustment programmes often provoke hunger and food riots, inflicting a pain that has been far greater than is necessary. In this way a backlash has been created. There is a growing divide between the haves and the havenots across the world. Over the last decade of the twentieth century, the numbers living in poverty increased by 100 million. The gap between the rich and poor has been growing and those living in abject poverty (less than $1 a day) have been increasing. They amount to 1.2 billion people and it is worth noting that 2.8 billion people – some 45 per cent of the world's population – live on less than $2 a day (2002: 24–5). Terrible poverty has, for example, been brought to Russia. Stiglitz devotes a whole chapter to the disastrous policies of the IMF here, noting that in 1990 China's GDP was 60 per cent of Russia's, by 2000, the figures were reversed (Stiglitz, 2002: 6).

In Russia, income is lower than it was a decade ago and poverty is much higher. The devastation – the loss in GDP – was greater than Russia had suffered in the Second World War. Wage payments have fallen into massive arrears and the workers are often paid with bartered goods rather than rubles. The IMF unwittingly connived with a new and wholly unscrupulous elite. The billions of dollars loaned to Russia showed up in Cyprus and Swiss bank accounts. The experience for the region has been a disaster. If Russia's GDP is two-thirds of what it was in 1990, Moldova and the Ukraine's is just one-third of what it was ten years ago. While in 1989 in Russia only 2 per cent of the population were in poverty, this had soared to 23.8 per cent in 1998 (less than $2 a day), and some 40 per cent are earning less than $4 a day. While a few friends and associates of former President Yeltsin became billionaires, the country is unable to pay pensioners $15 a month (2002: 133–65).

Stiglitz also provides a detailed analysis of the rigid policies adopted towards Ethiopia, which were eventually reversed under pressure from the World Bank (2002: 33). Capital market liberalization in East Asia gave a head to the irrational exuberance and pessimism of international investors and in Korea the policies of the IMF made the recession far worse (2002: 106). As the only shareholder in the IMF with veto power, the US was opposed to the formation of an Asian monetary fund (2002: 112; for a detailed analysis of the Asian crisis, see Barry Jones, 2000: 233–56). The role of government – indispensable in tackling problems of inequality, unemployment and pollution – has been ignored: yet in East Asia, governments have helped to shape and direct markets (2002: 92). Governments have an essential role in mitigating market failure and ensuring social justice (2002: 218). The IMF's imposition of rigid conditions has often made repayment more difficult and has strayed into explicitly political areas, as in the situation, for example, when the IMF demanded the 'independence' of the central bank in Korea (2002: 45).

The dogmatic approach of the IMF reflects thinly veiled vested interests. The liberalization of financial markets often serves the narrow interests of the financial community in the US (2002: 64). A Washington consensus, incorporating the US Treasury, has developed and the elitist attitudes of the IMF have been expressed in their methods of working. While the World Bank seeks to ensure that a substantial fraction of its staff live permanently in the country they are trying to help, IMF representatives go on short visits and stay in the capital of the countries they 'assist' (2002: 23). All too often, the Fund's approach to the developing countries has the feel of a colonial ruler (2002: 40). The Fund operates in considerable secrecy: democratic procedures and values are notable by their absence.

Whereas the industrialized countries – and notably the US – have ignored the IMF's prescriptions, the developing world has had little choice but to accept its policies. Developing countries are forced to open their markets and yet industrial countries keep their own markets protected, with the consequence that the rich get richer. The US has been one of the prime culprits of hypocrisy in terms of its trade policy – quotas have been kept on a multitude of goods from textiles to sugar (2002: 7). Monbiot points out that the General Agreement on Trade in Services (GATS) prevents poor countries from defending their indigenous businesses, although that is precisely what the current industrial powers did during their major phases of development (2002: 15).

Stiglitz is not opposed to market forces, but argues that IMF policies are likely to impair the overall efficiency of the market (2002: 128). 'Labour market flexibility' has simply been code for lower wages and less job protection and the MNCs have to learn that providing better working conditions may actually enhance worker productivity and lower overall costs (or not raise them much) (2002: 68–9). A penchant for premature trade liberalization and a refusal to look at the broader social context in which policies work, has meant that the IMF have ignored the fact that privatization only makes sense when an adequate regulatory and competitive framework is intact. Sequencing has been ignored (i.e., the need to undertake reforms at a particular pace and in a particular order) and trade liberalization has been pushed before safety nets are in place (2002: 17). Not surprisingly, the IMF's record has been dismal. Close to 100 countries have faced crises and the policies of the IMF have contributed to global instability. Poverty and social and political chaos have resulted. Even where countries have experienced limited growth, benefits have only accrued to the very well off: the top 10 per cent (2002: 18). It is painfully clear that trickle-down economics does not work.

Stiglitz argues that the problem is not with globalization *per se*, but with how it is managed. International economic institutions need to be reshaped. Global public institutions are required to set the rules (2002: 215, 222). The UN focuses on issues of global political security while institutions like the IMF are supposed to focus on global economic security. Globalization has enhanced the need for global collective action and global public goods (2002: 223–4). We have a system that might be called global governance without global government in which a few players dominate the scene. Globalization needs to be democratized, with a change in voting rights so that it is not just finance and trade ministers whose voice predominates at IMF and World Trade Organization (WTO) meetings. Given the fact that the IMF and World Bank are not directly accountable to the public, there should be more, not less transparency. Secrecy allows special interests full sway. Surveillance ought to be done by others. A more balanced agenda for the WTO is crucial (2002: 214–52).

Stiglitz's critique of the IMF is well judged and authoritative. He is highly critical of market fundamentalist versions of globalization, and he indicates implicitly that the market can only flourish when it is humanely and governmentally regulated, and thus subject to a process of gradual and long-term transcendence.

The Challenge of Global Government

If globalization is to be positively conceived, then we must tackle abstract analyses which are, alas, far too common. Barry Jones argues that globalization might prompt the reassertion of diversity – a dialectic of difference – rather than the smooth emergence of similarity (2000: 112). But this supposes that diversity can only take the form of antagonism. It is true that the free market does impose an abstract similarity upon the world as a whole, but that is a distortion of globalization. If we mean by globalization a sense of interconnectedness between all the peoples of the world, then it has to be argued that free market policies privilege the haves over the have-nots and in reality impose the life styles and values of an elite upon the world in general. This is not globalization in reality, but 'Westernization' or 'Americanization' – the kind of pseudo-globalization that inevitably creates a fundamentalist reaction.

This is why it is crucial to stress the multi-faceted character of globalization, a phenomenon that is not simply economic, but also cultural and political in its consequences. It is not simply that states are losing economic power: the claim by the state to impose a monopolistic outlook upon a particular society is radically challenged by a growing sense of diversity and difference – not only between societies but within societies as well. The value of the Stiglitz critique is that it explains why international institutions like the IMF have discredited globalization by making it appear synonymous with neo-liberalism and devastation.

The problem is that the notion of governance is often used without consideration being given to the type of sanction employed. Thus Barry Jones generally sees public governance as synonymous with the work of the state, although he does consider the UN an example of public governance (2000: 176–7). It has to be said that Barry Jones' own list of the functions of governance – the provision of collective goods, the management of general externalities and the satisfaction of minority needs – do not require institutional force as a sanction (2000: 178). In my terminology, these 'functions' are governmental rather than intrinsically statist in character. Politics is, in Barry Jones' view, quintessentially a matter of debate about the nature of conditions that should be defined as collective goods or pertinent externalities (2000: 188), so that the question arises: is a global politics, governance or government possible?

The first point that is crucial to the argument is clarity about the nature of the state. The state is not synonymous with government and, by confusing the two, we make it impossible to chart the way towards a global regime. Barry Jones refers continually to the state or 'its functional equivalent' (2000: 189), but the state has no functional equivalent. It is distinctive and specific and its use of force as a method of tackling conflicts of interest is logically and conceptually quite different from the governmental role that states may play. The reason why the demise of the state fills writers with fear of a world of chaos and 'anarchy' is of course that they equate the state with government and therefore assume that without the state, a Hobbesian state of nature will necessarily ensure. Once we understand the distinctiveness of the state and the circumstances in which states are necessary, we can avoid both an abstract utopianism and an abstract realism.

An abstract utopianism sees global government as a substitute for the state. It argues that cosmopolitan government must somehow replace the state, the argument being that the state has become redundant. Sharp has distinguished between the 'no change' school, which assumes that only professional diplomats as state functionaries can be taken seriously, and the 'all-change' school, which assumes that state sovereignty is now irrelevant. The sovereign state system is depicted as a town whose buildings have been burned down to shells (2001: 16). This is a valid point. It is clearly a false choice to assume that *either* we accept a realist view of the state *or* we assume that state sovereignty exists only in the past.

Barry Jones contends that the 'traditional' state constitutes the 'best institutionalised form of public governance in the contemporary world' (2000: 205). But an institution claiming a monopoly of legitimate force for a particular territory is in fact a serious obstacle to effective global public governance. Barry Jones takes it for granted that global government must supplant the state, since it is only possible for one monopolistic institution to exist! He assumes, therefore, not only that global government must take the form of a state, but that the inauguration of global governance involves the 'collapse' of the nation or the traditional state. Setting up the argument in this manner, he finds unsurprisingly that the record of international institutions and associations is far too mixed to support unqualified optimism (2000: 209).

If, as Barry Jones rightly suggests, we are moving to a world of 'complex, multi-layered' public governance (2000: 270), then it is crucial that we must challenge the monopolistic pretensions of the state and also a statist mode of thinking, in which diversity is construed as fragmentation and set against a 'common popular response' (2000: 225). The challenge of global governance can only be met if we reject the statist assumption that global politics has to become the politics of a global state in which the nation state must simply disappear if global governance is to exist.

States will remain for the foreseeable future, since it would be naive to suppose that the conditions that make them necessary will suddenly disappear. The case for global governance is one in which states become less important and increasingly devote their energies to governmental activities, thereby gradually transcending themselves. But it would be utopian indeed (in the abstract sense of the word) to imagine that states will vanish within any particular time-scale, although in terms of the world's well-being, the sooner this happens, the better!

The UN and the EU

Kant is often cited in the literature on cosmopolitanism but his celebrated case for perpetual peace rests upon the notion of a federation of states. Kant was a liberal republican – he certainly did not subscribe to a notion of global citizenship reaching beyond the state.

The principles driving many of the institutions considered as the instruments of global governance are, as Faulks points out, those of neo-liberalism and state sovereignty (1999: 194). Like the IMF and the WTO, international institutions currently represent the interests of the dominant few and operate in a divisive and inegalitarian manner, leading to Stiglitz's observation (noted above) that what is needed is not global governance, but global government (i.e., institutions that seek to empower rather than diminish the people of the world). As Faulks points out, while institutions like the IMF seek to manage the world economy, to say that organizations like these taken collectively constitute 'a de facto world government' (1999: 195), is to identify this global regime with the interests of the rich and the powerful.

But what of the UN, which is regarded by its most enthusiastic admirers like Johnston, as a supranational political authority (1993: 1)? The problem with Johnston's analysis is that he sees the UN as a federal world state, with the security council acting as the UN sheriff, in which Article 42 provides the force necessary to act in the 'common interest' (1993: 2). The concept of international law is dismissed by Johnston as humbug because it is not the law of a world state. He interprets the Charter (rather eccentrically perhaps) as giving sovereignty, which he sees as the power to use overriding force, to the UN. It is international law that stands in the way of world citizenship by limiting individuals to a nationality (1993: 15). Not surprisingly, he regards my own critique of the state as mere anarchism, an argument taken to 'a questionable extreme' (1993: 16).

It is certainly true that the UN enjoys almost universal membership and allows each state equal voting rights in the General Assembly. But it does seem, despite the Johnston thesis, that the UN is an organization with two souls. The one is certainly globalist in scope, since the Preamble to the Charter refers to the UN's faith in fundamental human rights, tolerance and the solution of international problems of an economic, social, cultural or humanitarian character (1993: 1). Article 1 of the Charter speaks of universal peace for the peoples of the world based on self-determination and equal rights (1993: 3).

But although Article 2 speaks of the principle of sovereign equality, it is clear that this sovereign equality is for its member states and the famous Article 2 (7) declares that no intervention is to be allowed in the 'domestic jurisdiction' of any state (1993: 5). The UN is given a 'vital and central role in global governance' by the Commission on Global Governance in their report (1995: 225), although it is conceded that the UN has never really been considered as belonging to the people of the world. Rather it is seen as the property of states (or a few of them). The General Assembly can only recommend, not determine and of course the Security Council, despite the principles endorsed of universality and equality, allows the five permanent members veto power over security council resolutions. Since the end of the Cold War, the Security Council has become much more active in peace-keeping activities. But its unrepresentative character (in 1963 the number of non-permanent members was raised from six to ten) has led to what the Commission on Global Governance calls 'a crisis of legitimacy' (1995: 237). This crisis can only be aggravated by the cavalier manner in which the US (and the UK) have gone to war against Iraq despite the fact that they have no UN authorization for their action.

The Commission proposes that the Security Council should be increased to twenty three members, with two coming from the industrialized countries and three from the developing world, with the veto of the permanent members phased out by 2005; it being used in the intervening years only 'in extreme cases' (Commission on Global Governance, 1995: 240–1). This crisis of legitimacy is linked directly to the predominance of statist attitudes within the UN. It is true that peace-keeping has played an important role in seeking to keep warring sides apart (most of the violent conflicts in the world have been within nations), but although this activity has dramatic potential, the UN has been selective in the way its peace-keeping role has been enacted. Resolutions on the abuses of human rights by Indonesia in East Timor and by Israel in Palestine have been consistently vetoed. Weaker countries understandably feel that the UN only acts when it serves the interests of its most powerful members (Faulks, 1999: 198).

The journal *New Internationalist* devoted a special issue to the UN in 1994, in which they noted that there was a sharp increase in peace-keeping costs, but that development outlays for the so-called 'third world' had fallen. The issue is scathing about the UN's intervention in Somalia, warning that a militaristic approach leads to ignoring community leaders and a needless loss of life. It is here that the statist soul of the UN becomes most apparent. The statist conceives of order in traditional terms – dissonance has to be suppressed from on-high through overwhelming force. The democrat conceives of order as conflict which involves differences that need to be addressed by negotiation, resources, mediation and empowerment. United Nations agencies like UNICEF – which tackles the problems of children – or the World Health Organization (WHO) – that tackle problems like small pox and diarrhoea – seek to create order through resource provision: agencies like these represent the developmental or democratic soul of the UN.

What prevents the UN from contributing much more vigorously to a global government is its statist (and patriarchal) character. The veto system and the relative weakness of the General Assembly expresses the domination not merely of states in general, but of particularly powerful states that, like the USA, pay their contributions only when they feel that the UN can advance their (narrowly conceived) national interests. Although the radical transformation of the UN that Held proposes is positive, the conflict between a global outlook and an uncritical acceptance of institutions claiming a monopoly of legitimate force needs to be tackled. Global governance must become global *government* (as I have defined it) if nationalist prejudices and distortions are to be a thing of the past. The decision by the newly established International Criminal Court (ICC) to allow immunity to US officials and members of its armed forces demonstrates the problem of a dominant superpower bullying a somewhat nervous international community. It could well be argued that instead of a military pursuit of 'weapons of mass destruction', Saddam Hussein should have been arraigned before the ICC for human rights abuses, with military power far better deployed (as a weapon of last resort) for his arrest.

Regional security organizations operate in terms of the interests of states, while regional trading blocs seem more positive, in terms of promoting an inclusive citizenship, because they cement common interests. Faulks notes that the number of such organizations has grown enormously in the post-war period, and represent an aspect of, rather than a reaction against, globalization (1999: 200). However, to the extent that they are dominated by neo-liberal ideology (and in general they are), they enshrine and exacerbate inequality and division, rather than work to overcome them.

The European Union (EU), on the other hand, is concerned about equalization and redistributive social policies. Richard Bellamy and Alex Warleigh's recently edited *Citizenship and Governance in the European Union* (2001) sees the EU and its concept of citizenship as a paradox and a puzzle. Is the Union seeking to establish a new kind of political entity or is it simply another (and larger) version of a state? The EU, it is argued, has two aspects: one is the market, the other is democracy. Neo-liberals may think of the two as synonymous, but that view is not shared by the contributors to Bellamy and Warleigh's volume, who rightly point out that citizenship is a political issue that necessarily transcends a market identity.

The argument advanced is that while the current rights of the EU citizen may at present seem somewhat limited, we should be concerned with unanticipated outcomes. Under the provisions of the Maastricht Treaty, European citizens have the right to stand and vote in local and European parliamentary elections even if they are not nationals in the states where they reside; they can petition the newly created Ombudsman as well as the European Parliament and they are entitled to diplomatic protection in third states where one's 'own' state is not represented (2001: 23).

Certainly, the EU was initially conceived as a transnational capitalist society, an economic union that is a free trade area, although it could well be argued that people like Jean Monnet had political objectives right from the start. However, universalist conceptions have a potential for development that often dismay liberals and usually outrage conservatives. It may well have been (for example) the *intention* of EU founders to confine sexual equality to the notion of a level playing field constituted by the cost of factors of production, but economic rights require a political and social context to be meaningful. It is the *potential* of EU citizenship that is important. It is this that links a rather passive, state-centred notion to a much more 'active, democratic citizenship' (Bellamy and Warleigh, 2001: 117), a move from a politics of identity – which implies a rather repressive homogeneity – to a politics of affinity, which recognizes and respects difference. This politics of affinity has broken with the pessimistic 'realism' of a figure like Aron who (cited by Heater, 1999: 150) declared in 1974 that 'there are no such animals as "European citizens". There are only French, German or Italian citizens'.

It is the great strength of Bellamy and Warleigh's collection of essays that they capture the sense of what I have called a 'momentum concept'. This is the idea that concepts like freedom and equality (for example) have an emancipatory potential that goes well beyond those who initially formulate them. Citizenship is seen (Bellamy and Warleigh, 2001: 143) as a 'surprisingly elusive concept' and the concept is an excellent example of an idea that compels us to think the unthinkable. Indeed, the very notion of citizenship was introduced, we are told, as an attempt to overcome the 'democratic deficit' – to combat the view that the EU is an alien body and that only nation states really matter.

Undoubtedly there is a 'dualism' at the heart of the concept of EU citizenship. On the one hand, the term is tied to states and markets. On the other hand, the European Court of Justice has interpreted the question of freedom of movement in broad social terms, as a quasi-constitutional entitlement, and not simply as a direct economic imperative. Thus, to take an example, the right to freedom of movement is linked to the right not to be discriminated against by comparison with host-state nationals (Bellamy and Warleigh, 2001: 96).

None of the contributors in the volume are satisfied with the current position. There is support for a basic income for all citizens (Bellamy and Warleigh, 2001: 127). Current rights of EU citizens are limited, but the point is that once the notion of citizenship is established, the anomaly of confining political rights to those who are already citizens of member states, becomes plain. Already, limited rights – like the right to petition the Parliament and refer matters to the Ombudsman – are bestowed on individuals even if they are not members of one of the constituent nation states and are therefore not 'citizens'. It is difficult to disagree with Heater's point that potentially, the EU is a sophisticated example of a new kind of citizenship, but 'at the moment, to be honest, it is a mere shadow of that potential' (1999: 129).

The European Ombudsman was introduced in 1992 as a result of Spanish enthusiasm for EU citizenship and Danish concern for administrative efficiency. The Ombudsman can deal with a wide range of issues including matters relating to the environment and human rights. Questions of administrative transparency and the use of age limits in employment have been vigorously pursued, and the Ombudsman should not be seen as a 'stand alone' institution, but one that co-exists with courts, tribunals, parliaments and other intermediaries at European, national, regional and local levels.

It is clearly wrong to think that there is somehow a benign historical trend towards giving more and more rights for European citizens. Clearly struggle is necessary and crucial to this struggle is patience and tactics. Unsurprisingly, people think in terms of nation states and the concept of the 'citizen' is still taken by most of the literature to mean membership of a state. It is very important that we do not think of a European identity as somehow in competition with other identities. On the contrary, European institutions add to and reinforce national and sub-national governance, although conflict and dialogue exist between these levels.

In other words, we need to encourage people to think less in the monopolistic and nationalist idioms of statist thought. This is a long-term project in which the tyranny of established concepts is gradually challenged, so that citizenship as an inclusive and a post-statist concept can be established. Doubtless, legitimacy is fundamental to every government. This is important for both the EU and its member states. If the latter want to increase their legitimacy, then they need to act, in my view, less and less like states – institutions that claim a monopoly of legitimate force for a particular territory – and more and more like governments or organs of governance, i.e., organizations seeking to settle conflicts of interest without the use of force.

This requires a movement both upwards and downwards that involves more and more people at every level. The crucial question facing the EU at the moment seems to be the status of residents who are currently excluded from EU citizenship. Here, as the Bellamy and Warleigh volume argues, a statist 'nationality' model currently prevails, with ethnic migrants being seen as vulnerable 'subjects' rather than as active and entitled members of the EU. Yet, Article 25, for example, of the draft Charter of Fundamental Rights, does allow residents who are non-citizens to vote and stand for EU elections (Bellamy and Warleigh, 2001: 198).

Enlargement of the EU poses another set of challenges. Might not the EU learn something from the legacies of the former Communist Party states, given the fact that some of these states have now been accepted as members of the EU? After all, the Marxist tradition does pose the question of the withering away of the state, even if its practitioners spectacularly failed to achieve this. Perhaps the EU offers the most developed example to date of how we can start the process of broadening the horizons of people so that they see citizenship rights as incompatible with old-fashioned institutions that claim a monopoly of legitimate force. Citizenship and governance are concepts with a future and the EU needs to assist states into converting themselves into governments involving people at every level.

European citizenship is both utopian and realistic. Instead of seeing these attributes in a dualistic and zero-sum (I am tempted to say state-centric) manner, we need to argue that they must become mutually reinforcing aspects as a new conception of politics struggles to be born.

A global civil society, as it is often called, is developing around the Non-Governmental Organizations (NGOs), which could be better called Non-Statist Organizations, given the fact that NGOs operate within and between countries in ways that help to cement common interests. NGOs like the World Wildlife Fund, Amnesty International, OXFAM, Human Rights Watch and Christian Aid seek to support a concept of order that stresses resource provision rather than military action, and they pose what has been called, a 'serious challenge to the imperatives of statehood' (Faulks, 1999: 202). Heater argues that Amnesty International is of special relevance in terms of world citizenship because it is confronting national governments with transgressions against the UN Charter and International Bill of Rights (1999: 144). In 1993 there were almost 29,000 International NGOs (Commission on Global Governance, 1995: 32).

Of course, NGOs (or some of them) suffer from problems of bureaucracy and elitism that afflict states themselves, but they are becoming increasingly influential and they do represent proof that alternative organizations can increasingly resolve problems without claiming to exercise a monopoly of legitimate force. They are no substitute (as Faulks points out, 1999: 204) for coordinated, collective global action to tackle the problems of global inequality, but NGOs make a significant practical and theoretical contribution to the development of a sense of global citizenship.

Global Government as a Multiple Citizenship

The danger of seeing the problem of citizenship simply through statist lenses is exemplified by Huntington's contention that globalization is leading to a clash of civilisations. He explicitly identifies his position with the realist theory of international relations (1996: 185) and argues that the tools of realism – a state-centric view of the world that must remain forever changeless – lead to seeing (violent) conflict in terms of cultural and what he calls 'civilizational' difference.

While he concedes that minorities in other cultures may espouse Western values – by which Huntington means the values of what he calls democratic liberalism – dominant attitudes in non-Western cultures range from widespread scepticism to intense opposition to Western values (1996: 184). Although almost all non-Western civilizations are resistant to pressure from the West – including Hindu, Orthodox, African and even Latin American countries – the greatest resistance to Western democratization efforts has come from Islam and Asia (1996: 193).

Civilizations, Huntington argues, are the ultimate human tribes and the clash of civilizations is tribal conflict on a global scale. Trust and friendship between the civilizations will be rare (1996: 206). He sees a deeply conflictual relation (Huntington takes it for granted that conflict is always violent), not simply between Islamic fundamentalists and Christianity but between Islam itself and Christianity. Conflict is a product of difference. In civilizational conflicts, unlike ideological ones, kin stand by their kin (1996: 209–10, 217). Thus, the Gulf War is interpreted as a war between civilizations (1996: 251). Religion is the principal defining characteristic of civilization, so that what he calls 'fault-line wars' are almost always between people of different religions (1996: 253). At the global level, the clash is between the West and the rest; at the micro or local level, it is between Islam and others (1996: 255). The longer a fault-line war continues, the more that kin countries are likely to become involved (1996: 272).

Huntington takes the view that it is futile and counter-productive for countries to integrate its peoples. A multi-civilizational United States, he argues, will not be the United States: it will be the United Nations. We must reject the divisive siren calls of multiculturalism (1996: 306–7, 310). Cultural identities inevitably collide in an antagonistic manner. 'We know who we are only when we know who we are not and often only when we know whom we are against' (1996: 21). Here is realism with a cultural twist! Nation states are and will remain the most important actors in world affairs, but their interests, associations and conflicts are increasingly shaped by cultural and civilizational factors (1996: 36).

Huntington is a fundamentalist who believes that human history is the history of civilizations (1996: 40). Islamic civilization in particular and non-Western culture in general, is on the ascendant and it is wrong to assume that with 'modernization', the world becomes more amenable to Western values. In fact, he argues, the world is becoming more modern and less Western (1996: 78). Of course, people are different, but for Huntington these differences can only lead to exclusion and antagonism. Thus he insists that religion posits a basic distinction between a superior in-group and a different and inferior out-group, and cultural questions (like the mosque at Ayodhya or the status of Jerusalem) tend to involve a yes–no, zero-sum choice. For self-definition and motivation, people need enemies (1996: 97, 130).

I accept that civilizational differences are real and important, but Huntington is wrong to see them as a necessary source of antagonism. It is true that many Muslims are not convinced by US attempts to present its demonization of political figures like deposed Iraqi leader, Saddam Hussein, as something other than raw hostility to Islam *per se*. But it needs to be remembered that it was a US-led NATO that intervened in Kosovo to defend the human rights of people of Muslim faith against their Serbian (and Christian Orthodox) oppressors. This hardly fits the clash of civilizations thesis.

Huntington himself links what he calls 'Muslim assertiveness' to social mobilization, population growth, and a flood of people from the countryside into the towns (1996: 102, 98). This is surely a social rather than a purely cultural explanation for antagonism. Moreover, only a realist schooled in state-centric analysis and rooted in American triumphalism could ignore the adverse effect of the insensitivity and arrogance of US policy makers upon others. It is not that the differences he speaks of are unimportant. Rather it is that he fossilizes them, fails to see the contradiction between the 'culturalist' and sociological dimensions of his analysis, and ignores the tensions within the so-called Western tradition between neo-liberal and social democratic strategies and values. His work is a good example of why, if a case is to be made for a universal and inclusive concept of citizenship, the question of the statism itself with its conservative and superficial assumptions has to be tackled.

The notion of global governance must not merely reject the argument for a global state. It must also question the idea that the assertion of rights and responsibilities at the global level contradicts loyalties at a regional, national and local level. An inclusive notion of citizenship implies that people in whatever area of government they are involved, are respected and empowered, so that people can increasingly 'change places' with others, whether these others are neighbours in the same block, people of their own nation and region, or members of the other countries in distant parts of the world. One of the most positive features of globalization is that people meet others of different ethnic and cultural origin and outlook, not only when they travel abroad, but even at the local level. The media (at its best) presents people suffering and developing in other parts of the world as though they were neighbours, so that it becomes increasingly possible to imagine what it is like to be the other. Modern conditions have contributed much to realize Kant's argument that 'a violation of rights in *one* part of the world is felt *everywhere*' (cited by Heater, 1999: 140).

Lister is surely right to link the notion of 'global citizenship' with a 'multi-layered conception' of citizenship itself (1997a: 196). Of course, international institutions need to be strengthened in the way that Held and others have suggested. States will obviously remain important as actors in this process, although the extent to which states must acknowledge the importance of human rights and international law will necessitate them dissolving their statist qualities into what I have called processes of government. Lister's notion of 'differentiated universalism' (1997a: 197) captures a respect for difference that is compatible with, and indeed strengthened by, a sense of being a citizen of the world. Chauvinist and xenophobic attitudes are not only militantly exclusive, but lead to a fragmentation within elite groups so that it is perfectly logical that the hostility towards the Jews in Nazi ideology was accompanied by a contempt for the masses (whatever their ethnic purity) and great suspicion even towards fellow leaders.

Each layer, if it is democratically constructed, strengthens the other. Global citizenship – a respect for others, a concern for their well-being and a belief that the security of each person depends upon the security of everyone else – does not operate in contradiction with regional, national and local identities. It expresses itself through them. As Lister puts it well, either/or choices lead us into a theoretical and political cul-de-sac (1997a: 197).

Heater argues that the 'singular concept' of citizenship has burst its bounds (1999: 117) and it is true that dual citizenship (which already exists in some states) represents a much more relaxed view of the question so that a person can exercise formal state-centred citizenship rights in more than one country. But it is with regard to the relationship between global citizenship and the state that Heater exhibits a measure of theoretical ambivalence by looking in two different directions at the same time. He argues that membership of a voluntary association in civil society can qualify a person for citizenship, so that we can legitimately speak of a person as the citizen of a church, a trade union, a club, an environmental group, etc. (1999: 121). It is worth noting that if citizenship is to be conceptualized as inclusive and emancipatory, then these groups must be open in principle to all members of a community – one cannot be a citizen of a racist group, since by definition, this has an exclusive membership. I think that Heater is right to insist that civil society offers a useful and even superior option to traditional state membership (1999: 121).

It goes without saying that world or global citizens cannot have rights and responsibilities prescribed for them with the precision that written (or indeed unwritten) constitutions prescribe for national citizens. Nor, as Heater shows at some length, is the notion of a world citizen a new one. He gives examples of cosmopolitanism in ancient Greek thought and quotes the words of the ancient Roman, Marcus Aurelius, that 'wherever a man lives, he lives as a citizen of the World-City' (1999: 139). But the problem here – as the somewhat exclusive language suggests – is that citizenship is still conceived as the membership of a state; indeed Marcus Aurelius is cited by Heater as saying that we are all members of a 'common State' and presenting the 'Universe' as if 'it were a State' (1999: 135).

If we accept the celebrated Kantian argument for world government as a loose confederation of states, we remain with a notion of politics that is inherently exclusive and repressive in character. The equation of world government with a world state leaves us prisoners of liberal discourse, for the point is that world government cannot be governmental to the extent that it is statist. Only by rigorously distinguishing between the state and government (or governance), can we develop a notion of citizenship that is meaningfully inclusive.

Heater is sympathetic to the notion of a global citizen, but his notion of multiple citizenship is severely compromised by his insistence that a universal polity must be a world state. He is suspicious of the state, but feels stuck with it! He writes (rather curiously) that 'a fully-fledged modern world state' might well require 'a transfer of civil allegiance from the state to the universal polity' (1999: 151), arguing that 'political citizenship, so intimately reliant on the possession of the means of force by the state, must remain absorbed in the state as the necessary catalyst for its vitality' (1999: 152). Yet the use of force by the state must divide and the assertion of a monopoly of legitimacy to justify this use of force can only impose a divisive sense of insider and outsider: those who are citizens and those who are 'enemies'.

Heater undermines his own argument for a 'multiple citizenship' by uncritically endorsing a statist model of politics – a model that necessarily privileges an exclusive form of citizenship over all others. He rightly notes that the intricate realities of the world of the twenty-first century are undermining the traditional uni-dimensional concept of citizenship (1999: 154). However, central to this process of theoretical erosion is the need to break with a state-centric view of citizenship.

SUMMARY

- The origins of globalization lie in capitalism's international scope, and even if these linkages are not new, quantitative increases have given birth to an interconnectedness that is new.
- While the development of globalization lies with capitalism, capitalism also undermines globalization by privileging particular countries and particular states.
- Stiglitz argues that the IMF has aggravated, rather than helped, difficult economic situations through its doctrinaire attachment to neo-liberalism. Globalization, he contends, can and must be rescued from the free marketeers's dogma and arrogance.
- The state stands as a barrier to the diversity and pluralism that globalization conveys. The UN seeks to tackle problems by providing resources and helping the vulnerable, while at the same time enshrining statism. The EU, on the other hand, offers a notion of citizenship, which although limited, has considerable potential.
- Huntington's argument is a good example of the deficiencies of a realist view of international relations and he graphically indicates the link between state-centric analysis, and a conservative and superficial view of world affairs.
- It is important that we see citizenship as multi-layered. Involvement in governance at each level can strengthen a sense and commitment to the well-being of people everywhere. A 'differentiated' universalism avoids the idea that either we are all the same, or we are all different, and argues that global government requires a sense of both difference and similarity at the same time.
- In arguing the case for a global citizenship, it is important not to allow statist institutions to slip through the back door. Central to a positive notion of globalization is a critique of the state and statist ways of looking at the problem.

Part Three
The Future of
Democratic Citizenship

8

Citizenship, Democracy and Emancipation

Citizenship and democracy, when detached from the state, are crucial to human emancipation.

The notion of emancipation is sometimes challenged by postmodernists who find it static and 'foundational' in character. It is true that emancipation was initially formulated in abstract terms as a concept during the Enlightenment. But it will be argued that the concept can and should be reconstructed to capture a dynamic sense of autonomy and self-government. This makes it incompatible with the state, but central to a coherent notion of democracy and citizenship.

A distinction will be made between static and hierarchical concepts and concepts that are egalitarian and 'momentum' in character. Emancipation, like democracy and citizenship, is of the latter kind, provided we are willing to reconstruct it, thus transforming its foundational and modernist heritage.

Emancipation can become a postmodern concept if it builds upon and therefore transcends liberalism.

The Problem of Emancipation

Emancipation is a concept closely linked to democracy and citizenship. To be a citizen is to govern oneself in a political community. It is also to be democratic and to be emancipated.

The term emancipation arises in the period of the Enlightenment. We have a series of terms like autonomy, reason, freedom and emancipation, which are so close to each other that it is impossible to adhere to one without adhering to all. 'Enlightenment', Kant declared, is a person's release from their 'self-incurred tutelage'. Tutelage is self-incurred when people impose upon themselves the direction of another. 'Have courage to use your own reason!' – that is the motto, Kant proclaims, of enlightenment (1959: 85).

Kant, admittedly, was patriarchal, elitist and abstract. The concept of emancipation is regarded by many (and particularly those calling themselves postmodernists) as blighted with an arrogance and an absolutism that it acquired in its origins. It is seen as exclusive – applying to men, people of property and people of Western Europe. The emancipated citizen is a rational male, rationality being linked to property ownership, the liberal persuasion and middle-class status.

The notion of emancipation extends back (by implication) to the ancient Greeks where, as we saw in Chapter 1 in our discussion on citizenship and the state, it was even more exclusive in character. The young Marx enthusiastically identifies himself with a tradition extending from Aristotle and that embraces Hobbes, Rousseau and Hegel (Marx and Engels, 1975a: 207). It is a tradition that stresses autonomy, citizenship and in its mature liberal phase, individuality, but its abstract universality betrays its concrete exclusiveness. It 'leaves out' women, the poor and non-Europeans. Yuval-Davis has noted the 'fraternal' character of the Enlightenment project – a project that confined women to the domestic 'private' domain (1999: 119).

It is not that the thinkers of the Enlightenment necessarily intended to be exclusive and liberals today are often astonished when the point is made that their own formulations are implicitly selective and elitist. Lloyd cites Condorcet's vision of the human race 'emancipated from its shackles, released from the empire of fate, and from that of the enemies of progress, advancing with a firm and sure step along the path of truth, virtue and happiness' (Lloyd, 1984: 57). But the idea that 'truth, virtue and happiness' are self-evident and timeless verities, discoverable by all rational people, is an abstract notion that embodies the concrete misery of the 'other': the victim crushed by prejudice and structure. If emancipation is presented in this absolutist way, then it negates the inclusivity that is crucial to the concept of citizenship we are seeking to expound.

But the weaknesses of the notion of emancipation historically arise from the weaknesses of the liberal tradition. But this is a tradition upon which we should build. The concept of emancipation is crucial to the discourse of inclusivity, provided we rework emancipation so that it embraces circumstance, situation and, a point that feminists in particular stress, takes account of body and gender. Lloyd herself emphasizes the importance of reworking, rather than simply rejecting, these traditions when she argues that we should point to the limitations of the Enlightenment concept of philosophy and reason 'without repudiating either Reason or Philosophy' (1984: 109; Hoffman, 2001: 54).

It is not emancipation that is the problem. It is abstraction, elitism, patriarchy and statism. Of course, we cannot ignore the way in which the market generates divisions which themselves create the violence that makes the role of the state seem natural. Melissa Benn (2002) has noted that inequality is increasing on a global scale (Sorensen, 2001: 183). Whereas the income of company directors in the USA ten years ago was 42 times higher than that of blue collar workers, now it is some 419 times higher (Benn, 2002). Is it any wonder that a sense of community is radically undermined by what is too often seen as the inevitable workings of the market?

Emancipation is impossible if people cannot 'change places'. Sylvester objects to the idea of looking to an 'emancipatory finale' (1994: 210). But why should we characterize emancipation as a timeless culmination beyond which no further development is possible? Emancipation involves greater control over our lives and thus an awareness of the malleable character of repressive hierarchy and domination. But it does not follow that emancipation will be 'realized' in some particular (and thus absurdly privileged) historical context (Hoffman, 2001: 68).

It is true that the concept of emancipation as formulated in the Enlightenment had this abstract and static dimension. This is why writers like Ashley, who see themselves as poststructuralists (or postmodernists – we will not make any distinction here), regard the concept of emancipation with suspicion. Ashley insists that, despite the many salient comments he makes about the state and state sovereignty, he is not undertaking 'an emancipatory critique'. He is not seeking to impose a standard or pass a judgement on the world (1988: 228). But why should we take the view that an emancipatory critique has to be arbitrary and historically insensitive?

The case for an inclusive citizenship does not assume that people should be 'emancipated' simply because we decree that this should be so. It rests upon an argument that in an interconnected world, the state has become archaic and the use of violence to tackle conflicts of interests increasingly counter-productive. Postmodernists sometimes see emancipation as an inherently 'foundational' concept i.e., that it rests upon moral and philosophical foundations that are timeless and thus dogmatic in nature. But this assumes that emancipation cannot be developed as a concept so that full account is taken of historical change and fluid context.

Postmodernism and Momentum Concepts

To reconstruct the concept of emancipation, we have to free it from the absolutism and abstraction that it inherited from the Enlightenment. To reconstruct a concept involves a critical process in which older concepts are not demolished, but they are creatively reworked.

Indeed, I would argue that an effective critique involves both demolition *and* reworking, deconstruction *and* reconstruction. One without the other is either nihilist or positivist – either a mindless destruction, or a triumphalist celebration, of the status quo. To avoid this kind of self-defeating one-sidedness, a distinction must be made between 'momentum' as opposed to 'static' concepts. Some concepts are inherently static, by which I mean that they cannot be reconstructed, because they are intrinsically repressive and exclusionary. They can only be discarded. Concepts like the 'state', 'patriarchy' and 'violence' fall into this category. This does not mean that such concepts must simply be erased because we deem them inherently exclusionary. They have to be understood, analysed and, above all, placed accurately in their historical context.

Static concepts are not all the same. We need, for example, to distinguish between liberal or modern patriarchy and pre-modern patriarchy: the latter explicitly separates men and women, the former does so implicitly. But the fact remains that all patriarchy, whether liberal or not, is repressive. The same is true of the state, no matter how modern. It is undoubtedly the case that the more liberal the repression the better, since hypocrisy (as is so often said) is the homage vice pays to virtue. This is why we regard concepts like the state, patriarchy and violence as static concepts. They are not, despite what conservatives sometimes think, part of the 'human condition' and they stand as barriers to emancipation and an inclusive citizenship. We need to look beyond them – so that like the notion of chattel slavery today, they come to be regarded as unacceptable concepts to rational and fair-minded people.

In contrast to static concepts are *momentum* concepts, which I define as concepts that *are* part of the human condition, and that are capable of further development. Momentum concepts can and should be reconstructed: static concepts cannot be reconstructed. Thus freedom and equality are examples of momentum concepts. The concept of freedom in ancient Greece is not a concept that applies to slaves. But we must build upon it. It is broadened by liberals to embrace the rights of former slaves and later extended (in a formal sense) to women and the property-less. But the notion of freedom, as developed by classical liberalism, although more inclusive than earlier formulations, is still exclusive and unsatisfactory, for its abstract character masks the concrete oppression of hapless others. But this is the problem with liberalism, not with freedom. Momentum concepts should be developed so that they apply to excluded others in a way that takes account of their particular oppression.

Momentum concepts have an egalitarian and anti-hierarchical 'logic', using the term 'hierarchy' to mean a differentiation that is repressive and divisive. This logic invites us to link the different phases within a concept's formulation in a progressive manner, so that, as we have seen, the 'movement' from ancient notions of freedom (for example) to liberal notions, constitutes a step forward. Momentum concepts are inherently progressive. They 'unfold' so that we must continuously rework them in a way that realizes more and more of their egalitarian and anti-hierarchical potential.

Tocqueville, a French liberal aristocrat, defines democracy as a momentum concept. In a famous passage he speaks of democracy as a concept whose universal and permanent progress is helped along by every event: 'is it wise', he asks, ' to suppose that a movement which has been so long in train could be halted by one generation?' The point he makes about democracy is that it forever progresses, outstripping earlier formulations with more advanced ones. To some, it seems a purely bourgeois concept, concerned with the rights of those who have capital. But beware! It is the kind of concept with no stopping point: why should democracy simply address itself to the middle classes and the rich? Why eliminate the hierarchies of feudalism, only to accept the rule of the capitalists (1966: 8–9)? Turner speaks of citizenship as a series of expanding circles pushed forward 'by the momentum of conflict and struggle' (1986: xii; see also 133–5). This is precisely the point that the momentum concept seeks to capture.

It might be argued, however, that the whole idea of a momentum concept is self-contradictory since it appears to presuppose a resting place – a point at which its egalitarian potential is 'realized'. Are not momentum concepts also static therefore, and have a foundational character? It is true that Tocqueville's formulation of democracy does, indeed, betray foundational and static features. He speaks of the democratic momentum as the product of a providence in which the people serve 'as the blind instruments in the hands of God'. To fight against democracy is 'a fight against God himself' (1966: 8–9).

What this shows, however, is not that the momentum concept is itself flawed, but that Tocqueville has developed the notion in a partial and inadequate way. To link a momentum concept with a notion of divine providence is to deny it consistent historicity, since it is tied to a 'God' whose conception is static, whole and complete. Such a God lies outside of the historical process it seeks to explain. It is this idea that is static, not the momentum concept itself. Tocqueville's own analysis of democracy in the USA in the 1840s is uncritical in the way in which it treats democracy as simply a synonym for the spread of property ownership; it regards blacks and native Americans (whose exploitation Tocqueville eloquently denounces) as 'tangents to my subject', and it does not see the exclusion of women from the franchise as a problem for America as 'an immense and complete democracy' (1966: 390–421; Hoffman, 2001: 24). Vogel argues when it comes to his analysis of marriage, Tocqueville affirms the medieval structures of the English Common Law as the requisite of a modern egalitarian order (1994: 82).

Contrary to Tocqueville's particular stance, the momentum concept itself is inherently subversive. It restlessly moves beyond the formulations of its supporters by drawing attention to those who are either thoughtlessly excluded or who are included in inadequate ways to the particular disabilities they face. What makes the notion of emancipation a 'momentum' concept is the idea that we can only move towards an emancipated society. Were we to say that an emancipated society had finally arrived, we would indeed have idealized a particular status quo, and abandoned the *infinitely* critical quality of the momentum concept. This is why I argue that politics itself will always exist. The fact that people are, have been and always will be different, means that conflict is part of society and since conflicts need to be resolved, politics is also part of the 'human condition'.

Many of those who call themselves postmodernists, have simply inverted static notions of truth and progress. Not surprisingly, they have ended up with a nihilism and a scepticism that is as abstract and absolutist as the positions they challenge. I have argued elsewhere that Ashley's rejection of the 'truth', like his rejection of emancipation, rests upon an inverted modernism that is as one-sided and uncritical as the positions he challenges. As Turner reminds us, postmodernity means 'after' but not 'anti' modernity (1994: 155), but the point is that if postmodernism means (as it should) a movement *beyond* modernity, then it must embrace the momentum concept. To do this, postmodernism must avoid being trapped in the 'either/or' logic of the modernist position. The replacement of a statically conceived notion of absolute truth by a (equally statically conceived) notion of sheer contingency does not represent a move forward, however much it may scandalize conservative academia.

Walker argues that the concept of citizenship will continue to 'name a political practice that is plausibly monopolised by the modern state'. Yet citizenship, he contends, 'is always already reaching beyond the state, reaching to a beyond, to an abstract humanity, that is constitutive of the state itself' (1999: 198). But this implies that no progress beyond statism is possible – that we cannot conceptualize a citizenship that is neither dualistic nor abstractly universal in character. This is a scepticism ultimately leading to despair and passivity.

Harding is right to ask the question: why should we assume that in giving up the goal of telling one true story about reality, we cannot at the same time strive to tell 'less false stories'? We can produce less partial and perverse representations of the real world 'without having to assert the absolute, complete, universal or eternal advocacy' of these representations (Harding, 1990: 100). In other words, the argument that we must *choose* – in this case between timeless absolute truths and no truth at all – rests upon a supremely modernist juxtaposition of opposites. It cannot be called postmodernist at all, and despite the 'newness' of its appearances, this kind of nihilism can be found, for example, in the work of David Hume, an eighteenth-century liberal sceptic!

Yeatman develops what she calls 'a postmodern emancipatory politics', which is rooted in the 'values of modern universalism, rationalism, justice and individualism' (1994: x). This is surely a correct approach, although it is important to emphasize that modern values need to be reworked and transcended if they are to serve as the basis of a postmodern project. We need to both deconstruct and reconstruct, and what has given postmodernism its nihilist image is the way in which some of its self-appointed practitioners imagine that it is possible to destroy without at the same time building, to deconstruct without simultaneously reconstructing.

Yeatman comments that instead of trying to overcome domination once and for all, we should seek 'on-going imaginative and creative forms of positive resistance to various forms of domination' (1994: 9). But there are two problems with this argument. The first is that Yeatman identifies her emancipatory postmodernism with 'an ideal state' but the very concept of an ideal state is a modernist abstraction that presupposes a gulf between theory and practice, ideals and reality. The state, it could well be argued, is an institution that moves incessantly between an 'idealized' view of community (which it vainly seeks to realize) and a 'realistic' view of human nature (which, alas, frustrates its communitarian ideals).

The idea that the universal constitutes an oppressive 'grand narrative' so that we can only attend to particularities, represents a concession to the dualism between the general and the specific: an argument much beloved by pseudo-postmodernists. Derrida's attack on the 'narrative of emancipation' (cited by Carter, 2001: 206) assumes that universality must suffocate that which is particular and diverse – the liberal position turned inside out. There is no contradiction between resisting various forms of domination (if by domination we mean control through violence) and domination itself, since it is by challenging domination in its particular forms that we can challenge domination *per se*. Yet, as her work elsewhere indicates, Yeatman ultimately accepts the need for a state and thus naturalizes violence (Hoffman, 2001: 191). It has to be said that an emancipatory politics can only move beyond modernism if it moves beyond the state, the naturalization of violence, and formulations that implicitly embrace the logic of dualism.

The assumption is not therefore being made that because emancipation, like citizenship, is a momentum concept, its egalitarian logic will ever be realized in a once-and-for-all manner. It would contradict its momentum status if we were to argue that our concept of inclusive citizenship has 'finally' included everyone in a wholly adequate way. We know that women, gays and the poor have been excluded from practical citizenship. But we are only now becoming conscious of the problems that prevent those with mental and physical disabilities from governing their own lives. It would be foolish and complacent to imagine that the road to emancipation or citizenship or equality (to name just three momentum concepts) has a sign at the end of it stating 'Goal attained; no further progress possible'.

This is the problem with Baumeister's argument (2000: 65) that the Kantian concept of imperfect obligations makes it possible to take account of situation and context. Perfect duties, she says, are universal: imperfect ones specific. We still have a dualism here – the conceptual expression of statism. The notion of a momentum concept seeks to move beyond all forms of dualism and abstraction.

Emancipation and Rights

A recent collection talks of the 'demands' of citizenship in order to stress that citizenship is not simply a right, but a duty, or in our terminology, an obligation (McKinnon and Hampsher-Monk, 2000: 1). Pre-modern notions of citizenship stress the relationships that exist between individuals and groups: it is true that these relationships are conceived in repressively hierarchical terms, but an emphasis upon relationships translates into a concern with duties. Classical liberals, by contrast, in constructing a notion of individuality bereft of relationships, stress the importance of rights. I want to argue that one should not be chosen in preference to the other. Emancipation requires both – otherwise it becomes a paradox, veering between anarchism (rights without obligations) and authoritarianism (obligations without rights).

The notion of right is, therefore, a modern concept. Pre-modern notions stress the duty to participate in public life for the elite who are deemed citizens. The idea of a right *against* others arises historically from the assumption that property ownership is an absolute entitlement and no-one, whatever their status, should interfere. This negativity is important but one-sided. It is true that the exercise of autonomy implies the right for individuals to determine their own lives, but the point is that one individual cannot be said to exercise their own rights if others are repressed as a consequence. Built into a coherent notion of negativity is positive respect for the rights of others.

Indeed, the term 'right' came to acquire a more positive connotation with Marshall's celebrated argument (which was explored in detail in Chapter 5), that citizenship involves not merely civil but political and social rights. Even civil rights depend upon access to resources, since in a capitalist society legal rights are problematic if a person cannot afford to hire the services of solicitors and barristers. Rights are entitlements, and the more explicitly social they become, the more negative rights and positive rights are mixed together.

The argument that rights are collective should be looked at with caution. To say that collectivities have rights is contestable if by this is meant that individuals within those collectivities have their rights exercised by those apparently acting in their name. Surely rights should be seen as individual *and* relational so that rights are always exercised by individuals as part of groups – but these groups are fluid and pluralistic in their composition and structure. Isin and Wood (1999: 34) speak of the need for group rights, but the danger is that these 'rights' would be entitlements exercised at the expense of constituent individuals.

Of course, rights can become dependencies. But this arises because one right is abstracted from others, so that the question of access to resources is stressed at the expense of the right to self-government. If, as the New Right argue, welfare rights have led to dependency upon 'the state', this is because rights are treated in an abstract and statist manner. The right of a citizen cannot logically be construed as the right to exploit another, but because we often (and wrongly) allow 'rights' which have harmful consequences, we assume that people can have too many rights or the wrong kind of rights. It is no more a person's right to abuse a welfare system than it is their right to abuse another individual.

Indeed, the notion of emancipation turns into its opposite if we allow for an abstract concept of right, which juxtaposes it to duty. What has made emancipation seem problematic to millions of citizens in former Communist Party states, is the idea that emancipation is 'a right' that can be imposed from on-high. People have to emancipate themselves, so that there is – to put the point philosophically – both relativity and absolutism in the exercise of rights. No person can emancipate themselves by oppressing another – that is the absolute character of rights. But how they perceive their behaviour depends upon historical circumstances, which necessarily change. Women today demand rights that their predecessors would have been unaware of. The right, for example, not to be sexually molested by a marital partner is still not recognized in many societies and many women themselves do not recognize this as a right.

To be emancipated, one must exercise rights that enable a person to govern themselves. Any attempt to privilege one right over another, or to stress duties at the expense of rights, undermines the emancipatory thrust inherent in an inclusive notion of citizenship. It is frequently noted that liberalism, as it is presented by Rawls, prioritizes the right over the good – as though substantive questions are alien to the liberal state and proce-dural questions alone prevail. But this is abstract and one-sided. To recognize the rights of all is itself a particular good, and unless this parti-cular good prevails, rights themselves are in jeopardy. Because liberalism naturalizes the state and therefore violence, it cannot sustain the tolera-tion and fairness that it professes as its guiding principles. Rightful pro-cedures require resources and recognition if they are to operate meaningfully: to argue that the recognition of rights is not a substantive question (a particular 'good'), implies an abstract individuality that in practice sacrifices the freedom of the many for the privilege of the few.

The enjoyment of rights occurs, and can only occur, in a social context. No-one has the right to abuse others or indeed themselves. Rights, there-fore, imply duties, since rights are necessarily conditional and historical. It is this sense of context that imposes restraint and thus duty. Rights can only exist in the context of relationships; once this point is grasped, then the notion that rights can be anti-social or abusive, falls away. Emancipation neither implies dependence nor (if this is conceived in an abstract fashion) independence. It assumes *interdependence* i.e., the exer-cise of rights in a social context with an awareness that it is only possible for one person to exercise a right if others do as well. An exclusive eman-cipation is a contradiction in terms.

If people resort to violence so that counter-violence is necessary, then it is far better to provisionally justify the exercise of violence as an activity that necessarily erodes the rights of both the victor and the victim. This is why the state is crucial to the argument, for once we assume that states are time-lessly necessary and unproblematically natural, then rights will be treated abstractly and atomistically. This will inevitably lead us to argue that rights ought to give way to duties, or that we have a right to act in ways that harm others or ourselves. It may be necessary to incarcerate brutalized people: but it is an illusion to think that this activity is a 'right'. If we have to act violently towards others, then this can only mean that conditions do not exist (to this particular extent) that make rights and emancipation possible.

Democracy and Emancipation

Democracy, as we made clear in the discussion with Tocqueville, is a momentum concept, which is closely linked to the question of emancipation. But precisely because democracy is a momentum concept, it transcends the state, and, as discussed in Chapter 2, the case against democracy is in reality an argument against the repression of the state. It is not democracy that allows the rights of minorities to be violated: it is the state. In the same way, it is not emancipation seeking to impose a homogeneity from on-high, it is the state. Clearly a tyranny of the majority is, as Mill argued so well in *On Liberty*, no improvement over a tyranny of the minority, but it is crucial to be clear that such a tyranny is not itself the product of democracy.

Delanty speaks of a danger today that democracy may become disconnected from citizenship and the rule of law (2000: 3). But this is to use the term 'democracy' in a formalistic and superficial way. Of course, not everyone wishes to be emancipated. Can we emancipate someone against their will? There are two mistakes often made when linking democracy and emancipation. The first is to assume that 'everyone' deep down seeks to govern their own lives and that an act of external liberation will be gratefully received. Oppression brutalizes both the oppressor and the oppressed. What gives naturalism (i.e., a static and abstract view of nature) its superficial plausibility is the fact that people can internalize oppression and regard themselves as worthless. Emancipation remains a problem because significant numbers of people feel threatened and not empowered by the notion of emancipation.

There can be no short-cuts. By this we mean that any attempt to impose emancipation upon others in a violent way is self-defeating. If people are to be respected, then this respect must extend to unemancipated attitudes and activities. It is shameful that people smoke, drink excessive amounts of alcohol, drive cars as a leisure activity and have a consumerist attitude towards sexuality. This is just a tiny sample of activities that are contrary to human development. Let us agree that the activities, instanced above, are in conflict with emancipation. It does not follow that more enlightened activity can be imposed from on-high. As Tully puts it, 'it is the people themselves who must experience an identity as imposed and unjust; they must come to support a demand for the recognition of another identity from a first-person perspective' (2000: 225). To impose emancipation upon another is to act in a contradictory and self-defeating manner.

It has long been pointed out that a perceived gulf between emancipation and activity may arise from lack of information. There is certainly evidence to suggest that people are often ignorant of the consequences of smoking, driving cars when they could walk, casual sexual activity, etc. But not always. People may be aware of the negative consequences that flow from particular activities and yet still persist with these activities: what then? We have many sanctions short of force, which can and should be used to discourage activities that are not emancipatory. Persuasion, ostracism, and if these do not work, condemnation and criticism. We need to emphasize that unemancipatory activities are practically harmful – not merely that they contravene ethical norms. Not all activities are harmful in the same way and we may find some activities distasteful, even though we cannot say that strictly speaking, they are harmful at all. Mill's *On Liberty* offers a way of judging. But even when activities are harmful, there are many ways of bringing pressure on people, which fall short of force. This is why coercion is compatible with emancipation in a way that force is not.

But if we should resist the temptation to emancipate others – an absolutist error – we should also resist the relativist error of assuming that emancipation does not exist and, as the positivists say, it is a pure 'value judgement'. If absolutism leads to autocracy, relativism generates pessimism and despair. So the second mistake to avoid in tackling the question of emancipation is to assume that people cannot change and that those who feel threatened by emancipation today will always feel so threatened. One point is often overlooked by pessimists and relativists. Even those who feel threatened, act in ways that demonstrate the momentum nature of emancipation. Indeed, reaction can be a kind of inverted progress – a recognition that something which a person finds threatening, is inevitable. A backlash to developments like feminism and traffic regulation, should be seen as the defence of that which has become indefensible, so that those who *react* when faced with emancipation, are acknowledging in an inverted way that the tide is against them! But patience and persistence remain crucial. Indeed, to try and impose emancipation from above, has the effect of discrediting and delaying real progress towards emancipation. This is not a question of 'condoning' unemancipated activities: it is a question of working effectively to overcome them.

The notion of emancipation, like democracy, is an on-going activity. One can no more reach a final state of emancipation than one can say that a democratic society has been reached – a society that has exhausted all potential for further democratization. Converting statism into governmental activities is essential if we are to progress towards emancipation. But emancipation would instantly become an oppressive theology – a statist dogma – if it ever actually arrived.

Citizenship as a Momentum Concept

Citizenship is undermined by the state, nationalism, sexism and dogmas that exclude 'others'. But it does not follow that (a) inadequate and partial formulations of citizenship should be rejected, or that (b) a solution exists that should put an end to contention and controversy. Bankowski and Christodoulidis put the matter well when they say that what is important about a horizon is that 'you never get there, because each time you approach it, it expands and new vistas and possibilities open up' (1999: 103).

I have already argued that a liberal conception of citizenship is closer to emancipation than a pre-modern or archaic notion. Moreover, we should not reject advances simply because those making them do not embrace our view of citizenship. The recognition by modern liberal societies of the value of diversity is positive (even if often muddled). Just as feminists, for example, recognize that the acquisition of the vote represented an important step forward for women, so the fierce debate raging over citizenship is itself positive in that it recognizes that old definitions are not satisfactory.

States are increasingly sensitive to restrictive and ethnic notions of citizenship. If people can acquire citizenship through residence rather than through a (extremely vague) set of ethnic credentials, that is a crucial step forward on the road to inclusivity. Delanty is right to stress the importance of defining citizenship in terms of residence rather in terms of birth (2000: 121). If individuals can enjoy dual, or better, multiple citizenships, that too is an important advance. If being a citizen entitles you to material resources – like social security payments – that too is an advance toward emancipation, provided as always this right empowers rather than degrades. The momentum concept seeks to break with the dualistic view that either nothing changes or everything has to change – all at once! This is why the traditional notion of revolution is problematic. It is premised upon a rejection of continuity in favour of discontinuity as though we can have one without the other.

Tully goes some of the way to capturing the dynamic character of the momentum concept when he argues that a sense of citizen belonging is engendered more by struggles over recognition than by 'the actual end-state of gaining this or that form of recognition' (2000: 229). But there is a danger here. It is rather like the celebrated Bernsteinian formula that the end is nothing and the movement everything. We should neither absolutize or privilege means over ends or ends over means. Recognition does need to be gained, but the 'end-state' here is not an end to end all ends. Recognition is a process that has infinite depths to it.

The notion of citizenship as self-rule is a profound one, and Rousseau is right to see that legitimacy requires that we are governed by laws which we have imposed upon ourselves. The problem with the classical liberal tradition is not the 'ideal': it is the statist assumptions that accompany the argument. Once we naturalize the use of violent sanctions to enforce the law, then citizenship is problematized. Free citizens become those who rule over subjects – the irrational and inferior others who break the laws and whose own identity has to be submerged. This is surely the answer to the problem as to whether we define citizenship 'thinly' as the relatively passive enjoyment of rights, or 'thickly' as the robust exercise of socially responsible obligations. The question is not a choice between two rival notions, but a movement towards and beyond the 'thin' conception. The 'thin' conception is a significant advance for those who have no citizenship: the 'thick' conception is obviously one to work towards when the 'thin' has been obtained. Citizenship must be conceived in process, momentum terms.

Citizenship becomes a homogenizing rhetoric when, in classically statist fashion, we set up abstract ideals against divisive realities. Sperling speaks of incorporating women as full citizens, but while she makes an eloquent case for the inclusion of women, her argument ultimately relies upon a statist sense of the ideal (2001: 192–3). Butler has rightly argued that there 'can be no final or complete inclusivity' and adds: 'for democratic reasons', there ought never be (cited by Sylvester, 2002: 246). Bankowski and Christodoulidis' correctly argue that home and community are fluid concepts, which are forever reaching beyond themselves (1999: 89, 92). Like citizenship, the community must be conceived as both local and universal (1999: 98). Walker defines citizenship as 'an expression of historically specific, and historically variable relationships' (1999: 172) and it is this relational emphasis that is central to the case against exclusivity.

Precisely because citizenship is a momentum concept, it allows for both degrees of citizenship and citizenship as an activity that is distinct in kind. The notion of the 'second-class citizen' captures this problem well. One could not say of blacks under apartheid, or women under the Taliban or slaves in ancient Greece, that they were 'second-class' citizens. It was made brutally explicit by the rulers of these societies that blacks or women or slaves were not citizens at all. Becoming a second-class citizen suggests formal entitlements which structural pressures undermine. It is better to be a second-class citizen than no citizen at all. But at the same time, it is not enough. More is attainable.

Vogel finds the term 'second-class citizen' curious, since it suggests membership of a political community that is both universal and hierarchically ordered. She is right to stress that second-class citizens are those who are, on the one hand, recognized as members of the community in some regards yet are treated, in important respects, as if they were not. She gives examples of blacks, members of ethnic minorities and women – all groups whose access to money, time, health, education, linguistic skills and those with power and influence is problematic. Second-class citizens suffer the burden of a long history of dependence and subordination while being deemed formal equals within modern liberal democracies (Vogel, 1994: 76–7).

When Tully argues that citizenship is an identity that we acquire by being 'free citizens', by engaging in the institutions of self-rule of a 'free people' (2000: 214), one can agree with this, provided we understand that self-rule is something we aim at; increasingly realize, but never actually reach. Tully's definition becomes treacherously divisive if we link the 'free citizen' to the state, to particular nations, or to particular people within these nations. We say to Tully, what Tully says to the liberals: the liberals are right to stress the need for constitutional provision, but wrong to assume that these conditions 'adequately' account for citizenship (2000: 215). In the same way, we have to say to Tully that he is right to emphasize the importance of self-rule, but this welcome formula becomes woefully inadequate if presented in a statist and static way.

The Question of Exclusivity

It was argued in Chapter 1 that citizenship should be confined to adults, but this does not mean that children, animals and nature in general should be left out in the cold. On the contrary. An inclusive notion of citizenship can only be sustained if the interests of citizens as adults are linked to what we will call a developmental attitude towards non-citizens.

Children are the citizens of tomorrow. A democratic attitude towards children is crucial if children are to grow up with respect for human rights and a critical attitude towards repression. Post-statist attitudes can hardly be instilled if adults, whether teachers, parents or relatives feel free to use violence as a method of trying to resolve conflict, and it is sickening to read how those who brutalize and torment others as adults, have been maltreated in their youth. This does not mean that there is a case for children as such assuming the rights and responsibilities of citizenship. In fact to impose citizenship upon children would be unnatural – by which I mean that it would actually impede the development of a young person and undermine their preparation for adulthood.

A developmental attitude or ethic requires sensitivity to a person's precise position. To allow a five-year-old to cross a busy road unaided is no more helpful than insisting that a fifteen-year-old can only cross a road when 'guided' by his or her parents. It is true that this developmental ethic is central to all social relationships since we cannot empower others if we ignore their particular interests and identities. But there is a significant gulf between youth and adulthood, which is captured by the argument that adults can and should be citizens in ways that children cannot or should not. The case for citizenship studies at school level is overwhelming (as will be discussed in Chapter 9), not because school students should be deemed citizens, but because they are in a process of *becoming* citizens, and a respect for others, the need to be assertive rather than aggressive and a basic understanding of the political institutions regulating their lives, etc., is crucial for an inclusive citizenship. Indeed, it is as crucial as the knowledge about bodies and emotions, which ought to be presented in sex education.

Van Steenbergen has suggested that there are good arguments for extending the notion of citizenship to parts of nature other than humans. All 'living beings', he contends, should be seen as having 'rights' (1994: 145). But this argument is at once too narrow and too broad. It is too narrow because an inclusive citizenship requires respect not only for animals and 'living things' but for nature as a whole. Humans derive their identity from an evolutionary process, which means that they are natural beings in human form, and while this form is not unimportant, it is impossible for humans to develop if a purely negative attitude towards nature in general is taken. To respect animals but not inorganic nature is counter-productive and the social problems that afflict us today are linked in no small part to the hostile attitude we have inherited towards the world of nature.

But Van Steenbergen's position is also too broad. To argue that all living things should have rights empties the concept of right of its meaningful content, since to demand of animals, for example, that they have responsibilities and obligations is counter-productive. Indeed, it is, to use a word that Van Steenbergen himself employs, 'anthropocentric' (1994: 144), since the notion of punishing a cat, for example, for 'murdering' mice is truly grotesque. Van Steenbergen is not quite clear whether at the end of the day one of the rights, which all living things have, is that of citizenship (1994: 151).

But the point is this. If we are to develop emancipatory and egalitarian attitudes towards non-citizens, then we cannot merely invert authoritarian attitudes that treat nature as something for humans to exploit. We must go beyond conventional theology, which imposes a repressive hierarchy upon the world in general. In fact, it is not difficult to see that those who would naively extend citizenship and rights to all living things, are still operating (critical declarations notwithstanding) with the abstractions of modernist discourse. They assume that equality means sameness and democracy involves treating everything and everyone in an identical way.

An inclusive theory of citizenship requires respect for diversity. The case for human rights is premised on the assumption that humans are not only the same, but different. The argument against violence, the distinction between nationalism and national identity, the view of natural as developmental rather than timeless or ahistorical and the support for a feminism informed by postmodernism arises from the view that people can only be respected as equals when we acknowledge their particular (and thus differentiated) identities.

But it would be curious indeed if we did not extend this dialectic of difference and sameness to the relationship of humans to nature. Just as humans are not simply replicas of each other, so too must we insist that nature is different, and we do not acknowledge this difference, if we thoughtlessly extend to nature rights and responsibilities that exist for humans. This is why, as I have argued elsewhere (2001: 201), 'deep ecology' or 'ecocentrism' is profoundly modernist in the way it imposes human values upon nature. Although the intention is not to dominate or exploit (as it is in conventional modernist discourse), the effect is the same, since inverting oppression still leaves a theorist prisoner to authoritarian premises.

A momentum view of citizenship must make distinctions. I have argued the case for differentiating liberal from openly and explicitly exclusive notions of citizenship, just as I have argued that steps in the direction of a more inclusive notion of citizenship linked (for example) to residence and plurality should be welcomed. In the same way, an inclusive view of citizenship requires differentiating today's citizens from tomorrow's citizens, and citizens from non-citizens. Paternalism involves treating people oppressively: it is not synonymous with the distinction between adult and child! The fact that the notion of a 'non-citizen' has been used historically against other adults on racist, sexist and nationalist grounds, does not mean that the distinction itself is invalid.

On the contrary. To take democracy and emancipation seriously, we must differentiate. An inclusive theory of citizenship, which refuses to make distinctions, will be inclusive only in name. In reality it will merely replicate the repressive hierarchy of divided societies. This is why Turner is wrong to argue that children and animals should be regarded as citizens, as though this is the only way in which they can be treated with respect and equality. There is a significant difference – although Turner does not recognize it – between the abstract and the universal (1986: 98, 100). A universal view of citizenship is one that respects difference, rather than ignores it. Turner argues that whereas individuals require particularity, citizens require generality (1986: 133). Yet, it could be countered that citizenship requires overcoming the binary divide between generality and particularity, which Turner takes for granted.

Emancipation and Representation

Citizens need to be active in pressing their demands and taking responsibility for policies that have been democratically decided. But must a democratic notion of citizenship avoid representation, on the grounds that representatives act as substitutes for citizens and, therefore, undermine the participatory activism of citizens themselves?

Rousseau, in a famous passage in *The Social Contract* links emancipation and sovereignty to direct involvement, arguing passionately that to be represented is to give up – to alienate – powers that individuals alone can rightfully exercise. Deputies are acceptable since they are merely the agents of the people. Representation, on the other hand, an odious modern idea, involves a form of slavery – a negation of will (1968: 141).

Rousseau's position is untenable. He sees the individual as autonomous in a purely abstract sense and thus denies that hierarchy of any kind is tolerable. Once you consider individuals in relationships (and it is only through a relationship that a person can be an individual), then hierarchy – of a fluid, interpenetrating kind – is natural, and autonomy can only mean that individuals seek to govern their own lives in a relational context. Of course, as was noted earlier, when Rousseau speaks of 'individuals', he is only talking about a rather select group of propertied males, and his notion of abstract individuality betrays its elitist character when seriously interrogated.

But the problem of representation is a real one. For emancipation and citizenship imply action – representation allows others to act on your behalf. The liberal tradition is, as always, ambivalent over the question. For the very notion of representation as a re-presenting of the individual, arises from the classical liberal view that citizens are individuals: the notion must have an egalitarian core to it. Representatives can only act on behalf of those they represent if they understand their problems and way of life.

But it is important not to fall into the modernist trap of juxtaposing representation to direct democracy. It is revealing that the Burkean argument that representatives simply act in what they see (in their infinite wisdom) is the real interest of their constituents, inverts the Rousseauan view that representation is necessarily alienation. Emancipation, as we have defined it, involves a relational notion of autonomy so that those who have neither the time nor resources to make laws directly, authorize others to do so on their behalf. I have argued elsewhere that only through a combination of the direct and the indirect – hands-on participation *and* representation – can democratic autonomy be maximized (Hoffman, 1995: 207). Of course, there are dangers that representatives will act in an elitist manner: but this is also true of 'deputies'. Once we place individuals in a social context in which they relate to others, then representation in some shape or form is inherent in the governing process.

The notion of 'mirror' representation suggests that exact percentages of groups within the population at large need to be 'reflected' in the composition of representatives. If the population of a particular city (like Leicester) contains, say, 40 per cent of people with black faces, then an inclusive notion of citizenship demands that there should be 40 per cent of representatives who are black. It is not difficult to see the problem with this notion. If there are problems with homogenizing society at large, there are also problems with treating ethnic minorities as all the same. Black people in Leicester are divided ethnically, regionally, along class and gender lines, etc., and it is wrong therefore to assume that one black person is the same as another. Moreover, it does not follow that black representatives will necessarily represent the interests of black constituents, any more than we can assume that women representatives will necessarily represent the interests of women.

The 'mirror' theory is basically statist in character. It assumes an oppressive notion of sameness and denies the particular role and responsibility of the representative. Representation involves empathy – the capacity to put yourself in the position of another – and while it is impossible to be another person (hence the dangers of representation), it is necessary to imagine what it is like to be another. Accountability is 'the other side' of representation (Kymlicka, 1995: 149): one without the other descends into either unreality or elitism.

The notion of empathy points to the need for some link between representatives and constituents. Unless representatives are in some sense a reflection of the population at large, it is difficult to see how empathy could take place. Women who have experienced patriarchal oppression at first hand are more likely to have insight into the problems women face than men who – however sympathetic they may be – may have never been the recipients of that particular form of discrimination. The same is true with members of ethnic and sexual minorities, etc. To have experienced humiliation directly as a disabled person makes one far more sensitive to questions of disability. While the 'mirror' theory is untenable, the notion of difference cannot be seriously considered unless representatives 're-present' individuals in a way that sensitizes them to the particular identities and problems of those they represent.

Citizenship cannot be inclusive unless those represented feel comfortable with those who represent them. This is only possible if representatives are, broadly speaking, 'representative' – i.e., they contain significant numbers of people who are the same colour, gender, sexual orientation, etc. – of the population at large. This is crucial for emancipation, for statist attitudes thrive on a view that those who need to be 'governed' are unruly others and quite different from the sane and sensible people who make laws.

SUMMARY

- Citizenship is closely tied to democracy and emancipation. Emancipation – like the notion of freedom, equality, individuality, self-determination etc. – is initially explicitly formulated in a modernist idiom. Just as we must move beyond modernism, so we must reconstruct the notion of emancipation.
- Many self-styled postmodernists, by rejecting modernism rather than transcending it, place themselves in a sceptical cul-de-sac, which is best described as an *inverted*, rather than a *post*, modernism.
- Where concepts are universalistic, we should seek to render them concrete. This is what is meant by reconstruction. Concepts that are divisive, like patriarchy, force or state, cannot be reconstructed and should be rejected.
- Emancipation, like citizenship and democracy, is a momentum concept. But momentum concepts can only be conceived if they are not thoughtlessly idealized, i.e., presented as though they could be realized in some final and supra-historical fashion.

- Being a citizen involves governing oneself, an argument that is rooted in the past and yet looks to the future. Although violence and the state represent clear and manifest barriers to an emancipatory citizenship, moving beyond statism is merely a step along a road infinite in its depth and length.

- An inclusive theory of citizenship must make distinctions – between the citizens of today and the citizens of tomorrow, between human citizens and natural non-citizens. To treat equality as sameness and democracy as mere identity, i.e., an abstraction, is to perpetuate the dualistic attitudes linked to the state, modernity and the discourse of liberalism.

- Emancipated citizens need to be comfortable with those who represent them and this is only possible if representatives are empathetic. This empathy cannot be developed and sustained unless representatives are both different and the same as those they represent.

9

The Problem of
Agency and Realization

Who is to carry through the changes advocated here and is the notion of
an inclusive citizenship an ideal to be realized?

The first issue deserving of attention is the relation between theory
and practice, ideals and reality. It will be argued that we need to distinguish the gulf between theory and practice, which is positive and developmental, and one that is frustrating and disillusioning. A disjunction is
inevitable. But we should separate a disjunction from a dualism. Dualism
implies an unbridgeable divide and arises from an uncritical view of the
state.

The contribution Marxism makes to the argument for an inclusive
citizenship is substantial but not complete. On the one hand, Marxism has
a concept of a transitional state which is fruitful and that I have drawn
upon. There is also the question of what Geras calls the 'democratic
deficits', which have authoritarian consequences and prevent the Marxist
state from withering away. Even if we find a way around the inevitability
argument; the privileging of the proletariat and the problem of moralism,
there is still the question of revolution.

Anarchism appears promising as a doctrine that underpins an inclusive citizenship because of its hostility to the state. But crucial to my critique of anarchism is the argument that one can oppose the state but still
embrace statist assumptions. These lead to a doctrinaire view that coercion and force are equally objectionable, as is both government and the
state. Anarchists embrace a concept of the individual and social transformation that is fundamentally abstract in character and therefore its policy
prescriptions are inevitably anti-liberal rather than post-liberal.

New social movements have a crucial role to play in the struggle
for an inclusive citizenship. New social movements are those which are

concerned with emancipatory objectives so that (in an often implicit way) they seek to go beyond the repressive hierarchies linked to class division and the state. But it is important not to assume that these movements have simply supplanted the older vehicles of struggle – like the political parties – or that the struggle is no longer concerned with the state.

Newer perspectives enrich and enliven older ones and are an important resource in our attempts to resist the notion that citizenship is a static ideal, to be enacted wholesale at some particular historical vantage point. Struggles should not be confined to 'civil society', as opposed to the state, since both are abstract conceptions and we will never create a 'hegemony' for an inclusive citizenship unless we transcend both.

The Crick Report will be examined as an example of a growing concern that citizenship needs to be taken more seriously. The Crick Report is right to argue that a tolerant and democratic society is not something we can take for granted. We have to work consciously towards it. At the same time, as critics of the report point out, we must focus on the problems posed to young people in general, and the members of ethnic minorities in particular, by structural disadvantages. We cannot assume that minorities must simply 'blend' in with majoritarian norms, and that citizenship of a static kind needs to be 'extended' to them. The Crick Report demonstrates the limitations of a statist approach to the question of citizenship and the implicit nationalism that invariably accompanies this approach.

All who suffer from statist notions of citizenship are allies in the struggle to eradicate exclusiveness, even if they suffer in different ways. A relational position must mean that when one is deprived, all are insecure. Common interests can only be cemented when we assume that potentially, an inclusive citizenship should appeal to everyone, since, as in Hobbes' state of nature, no-one has a long-term interest in the increasing violence and destruction wreaked by the market and the state. Although more vulnerable people will particularly favour the struggle for a more inclusive citizenship, no-one is, in principle, excluded.

Theory and Practice: Why the Gulf?

Sandel argues that our principles seem unrealizable – our ideals typically flounder on the gap between theory and practice (1992: 12). Of course, there is a gulf between theory and practice. Theory will always oversimplify reality – it always has and always will – because we are part of an historical process that we can only ever partially grasp. This is not to deny that our theories contain truth, but it is important to remember that this truth is both absolute and relative. We can speak of an analysis seeking a deepening grasp of reality – a growing conformity of theory and practice – without suggesting that a day can ever arrive when theory and practice, ideals and reality, match completely. For such perfection takes us outside of the historical process that is both our source of strength and our source of weakness.

The gulf between theory and practice is positive and developmental. It is a spur to progress and it encourages us to dig deeper. This lies behind the notion of citizenship as a momentum concept as defined in the last chapter, for while we can identify particular barriers to the development of citizenship – violence, inequality, nationalism, sexism etc. – we cannot say that removing these barriers will see the 'final' realization of our concept. A gulf remains – and it always will – between theory and practice.

Such a gulf should be distinguished from the stark chasm that arises when we formulate our theories in ahistorical and perfectionist terms. Disappointment and frustration inevitably results. The notion that there is an 'ideal world' permanently out of reach to mortals on the ground, arises from conventional theology and the 'theological concept' – the mortal god – that is institutionalized in the state. The notion that static ideals can be realized at a given point in time – or the idea that a chasm remains between theory and practice that is tragic and frustrating – stem from the same source: an uncritical view of the state. This uncritical view means that one becomes the prisoner to the state's abstractions and the theoretical dualisms that lie at the heart of the state's practical activity.

Kant makes this point graphically clear when he argues that what is valid in theory (as demonstrated by reason) is valid in practice. There is no gulf between the two because the citizen, an adult male with property, is the member of a state (Reiss, 1970: 75). Kant demonstrates the link between perfectionism and an uncritical view of the state and it is crucial that we do not simply invert perfectionism. We need to go beyond it.

This is why the struggle to deepen citizenship is both ideological and post-ideological. It is ideological in that it seeks to transform the state and is directed at state functionaries. We cannot work for the emancipation of women, for example, or move against the deepening inequalities within and between societies, without involving the state, and without drawing attention in particular to the tension between government and state. On the other hand, the struggle to make citizenship more inclusive is also post-ideological because it seeks to move in the direction of a stateless society so that conflicting interests can be resolved through non-violent sanctions.

Ideology should be defined as a theoretical system that focuses on the state. This statist focus for ideology helps to preserve the common view of ideology as a dogma that distorts political realities. However, where I differ from the normal case for ideology as a negative phenomenon is through the argument that to overcome ideology, we must overcome the state. The struggle for a more inclusive citizenship is ideological in that it not only involves a critique of the state, but appeals to political movements concerned with emancipation. As discussed in the previous chapter, in a society in which explicit authoritarianism makes even formal liberal citizenship impossible, a movement for citizenship must seek allies from all who are opposed to authoritarian rule. Thus the Movement for Democratic Freedom (MDF) in Zimbabwe links conservatives, liberals and socialists in unity against the tyrannical rule of Robert Mugabe and his ZANU PF. Clearly the MDF is ideological in character. A movement within Britain that opposes patriarchy, or seeks equal rights for gays, or wishes to protect the environment, or whatever, is clearly ideological, because it demands action from the state.

However, emancipatory movements are not simply ideological because they can only be sustained if they look beyond the state. Feminists do not (normally) believe that punishing aggressive men will in itself resolve conflicts of interest, even though statist action of this kind can contribute to changing a culture and set of values and practices, which help women to develop. In this same way, there can only be transitional steps to improving the environment or protecting gays involving the force of the state. Thus, emancipatory movements and indeed the programmes of political parties, must be post-ideological as well as ideological in character. Ideology, in the way I am using the term, embodies a chasm between theory and practice insofar as its supporters believe that they are struggling for a statically conceived ideal world. Activists within peace movements who see war as wrong because it is contrary to scriptural teachings, are ideologists because they see issues in terms of static ideals: environmentalists who project a world in static equilibrium with nature, have an ideology that involves a statist mode of thinking even though it does not necessarily involve the state.

Mannheim in his famous *Ideology and Utopia*, which first appeared in 1936, raises the question as to whether it is possible to talk about ideology without being ideological: this is only possible where we look beyond the state, since it is the state which makes compromise, negotiation and arbitration impossible to sustain. Although there are problems with Marx and Engels' views on revolution and class war, they correctly argue in *The German Ideology* that ideology is tied to the state as an illusory community, so that a post-ideological view must look beyond the state (1976a: 90–2). This is why the Mannheimian solution, which sees classless intellectuals as the ideology-transcending group, is naive, and the attempt by post-war social scientists to chart an end to ideology is no more persuasive than the New Labour argument that ideologies are by nature extremist and thus a thing of the past.

Crick argues that political thinking should be contrasted to ideological thinking, since an ideology means an end to politics (1982: 55). This would be fine were it not for the fact that Crick defines politics in statist terms (1982: 18). This means that ideology again becomes synonymous with anti-liberalism, despite the fact that liberals and liberal socialists and liberal conservatives take the state for granted. If to be non-ideological is to be 'adaptive, flexible and conciliatory', then we must seriously chart the way beyond an institution claiming a monopoly of legitimate force.

Citizenship, therefore, must be conceived as ideological insofar as changes are proposed in which state action is crucial. For when states are involved, there is inevitably a gulf between theory and practice, which assumes chasmic and frustrating proportions. What rescues the notion of citizenship from having a purely ideological character is the argument that citizenship is undermined by the state and that it is a concept which cannot be 'realized' in any kind of static and absolute way. It is an absolute value (like other momentum concepts), which can only manifest itself in historically relative terms. Our theory of citizenship is necessarily in tension with practical development but that gulf becomes an incentive to work at the problem, since it is entirely predictable and derives from the fact that citizenship will continue developing long after the state itself has been surpassed.

Agents of Transformation: Marxism and Anarchism

Marx and Engels use the term 'ideology' in a negative way, but it is arguable that in practice, they are opposed not to ideology *per se* – i.e., a theory of state action – but to idealist ideologies. Ideologies presenting a topsy-turvy view of the world are distorting and vulnerable because they ignore the real conditions that make history possible. There is an analogy here with the way in which Marx and Engels use the term 'philosophy'. They are opposed to 'philosophy' in the sense of idealist theory, i.e., theory that does not recognize the premises of historical materialism, but at the same time they are not opposed to the need for a theory of knowledge and a theory of being.

The problem with the Marxist view of agency in relation to citizenship is not that it is ideological. Indeed, Marxism poses the need to move beyond the state and therefore apparently captures the argument developed above. We need to have a role for the state, which is transitional and self-annulling, so that the struggle for an inclusive citizenship is both ideological and post-ideological. There are elements within classical Marxism that seem promising and helpful. Not only is there the notion of a transitional state, but there is also the view that history is a continuous process and that communism is a phase within this historical process, rather than the 'end of history'.

It is true that the celebrated comment of the 'young' Marx that 'communism is the riddle of history solved' (Marx and Engels, 1975b: 296–7) makes it sound as if communism is the realization (in some kind of absolute sense) of history. But arguably this would be a glaring and pretty obvious inconsistency for a theory that stressed the 'present as history', and Marx's view is (I think) more accurately presented in the comment which occurs at the end of the *Poverty of Philosophy*, that in the classless society, social evolutions will cease to be political revolutions – the clear implication being that change will continue, but without the need for revolutionary upheaval (Marx and Engels, 1976b: 212).

The real problem is that the notion of revolution and class warfare introduce into Marxist theory anti-liberal elements that undermine what

I have called the 'post-liberal logic' of the theory (Hoffman, 1995: 132). Geras has spoken of three democratic 'deficits' within classical Marxist theory, all of which have authoritarian consequences and help to explain why the 'Marxist state' stubbornly refuses to wither away. The first is that emancipatory communism is seen not simply as a possible end, but as an inevitable one, a 'unique destination' in which the inexorable laws of history guarantee the working class victory (Geras, 1994: 80).

But it could be argued that the 'inevitability' reading of Marx is a dogmatic perversion of Marx's real position since Rosa Luxemburg warned that barbarism rather than socialism might triumph, and the *Communist Manifesto* itself notes that class struggle might end in the common ruin of the contending classes. But even if we accept this argument – which Geras rebuts on the grounds that communism remains the only thinkable option (1994: 80–1) – we have the second democratic deficit to contend with. This also has authoritarian and thus exclusivist implications. This is the argument that the agency of change is the proletariat. The notion that a leading role has to be played by the industrial workers (who create surplus value) is too narrow and uncritical to serve as a framework for an inclusive view of citizenship. It is true that the workers are exhorted to build a popular movement 'of the immense majority', but as a particular class they still have a predetermined destiny to construct socialism. To 'privilege' this particular class can only make it easier to justify authoritarian measures against non-proletarians in general or against workers who do not accept the role that Marxism prescribes for them (Hoffman, 1995: 142). Nor is it wholly satisfactory to argue that intellectuals can become leaders of the proletariat (like Marx and Engels) because they supposedly have the capacity to see the struggle as a whole. This might seem to be an elitist formulation encouraging dogmatism and dictatorship.

In regard of the point about 'privileging' the proletariat, it could be countered that increasingly people have to rely upon paid employment to make ends meet, so that the gap between the popular movement and the working class has more or less disappeared. Everyone, except the very rich, is in fact a 'proletarian' and therefore Marx and Engels' position is much more democratic than it sounds. As for the intellectuals, where is the emancipatory movement that does not rely for its leaders in significant part upon those who have been trained to see the movement 'as a whole'?

But even if we accept the case for a 'broad' notion of workers within Marxism, we still need to take account of the third of Geras' democratic deficits – the unwillingness of Marx and Engels to justify the struggle against exploitation in *moral* terms. The case for an inclusive citizenship has a crucial moral dimension to it – a morality rooted in an ethic of development – and yet Marxism suffers from a chronic 'moral constipation' (as one writer has called it; Hoffman, 1995: 142), a reluctance to explicitly endorse moral principles.

The invocation of historical necessity has been used to reject concepts of justice, and yet, as Geras has pointed out (1994: 83), what makes exploitation oppressive is not the technical fact that workers create surplus value for capitalists, but the disparity between effort and reward, suffering and enjoyment, which an inegalitarian society involves. If morality is simply tied to an abstract notion of class struggle, then it falls victim to the quandaries of a kind of 'relativism', which can justify injustice and the violation of human rights provided such actions are deemed to serve the so-called laws of social development. There is proletarian morality and bourgeois morality and never the twain shall meet!

It could be argued, however, that morality is de-emphasized by Marx and Engels for the same reason that philosophy and ideology are apparently rejected. Morality is seen as something absolute and supra-historical and, therefore, incompatible with a theory that stressed the changing nature of context and situation. Engels, towards the end of his life, warns against dogmatic and reductionist views of Marxism and concedes that he and Marx had rather overdramatized the discontinuity between their theory and that of their idealist and liberal rivals (Hoffman, 1995: 143). The view that their theory has broken with morality, oversimplifies an argument that clearly has moral implications, but which locates morality within a new theoretical structure.

But whatever one thinks of these defences against Geras' three democratic deficits, the major problem remains. Marx and Engels believe that a revolutionary transfer of power is necessary and that this is the reason why workers need their own state. One class displaces another class and hence special measures are necessary to protect the new order. This view – which is incontestably part of classical Marxism – creates insuperable problems for a notion that citizenship must be continuously deepened and extended. For if society develops through polarization and war, then it is not just a question of problematizing the citizenship of those who are the enemies of the 'people'. There is also the problem of their 'supporters' and 'apologists'. We remain the prisoners of a language of division in which differences denote an absence of common interests and conflict involves force.

Gramsci's very lack of orthodoxy demonstrates the problems of the classical Marxist position. Although he argues for the importance of culture in politics – and his celebrated notion of hegemony stresses the role of intellectual and moral factors in political leadership – it is often forgotten that his strategy for the societies of the West is a *war* of position. Hegemony is, in the last analysis, a concept of class control and dominance (Hoffman, 1996: 70). It is true that democracy and hegemony cease to be statist concepts as a 'morally unitary social organism', a classless but 'regulated' society develops, but in Gramsci, there is (rather more than in Marx and Engels' work) stress upon an emancipated society as a static ideal, in which freedom vanquishes necessity, theory becomes one with practice and the law ceases to be external to consciousness. No wonder Gramsci called this self-governing ideal an 'ethical state' (Hoffman, 1996: 72).

The problem with the Marxist concept of agency is that it has not fully jettisoned statist elements, and the notion of class war, revolution and of course the need for a new state, make it problematic as a theory to tackle the problem of agency in the struggle to make citizenship more inclusive.

But what of anarchism, which is, after all, a theory that explicitly rejects the need for the state? Surely anarchism has respect for the kind of egalitarianism crucial for a theory of inclusive citizenship? The problem with anarchism is that it may reject the state, but its theory is still premised upon statist assumptions. The 'philosophical anarchists' like Godwin and Stirner have an abstract view of the individual, which involves a kind of liberalism without the state, while Bakunin's stress upon sociability as an instinctual attribute leads in practice to a position that can only vindicate authoritarianism and violence. If both sociability (in the sense of equality) and atomism are natural instincts, then only the radical will-power of an elite can harness the first and crush the second. Indeed, it could be argued that the anti-liberal (rather than post-liberal) character of anarchist thought, makes it particularly prone to violence, since the rejection of constitutionalism means that politics becomes a question of the abstractly conceived will. There is no place for procedures, negotiation and accountability.

Certainly, the belief that coercion, constraint and government are themselves oppressive means that a relationship between individuals gives way to spontaneous expression of group or individual emotion. The distinction between state and government, force and coercion is crucial if we are to chart a path beyond the state that is realistic and achievable. The need to compromise and conciliate in order to achieve consensus and resolve conflicts of interest come into collision with anarchist abstraction. The liberal view of citizenship is a necessary, though clearly not sufficient, step towards a theory of inclusive citizenship. We need a view of the state that sees it as transitionally necessary until a time that common interests are sufficiently robust to rely solely upon arbitration and negotiation to tackle conflict.

Neither Marxism nor anarchism can provide an answer to the problem of agency in a theory of inclusive citizenship.

New Social Movements: A Vehicle for Developing Citizenship?

The new social movements (NSMs) can be presented as a way of developing citizenship capacity and responsibility. An embryonic global public sphere is opening up that allows public space and voice to social movements, non-state actors, 'global citizens' and international organizations (Cohen and Rai, 2000: 13). Is this the way forward for the project of an inclusive citizenship?

It is argued by Cohen and Rai that whereas the old left is preoccupied with rights/emancipation politics, new social movements want changes in life styles and social values (2000: 5). The problem here is to welcome the new, not by repudiating the old, but by enriching it. The notion that social repression and economic inequality, civic and political rights are the 'old' emancipation agenda (2000: 6), fails to see that changes in life styles and the adoption of new social values have an important link with this 'old' agenda.

It is true that the new social movements have significant post-statist implications, which are implicit in their critique of conventional politics, but it is important not to throw the baby out with the bath-water. Touraine's analysis of the new social movements is a classic case in point. In our type of society, he contends, social movements are more than ever the principal agents of history (1981: 9). There is almost a complete rift between party policies and social movements (1981: 23). Social movements are the collective action of actors at the highest level fighting for social control of historicity (1981: 26).

Touraine is certainly correct to stress the importance and the centrality of the new social movements. He describes them as being the 'fabric of society' (1981: 29), but radically weakens his argument by contending that the action of these social movements is not fundamentally directed towards the state (1981: 80). Indeed, Touraine's argument is curiously conservative since the strategy he proposes would leave the power of the state intact. He assumes that if the state is targeted, then its power is perpetuated. The struggle of the new social movements, he rightly insists, cannot be identified with political action for the conquest of power (1981: 80), but why should we assume that political action has to be geared to the 'conquest of power'? This is a notion which implies that only a revolutionary strategy (with strong militaristic implications) can tackle the state. The state either has to be 'captured' or ignored. That is the choice.

Of course, political action must be focused on the state. But politics is far more than (and is actually in tension with) state action. Politics involves the resolution of conflicts of interest, and this is why, if politics is to flourish, we need a strategy for moving beyond the state. Touraine argues that it is in the space between social domination and state order that conflicts, movements and negotiations occur (1981: 52). This is, however, a most curious way of putting it, for it implies that social domination and the state remain intact, and the new social movements operate in the space between them! There is nothing in this argument that points to the way in which new social movements (for peace, for 'racial' equality, for women's liberation etc.) turn the assumptions of dominant social groups and the state *against* themselves, insisting that universal-sounding norms must become social realities.

Touraine seems to identify difference with repressive hierarchy since he contends that difference is nothing but the absence of relationships and that no relation exists that is based upon equality. Conflict always occurs (1981: 33), but this suggests that conflicts cannot occur between equals. Since relationships are inevitable, equality can only be, according to

Touraine, a chimera. We can only have violent conflicts; he underscores this point by contending that one can imagine a classless society only by accepting a society without historicity (1981: 60). Where is the conservative theorist who would disagree? It is one thing to contend that the incessant struggle for the control of historicity is the class struggle (1981: 29). Theorists going back to Aristotle have held to this proposition. The challenge Marxism first posed (albeit in a rather unsatisfactory way) is whether we can transcend divisiveness, for the argument here is that class and state operate as barriers to an inclusive citizenship. It is hard to see Touraine's new social movements contributing positively to this struggle.

Melucci does at least argue that the new social movements are based on principles of democratic rights, equality and citizenship (1989: 8), and I accept the point that movements seeking to restore or defend traditional hierarchies (like Britain's Countryside Alliance or Anti-Abortion Movements) cannot be called 'new social movements' since they do not have emancipatory objectives. Nevertheless, Melucci sees new social movements as acting at a distance from the world of official politics (1989: 6). He embraces a traditional and statist view of politics, arguing that contemporary social movements have shifted towards a non-political terrain. They have, he argues, a conflictual and antagonistic, but not a political, orientation, because they challenge the logic of complex systems on cultural grounds (1989: 23).

Although he counts citizenship as one of the 'values' of the NSMs, he argues that the struggle for citizenship is linked to the old idea of historical agents marching toward a destiny of liberation (1989: 19). But there is far more to citizenship than the right to vote (which is what Melucci seems to be referring to here). When he says that today, struggles for the extension of citizenship affect diverse constituents (1989: 19), he indicates precisely why we should not accept citizenship as an essentialist goal to be obtained. Rather we should see it as an ongoing concept that can never be simply and finally realized.

Melucci is surely right to insist that we need to go beyond a dualism of structure and individual action (1989: 20). Social movements do not act within a scenario whose finale is predetermined (1989: 25). Contrary to spontaneist or elitist views, individuals define themselves as collective actors by means of a variety of negotiated interactions (1989: 32). This is so, but these propositions have enormous implications for citizenship and the state. They point to the need to have organized relationships, which at best use repressive hierarchies provisionally and transitionally in order to bring about the kind of common interests that make it possible for us to negotiate and compromise in order to resolve conflicts of interest.

Elsewhere, Melucci seems to take this point, for he argues that as a unitary agent of action and intervention, the state has dissolved, to be replaced by transnational relationships and partial governments from below. But alas this dissolution (which anyway can only be a gradual process and is not an 'event') appears purely analytical in character.

Nothing Melucci suggests can be taken to mean that institutions claiming a monopoly of legitimate force no longer actually exist: it is rather that (as noted above) in his view, social movements are not state-focused and (in this sense) political in character (1988: 256). Hence new social movements are not primarily concerned with citizenship (1988: 247) since it is impossible to deal with the issue of citizenship without raising the nature of the state.

When Melucci says that social movements fight in the present – hence they are neither left nor right (1988: 256) – he reveals the extent to which he is a prisoner of modernity. He merely inverts the traditional notion of a movement marching forwards (or backwards) to a statically conceived goal. While it is true that one can only 'fight in the present' (an action by definition takes place in the here and now), it does not follow that social movements do not have implications for a world of the future, or that they are neither left nor right. The environmental movement (just to take one example) is rightly concerned about the kind of world that our children and grandchildren will inherit, and to the extent that ecologists are seeking to develop egalitarian norms between humans and nature, they are left-wing in character.

Melucci himself suggests that social movements cannot realize their goals in any finite way. He says that representation means the possibility of presenting interests and demands, but at the same time it means remaining different and never being heard entirely. Participation also has a double meaning. It means taking part and it also means identifying with the 'general interests' of the community (1988: 259). But both these comments suggest not only that the struggle involves going beyond the dualism of representation and participation, but that neither dimension should be conceived in terms of static goals which can be finally realized. This means not ignoring the state and traditionally conceived ideologies, but going beyond them.

Sader has recently provided a critical appraisal of the Social Forum that took place at Porte Legre in Brazil in 2002. He warns that those who emphasize that struggles occur within civil society run the risk of rejecting a potential weapon in the radically unequal contest – the power of the state and 'traditional' political organizations. There is a danger that the new social movement thus distances itself from the themes of power, the state, public sphere, political leadership and even ideological struggle. Aspirations are confined to a local or sectoral contest. An alternative hegemony is given up, as are global proposals to defeat world capitalism's neo-liberal project (2002: 92).

The point that Sader makes is vital for the struggle for an inclusive citizenship. It is crucial, as he puts it, to insert oneself in the liberal critique of the state's actions. In other words, we have to take seriously the liberal norms of the modern state, parties and pressure groups, and develop a critique from within, showing that, for example, one cannot be an 'individual' if one is subject to discrimination, ill-health through pollution, the threat of nuclear obliteration etc. It is no use merely demonizing the state and assuming blithely that the loss of power and political debility of the nation state is something to be taken for granted (2002: 93).

Struggles that seem radical fail to postulate an alternative society and policies and proposals are confined within the limits of capitalism. Liberal democracy (or what is better described as the liberal state) is seemingly accepted as a fact (2002: 97). The Social Forum can only chart a radical and realistic way forward if it goes beyond the notion of civil society (and in my view the dualism between civil society and the state). In order to really challenge neo-liberalism, we must, as Sader suggests, propose an alternative globalization (2002: 97).

The new social movements have an important role to play in the struggle for an inclusive citizenship. Their values are radical; their objectives emancipatory and their organization post-statist. But they are not a substitute for traditional organizations like parties and they must be judged on the real inroads they are able to make into the state. Like all new developments, we should celebrate their strengths while noting their (often anarchist-inclined) weaknesses. They have an important but not exclusive role to play in the struggle for a citizenship which is not only all inclusive, but also enables people to increasingly govern their own lives.

An Evaluation of the Crick Report

In 1997 a document entitled *Education for Citizenship and the Teaching of Democracy in Schools* (Crick Report, 1997) was produced by the Department for Education and Employment, which has generally come to be called the 'Crick Report' after its chair.

The report takes the view that there are worrying levels of apathy, ignorance and cynicism about public life (1997: 8) and what is needed is 'a common citizenship with democratic values'. A course on citizenship needs to be phased into different levels of the national curriculum as a statutory entitlement, with a standing Commission on Citizenship Education to monitor progress and, where necessary, recommend amendments to entitlements (1997: 24).

Although the report is in favour of citizenship studies in England continuing after students have reached the age of 16, this question is outside their remit (1997: 28). The report seeks to supplement an existing Personal and Social Education programme, which it sees as a necessary, but not sufficient condition, for good citizenship (1997: 65).

There is much in the report that is positive. It argues that things are inexcusably and damagingly bad and could and should be remedied (1997: 16). What is required is a change in political culture both nationally and locally (1997: 7). The report speaks of the need to find a place for the plurality of nations, cultures, ethnic identities and religions long found in the United Kingdom (1997: 17). We need to learn more from each other and that citizenship at the global level needs to be looked at (1997: 19). It is surely right to argue that socio-political (indeed philosophical) issues must be considered before assuming that the new computerized media can facilitate a more democratic, participative approach to informed citizenship (1997: 70).

Politics is defined as the general process by which differences of values and interests are compromised or mediated through institutions in the general interest (1997: 20). But the problem is that Crick and his report locate the political process 'in the political tradition stemming from the Greek city states and the Roman republic' (1997: 7). Although a citizen democracy is very different from ancient polities, it is still confined by Crick and his supporters within the framework of the *state*, and it is here that the problems with the report become painfully and particularly apparent.

In the first place, there is a purely statist view of politics, so that although local communities are seen as linked to the state and public policy, civil society is seen as basically non-political (1997: 10–11). This means, as Osler and Starkey protest, that voting behaviour is seen as the sole indicator of political interest and engagement. In fact, if we adopt a broader view of the political process, evidence suggests that there are increasing levels of political activity by young people in England (2001: 289).

It goes without saying that voting is important, but Osler and Starkey are right to stress that lack of involvement by the young is better explained in terms of disillusionment with formal political processes, which may have arisen through structural disadvantage or through observation of certain politicians and public figures (2001: 297). It is too bland and facile to say, as the Crick Report does, that this lack of involvement stems from lack of knowledge or skills.

Statist analyses of citizenship shy away from structural problems because to recognize them, is to adopt a critical rather than a celebratory approach to liberal political culture. There is no acknowledgement in the report, as Osler and Starkey rightly complain, that experiences such as poverty or unemployment may lead to social exclusion and prevent full participation in the community (2001: 297).

It is true that the French pronouncements on citizenship in schools are explicitly statist in character and this leads to a neglect of the question of difference (2001: 290). There is a top-down, vertical view of citizenship, but at least the various documents of human rights are set before the pupils and there is an acknowledgement that politics also involves demonstrations and the right to strike! In the French textbooks there is little to suggest that minorities may be subject to discrimination except by the far right, and communitarianism is seen as 'inward looking' (2001: 302).

But explicit (albeit explicitly statist and nationalist) references to the politics of citizenship facilitates critical responses. Osler and Starkey are correct to argue that multiple identities are the norm in modern society and we should not insist, in statist fashion, that only one of these identities matters. The French approach fails to accept the possibility of combining a group identity with a French and Republican identity (2001: 302). Indeed, Osler and Starkey argue that the concept of citizenship does not have to be linked to nationality at all. Belonging to a community, the essence of citizenship, is experienced primarily at the local level through horizontal relationship with equals (2001: 295) – a relationship, I would argue, which is incompatible with an institution claiming a monopoly of legitimate force for society as a whole. But although the French position is certainly statist, its very explicitness places the question of human rights within a social or political framework rather than (as the Crick Report does) put it in a narrow legal framework (2001: 296).

Osler and Starkey argue that, by definition, citizenship is an inclusive concept (2001: 292) – a position that must have critical implications for the concept of the state. The Crick Report takes a quintessentially statist approach by suggesting that citizenship is an institution that already exists, as expressed in the laws of the state. It is not seen as something that we move towards through struggle and conflict, and we need to remember that conflict can be positive and developmental: it does not have to be violent.

As Osler and Starkey point out, the Crick Report assumes that it is the ethnic minorities who must change in order to realize a common citizenship. They, the minorities, must learn and respect the laws, codes and conventions, as established by the majority. The implication is that although the report says that 'we all need to learn more about each other' (1997: 18), minorities are to be assimilated with white British citizens who, for their part, need only learn to 'tolerate' ethnic minorities. It seems that the dominant group is to do all the teaching and the ethnic minorities all the learning!

Osler and Starkey, indeed, argue not only that there is a deficit model of minority cultures, but that a colonial approach is adopted towards black British communities, an approach that runs throughout the report. Such communities, it appears, have more need of citizenship education than the host community and the report thus appears to be flawed by 'institutionalised racism' (2001: 293). Issues of ethnicity are not discussed in relation to inequalities in power and community leaders appear to be those (unelected) leaders of minority communities – a notion that has colonial overtones. (2001: 297). These 'leaders' are assumed to speak as the voices of supposedly homogeneous minority ethnic communities. As Osler and Starkey put it, the egalitarian potential of the concept of multiculturalism is not fully exploited (2001: 294).

The Macpherson Report, which was issued in 1999, drew attention in its concept of 'institutionalised racism' to the structural character of discrimination. This is a vital concept, for the fact is that this institutional racism and unemployment may cause abstention among young people from ethnic minority backgrounds (Osler and Starkey, 2001: 289). The reference in the Crick Report to the problem of 'bullying and other differences' implies that only conscious and intended repression is a problem. The report ignores structural disadvantage (2001: 299). Where the report does refer to 'social disparities', this is in a global rather than within a UK context. Little attention is given to the impact of 'race', ethnicity, gender, social class or religion. The problem of discrimination against women – structural as well as interpersonal – is simply ignored (2001: 293).

Osler and Starkey complain that little is said about the problem of forging a UK identity in the context of a multi-national and ethnic society, and this is hardly surprising, given the statist lenses of the report. Colonial struggles are notable by their absence (2001: 298). The British state is here to stay – it is not something that arose out of the bloody conquests of subjugated peoples.

Although the report speaks of the fact that the whole community should be encouraged to find and restore a sense of common citizenship (1997: 9), it tends to downplay the fact that the school itself is also a community – a vital arena for school students to learn the rudiments of an inclusive citizenship. What role do pupils with physical and mental disabilities play in active citizenship? A statist view of politics, an assimilationist view of minorities, a lack of concern about structural disadvantages and a tendency to downplay the democratic potential of multi-culturalism all mar the report (2001: 303).

In my view, the Crick Report, for all its welcome features, demonstrates the problems of a statist (and nationalist) view of citizenship.

Agency and the Struggle for Citizenship

Touraine has rightly argued that we must reconstruct modernity. We must find a way of recombining universalism with particularism and instrumental rationality with a personal life project. If we do not combine the highly differentiated elements of our culture, democracy will be impossible and we will have a society in which 'citizenship will become a meaningless word' (1995). The problem that Touraine does not address, is the fact that we can only reconstruct modernity if we chart a way beyond its key elements – the state and market. Touraine speaks of limiting the 'absolute power of the market and of the decision makers who control it' (1995: 271), but if we are merely to *limit* the power of market and state, we can only moderate, rather than transcend, the dualisms and abstractions associated with them. The problem of agency is the problem of locating forces which will go beyond those barriers that cramp and confine our theory and practice of citizenship.

The Marxist approach is helpful here but also limiting. Clearly, we must seek to mobilize, in the first instance, all those who are excluded by contemporary institutions. This goes well beyond the concept of a 'proletariat', although those who are poor and have to subject themselves to the 'despotic' rules of employers are an obvious constituency in the struggle to govern one's own life. Here a broad view of politics is crucial because it is impossible to be a citizen if one is subject to aggressive pressures from employers and managers. Democratizing the workplace to allow greater security, transparency and participation is critical to citizenship, and all those who suffer from these problems are natural constituents in the struggle for a more meaningful citizenship.

People who are obviously 'different' from dominant norms, will be particularly at risk. We cannot assume that such people are all the 'same'. Obviously poor women are more vulnerable than wealthy women; poor African-Caribbeans and people of, for instance, Asian descent (in Britain) are likely to be more enthusiastic about extending citizenship than those who have property; wealthy immigrants are liable to be less committed to change than impoverished asylum seekers.

But all differences must be evaluated in a positive way. Wealthier people have confidence and resources that poor people do not: they may also be better educated and therefore (although not necessarily) in a position to dispute a crude prejudice that is manifestly in opposition to the facts. A struggle for an inclusive citizenship needs to avoid privileging a particular group. Gays and blacks often experience discrimination and therefore are not only concerned with their own rights, but sympathize with the suffering of others. But attitudes and resources will differ among them. All women have suffered stereotyping and patronizing attitudes of some kind, although these attacks on their self-esteem will clearly vary according to their social position and the wealth they command.

I have argued elsewhere that class is not simply one factor to be mechanically added to others. Vulnerability to market forces is likely to manifest itself particularly starkly through those who are 'different' from dominant norms, so it is hardly surprising that women are poorer than men, or that black people are more likely to be unemployed than whites. To govern your own life, it is necessary to be secure economically, politically and culturally so that the struggle for a more meaningful citizenship must avoid treating analytically separable dimensions as though they are empirical divides inhabiting different worlds. Class as an analytical tool cannot be separated from the gender, regional, religious etc. forms that it takes in reality. Security in one 'area' is linked to security in others.

But what about the beneficiaries of the market and the functionaries of the state? Are they the enemies of the struggle for a more inclusive citizenship, since they have 'made it'? It is a problem with classical Marxist and anarchist scenarios that they operate with a modernist logic which assumes a zero-sum game model of social relations. The world appears to be divided into those who are 'complete' citizens and those who are not. It is true that classical Marxism does allow for an element of mutuality in its concept of alienation, which extends from the proletariat to the bourgeoisie, but far more needs to be made of this question of mutuality. Once we break with an atomistic notion of social relations, it becomes clear that the freedom and individuality of each depends upon the freedom and individuality of all.

Those who drive cars are still vulnerable to the health problems associated with pollution. They suffer the nervous disorders linked to congestion and frustration on the roads. Inequalities whether within or between societies, make everyone insecure, and result in a futile and wasteful use of resources by wealthy people to 'buy' peaceful neighbourhoods. The point is that if everyone is not in a position to govern their own lives, no-one is in a position to do so.

It is becoming increasingly clear to 'establishments' in advanced industrial countries that if nothing is done about the divisions within the international community, then liberal traditions will be eroded, as tidal waves of refugees move around the globe. Although the victims of crime in, say, contemporary South Africa, are predominantly the poor who live in the shanty towns, this scourge does not simply affect those who are on the margins of society. Everyone can be the victim of crime. Patriarchy does not simply oppress women; it also prevents men from governing their own lives. Indeed, if one links patriarchy with conventional wars, then men may suffer directly and tangibly from a system that ostensibly benefits them. Patriarchal-minded judges have no compunction in denying men access to children when marriages break up.

A relational view of citizenship has important implications for the question of agency. We cannot exclude the wealthy and the 'beneficiaries' of the market and state from the struggle for a more inclusive citizenship, although it would be foolish and naive to assume that the 'haves' will be enthusiastic proponents for an inclusive citizenship!

The fact is that those who benefit from the present, do so superficially and in a short-term fashion. Although there is something in the Marxist proposition that the victors do not sympathize with their victims, it is important that we do not treat this proposition in a dogmatic fashion. We cannot assume in advance that wealthy people are incapable of looking beyond their noses: on the contrary, accumulating wealth, becoming educated, securing a leadership role in the present society may involve the capacity to take a long-term view of problems. It is vital that the interests of the 'haves' are also taken into account and the struggle for an inclusive citizenship is seen as just this – a struggle from which all will benefit.

In trying to coordinate struggles for a more inclusive citizenship, we should seek to isolate those who stubbornly take a short-term view of their own interest and act in ways that prevent others from having greater control over their lives. We need to make it as difficult as possible for the opponents of an inclusive citizenship to gain allies and adherents, using argument and sanction to this end. A critique of an opposing position needs to be 'immanent' in character, by which is meant a critique that comes from within. 'How can you continue a favoured life style if the environment becomes increasingly polluted, and insecurity and violence inexorably mount?' There is an interesting parallel here with measures taken to combat cholera in nineteenth-century British cities. The disease was no respecter of class or wealth: it was in everyone's interest that it was eradicated. What is the point of having wealth and power if your health is devastated?

Hobbes' concept of a state of nature is a useful one to build upon. For the point about the state of nature is that everyone is in the same boat. It is true that the equality is a rather negative one – the weakest can kill the strongest – but the point is that everyone has a common interest in leaving the war of all against all. The device is a good one for the argument here. No-one gains in any meaningful sense in a world in which citizenship is either thin or non-existent. Inequality, class division, the market and the state are part of the problem: as a result, conflicts of interest are tackled through a pervasive violence that, as in Hobbes' state of nature, leaves no-one secure.

The struggle for a more inclusive citizenship is a political one, fought on many fronts. Every step forward is a victory, whether it is the achievement of legal and political rights in authoritarian societies or inroads into the market in liberal ones. At the same time, it is important to see the struggle for citizenship as on-going, without a culminating point beyond which no further progress is possible. This is why it was argued in Chapter 8 that the concept of citizenship is a momentum one – it is progressive but has no stopping point.

A critique of the state is essential to sustaining this view of citizenship. An institution claiming a monopoly of legitimate force 'naturalizes' divisions and encourages the adoption of a static concept of human nature. It imposes rigidities upon our approach, so that it is impossible to combine utopia (in the sense of a radically different kind of future) with realism. Falk captures this link between utopia and realism well in his case for a global citizenship where he argues that a 'utopian confidence in the human capacity to exceed realistic horizons' needs to be rooted in 'the highly pragmatic conviction that what is currently taken to be realistic is not sustainable' (1994: 140). Statist attitudes encourage a realism that is myopic and limiting, or they embrace a perfectionist and impotent utopianism. This is why the struggle for an inclusive citizenship needs to move beyond the state. If common interests are to be cemented so that arbitration and negotiation can replace force, then no-one should be left out when we consider the question of agency for change.

SUMMARY

- The gulf between theory and practice can and should be a spur to develop more accurate and comprehensive views. This gulf only becomes frustrating and disillusioning when it is absolutized or romantically dissolved away – a dualism which occurs when we uncritically accept the state.
- Marxism appears promising as a theory to underpin the struggle for an inclusive citizenship, but it subscribes to a notion of class war and revolution that makes it impossible to conceptualize common interests and thus to tackle the problem of the state. Anarchism likewise is an anti-statist doctrine resting upon statist assumptions.
- We undermine the role that the new social movements can play in the struggle of an inclusive citizenship if we assume that they are cultural rather than political organizations. It is wrong to argue that because the NSMs are new, older forms of political struggle are now irrelevant.
- The Crick Report seeks to make citizenship a compulsory subject for secondary school students. However, underpinning the report is a statist notion of citizenship, which leads to a rather 'assimilationist' view of ethnic minorities and a tendency to downplay the structural problems afflicting those who are 'different'.
- The struggle for a more inclusive citizenship involves those who are exploited and who manifest their vulnerability through dimensions of 'race', gender, sexuality and region etc. However, we should not assume that the vulnerable are all the same, nor should we absolutize the division between the haves and have-nots. No-one really benefits from a society that is governed by the state and market, and it is important that we isolate those who stand against emancipatory movements and pressures.

Conclusion

The central theme of my argument is that the state itself is a barrier to citizenship. The state is defined by Weber as an institution that claims a monopoly of legitimate force. It is a paradoxical institution and increasingly scholars have come to recognize its problematic nature. This book stands or falls as an attempt to convincingly detach citizenship (and democracy) from the state.

It argues that the state tackles conflicts of interest through force. But the use of force is inimical to conflict resolution: only negotiation and arbitration can resolve conflicts of interest, since force crushes agency, and the agency of all the parties is essential if a dispute is to be successfully tackled. Two important points need to be added here. The first is that it may not be possible to employ negotiation and arbitration in particular circumstances, since the latter only operate as conflict-resolving mechanisms where common interests between contending parties exist. Common interests do not exclude differences, but they imply that such differences are amenable to compromise. Hence force may be necessary but my point remains: force cannot resolve conflicts – it can only suppress them. It is justified if it provides a breathing space, thereby allowing policies that *do* cement common interests, to be implemented.

The second point is that negotiation, although undermined by force, is compatible with coercion and constraint. The distinction between coercion and constraint, on the one hand, and force on the other, is of the utmost importance to my argument, since it would be naive (and contrary to all we know about stateless societies, whether domestic or international) to imagine that disputes can be resolved without the kind of pressures that I have labelled coercive and constraining.

The distinction between coercion (and constraint) and force translates into the equally vital distinction between state and government. States use force; governments employ coercion and constraint. This means that in seeking legitimacy, states increasingly rely upon negotiation and compromise to solve problems and when they do, they cease to be states, and act governmentally. This is a crucial point because it is only through the advance of government that states gradually die out.

Nationalism, Democracy and Gender

Distinctions between coercion, constraint and force and between state and government assume a relational (as opposed to an atomistic) view of the individual. This relational stance is also crucial in defending the linkage between citizenship and democracy. Liberal objections to democracy – that it tramples on the rights of minorities, that it suppresses individual difference in the name of majoritarian uniformity – only make sense as objections to the state, and central to my definition of democracy as self-government is the argument that democracy cannot be a form of the state. Indeed, the idea that democracies suppress individuals and minorities rests upon an atomistic view of the latter, so that violence towards individuals and minorities is not related to the freedom of the majority and the well-being of society as a whole. Liberal societies can only become more democratic if a critique of the monopolistic character of the state is developed.

This is why nationalism is inherently undemocratic. Unlike a national consciousness (which increasingly exists in plural form), nationalism privileges one particular national identity. The notion of the nation state is all revealing, for not only is the nation tied to an institution that uses national identity to provide cohesion to its claim to a monopoly of legitimacy and force, but the term nation is in the singular. When nationalism is involved, one nation in particular has pre-eminence over others. National differences, like all differences, are certainly a source of tension and conflict. But tensions and conflict can (and where possible should) be tackled governmentally through social rather than statist sanctions. A democratic policy must respect differences, not in a supinely relativist way (as multi-cultural policies are sometimes accused of doing), but in a way which strengthens democracy and therefore rejects practices that are exploitative and marginalizing.

One of the differences crucial to citizenship is gender. Women in liberal societies are still second-class citizens even when they have formal political rights. The public/private divide serves to keep them out of leadership roles and both nationalism and the state marginalize women. Women are both different from men and differ among themselves, but as long as these differences are dealt with by the state, violence will be normalized, and women will particularly suffer. An attempt to render citizenship more inclusive must address itself to the mechanisms that favour men and degrade women.

Capitalism, Participation and Globalization

Capitalism divides, and therefore like the state, is a barrier to an inclusive citizenship. Marx is right, however, to stress the positive and historically necessary role of capitalism, but his notion of class is too narrow and appears to exclude national, regional, gender divisions, etc. In my view, the notion of class needs to be expanded so that class exploitation always expresses itself in a culturally specific form, whether this is national, regional, gendered, religious, etc. The critique of the market in classical Marxism is helpful in that it emphasizes the mystifying character of abstraction – a real but confusing process.

The rise of the welfare state has seen real inroads into the market logic of capitalism and it is through the continuation and extension of these inroads that capitalism is transformed and the market itself overcome. The case is made for a citizen's income – a reform that would dramatically accelerate these inroads – and the rise of the New Right is seen as a neo-liberal reaction to these inroads. This reaction, although mostly negative, does at least have the merit of bringing the concept of individual autonomy to the fore.

Citizenship involves participation. With the rejection of the 'equiliberal' model of a low-participation society, radicals have rightly sought to make the case for greater participation. But how? Macpherson's argument is persuasive in that it seeks to show how consumer-minded citizens have to take an increasingly longer-term view of their interests (just to carry on as consumers). However, Macpherson (like other radicals) ignores the anti-participatory character of the state, and a case is made for compulsory voting as a way of popularizing the responsibilities of citizenship. Communitarians are right to stress the importance of community responsibility, but even where they avoid authoritarian and relativistic arguments, they ignore the psuedo- or anti-communitarianism of the state. Like republicans, liberal-minded communitarians are strong on the need to avoid domination but weak in their critique of force.

Globalization raises the prospect of a global citizenship. But to move in this direction, we need to defend a positive, post-capitalist version of globalization and not a 'market fundamentalist' one. The latter in fact strengthens inequality, nationalism and the need for the state, whereas the former must be guided by goals of social justice and the need for global institutions to work for a more equal world. The United Nations can only become a global government if it is democratized, and the concept of a European citizenship, although hugely positive, must win the argument for post-statism. A global citizenship does not involve obliterating differences, but rather celebrating them through a multi-layered form of government that involves people in governing their own lives at every level.

Emancipation and the 'Realization' of an Inclusive Citizenship

The notion of emancipation has become controversial. Many (self-styled) postmodernists regard emancipation as a modernist concept and it is certainly true that it is a concept with unambiguously modernist origins. But the concept can be reconstructed and, to this end, I propose a distinction between momentum concepts whose potential for change and development is infinite, and static concepts that are divisive and repressive. What makes emancipation a momentum concept is that it cannot be realized at any given point in time.

The notion of emancipation reinforces the self-governing attribute of an inclusive citizenship, since only the individual can emancipate him or herself. This is why the use of force is inimical to emancipation, although a whole range of social pressures (which I label coercive and constraining) can be brought to bear on behaviour deemed harmful. Self-government involves both direct action and representation by others, and it is important, here as elsewhere, that we do not surrender to a modernist logic of either/or. The need to embrace both sameness and difference becomes particularly salient with respect to distinguishing adult citizens from children as citizens-to-be, and humans from the rest of the natural world.

As for the problem of 'realization', we need to distinguish between theory and practice in a way that does not demoralize, but empowers. Although we would expect the victims rather than the beneficiaries of the market and the state to be particularly concerned with the struggle for an inclusive citizenship, all have skills they can contribute, and there is no *prima facie* case for excluding anyone. The classical Marxist view would narrow the question of agency down to the proletariat, while anarchists invert rather than transcend liberalism, by exalting spontaneity, and generally refusing to distinguish between coercion (and constraint) and force, or state and government.

New social movements must be seen as vehicles for transforming an inegalitarian society as a whole, while the Crick Report weakens its laudable aim of developing citizenship education in secondary schools, by defining politics in a traditional statist manner and treating citizenship in a nationalist way.

All members of society are potential agents for developing an inclusive citizenship. If we are moving inexorably towards a veritable Hobbesian state of nature, in which insecurity, violence and arbitrariness become all pervasive, then the relational argument is expressed in the most graphic manner. No-one benefits, and all have a vested interest in looking beyond the state to a world of democracy and inclusive citizenship.

Bibliography

Allen, J. (1990) 'Does Feminism Need a Theory of the State?' in S. Watson (ed.), *Playing the State* London: Verso, 21–37.

Anderson, B. (1991) *Imagined Communities* revised edn., London: Verso.

Arblaster, A. (1984) *The Rise and Decline of Western Liberalism* Oxford: Basil Blackwell.

Ashley, R. (1988) 'Untying the Sovereign State: a Double Reading of the Anarchy Problematique', *Millenium* 17 (2), 227–62.

Avineri, S. (1970) *The Social and Political Thought of Karl Marx* Cambridge: Cambridge University Press.

Bankowski, Z. and Christodoulidis, E. (1999) 'Bound and Citizenship Unbound' in K. Hutchings and R. Dannreuther (eds), *Cosmopolitan Citizenship* Basingstoke: Macmillan, 83–104.

Barbalet, J. (2000) 'Vagaries of Social Capital: Citizenship, Trust and Loyalty', in E. Vasta (ed.), *Citizenship, Community and Democracy* Basingstoke: Macmillan, 91–106.

Barry Jones, R. (2000) *The World Turned Upside Down* Manchester and New York: Manchester University Press.

Baumeister, A. (2000) 'The New Feminism' in N. O'Sullivan (ed.), *Political Theory in Transition* London and New York: Routledge, 49–69.

Beck, U. (1998) *Democracy Without Enemies* Cambridge: Polity Press.

Beetham, D. (1984) 'The Future of the Modern State' in G. McLellan, D. Held and S. Hall (eds), *The Idea of the Modern State* Milton Keynes and Philadelpia: Open University Press, 208–22.

Bellah, R. (1998) 'Community Properly Understood: A Defense of "Democratic Communitarianism"' in A. Etzioni (ed.), *The Essential Communitarian Reader* Oxford: Rowman and Littlefield, 15–19.

Bellamy, R. and Warleigh, A. (eds) (2001) *Citizenship and Governance in the European Union* London and New York: Continuum.

Benn, M. (2002) 'The Hour of Reckoning', *Guardian*, 30 January.

Bourdieu, P. (1998) *Acts of Resistance* Cambridge: Polity.

Breuilly, J. (1993) *Nationalism and the State* 2nd edn, Manchester: Manchester University Press.

Brown, W. (1992) 'Finding the Man in the State', *Feminist Studies* 18 (1), 7–34.

Brubaker, R. (1998) 'Myths and Misconceptions in the Study of Nationalism' in J. Hall (ed.), *The State of the Nation* Cambridge: Cambridge University Press, 272–306.

Bryson, V. (1992) *Feminist Political Theory* Basingstoke: Macmillan.

Bryson, V. (1994) *Women in British Politics* Huddersfield: Pamphlets in History and Politics, University of Huddersfield.

Bubeck, D. (1995) *A Feminist Approach to Citizenship* Florence: European University Institute.

Bull, H. (1977) *The Anarchical Society* London: Macmillan.

Calhoun, C. (1997) *Nationalism* Buckingham: Open University Press.

Canovan, M. (1996) *Nationhood and Political Theory* Cheltenham: Edward Elgar.

Carter, A. (2001) *The Political Theory of Global Citizenship* London and New York: Routledge.

Childe, G. (1964) *What Happened in History* Harmondsworth: Penguin.

Cohen, R. and Rai, S. (2000) 'Global Social Movements: Towards a Cosmopolitan Politics' in R. Cohen and S. Rai (eds), *Global Social Movements* London and New Brunswick: Athlone Press, 1–17.

Commission on Global Governance (1995) *Our Global Neighbourhood* Oxford: Oxford University Press.

Connell, R. (1987) *Gender and Power* Cambridge: Polity Press.

Connell, R. (1990) 'The State, Gender and Sexual Politics: Theory and Appraisal', *Theory and Society* 19: 507–44.

Coole, D. (1988) *Women in Political Theory* Hemel Hempstead: Harvester-Wheatsheaf.

Crick, B. (1982) *In Defence of Politics* 2nd edn, Harmondsworth: Penguin.

Crick Report (1997) *Education for Citizenship and the Teaching of Democracy in Schools* London: Department for Education and Employment.

Dagger, R. (1997) *Civic Virtue* Oxford: Oxford University Press.

Dahl, R. (1956) *A Preface to Democratic Theory* Chicago and London: University of Chicago Press.

Dahl, R. (1961) *Who Governs?* New Haven and London: Yale University Press.

Dahl, R. (1989) *Democracy and Its Critics* New Haven: Yale University Press.

Dahrendorf, R. (1998) 'A Precarious Balance: Economic Opportunity, Civil Society and Political Liberty' in A. Etzioni (ed.), *The Essential Communitarian Reader* Lanham et al. Oxford: Rowman and Littlefield, 73–94.

Davis, H. (1967) *Nationalism and Socialism* New York and London: Monthly Review Press.

Davis, H. (1978) *Toward a Marxist Theory of Nationalism* New York and London: Monthly Review Press.

De Jasay, A. (1985) *The State* Oxford: Basil Blackwell.

Delanty, G. (2000) *Citizenship in a Global Age* Buckingham and Philadelphia: Open University Press.

Department for International Development (2002) *Issues Paper 3* Kingston upon Thames: DFID Development Policy Forums.

Dickenson, D. (1997) 'Counting Women In: Globalization, Democratization and the Women's Movement' in A. McGrew (ed.), *The Transformation of Democracy* Cambridge and Milton Keynes: Polity and the Open University Press, 97–120.

Dryzek, J. (1999) 'Transnational Democracy', *The Journal of Political Philosophy* 7 (1), 30–51.

Dunn, J. (1979) *Western Political Theory in the Face of the Future* London: Cambridge University Press.

Eisenstein, Z. (1981) *The Radical Future of Liberal Feminism* London: Longman.

Eisenstein, Z. (1994) *The Color of Gender* Los Angeles: University of California Press.

Enloe, C. (1993) *The Morning After* Berkeley: University of California Press.

Etzioni, A. (1996) *The New Golden Rule* London: Profile Books.

Etzioni, A. (ed.) (1998) *The Essential Communitarian Reader* Lanham et al. Oxford: Rowman and Littlefield.

Falk, R. (1994) 'The Making of Global Citizenship' in B. Van Steenbergen (ed.), *The Condition of Citizenship* London: Sage, 127–40.

Faulks, K. (1998) *Citizenship in Modern Britain* Edinburgh: Edinburgh University Press.

Faulks, K. (1999) *Political Sociology* Edinburgh: Edinburgh University Press.

Faulks, K. (2000) *Citizenship* London and New York: Routledge.

Faulks, K. (2001) 'Should Voting be Compulsory?', *Politics Review* 10 (3), 24–5.

Freedman, J. (2001) *Feminism* Buckingham: Open University Press.

French, M. (1992) *The War Against Women* London: Hamish Hamilton.

Galston, W. (1998) 'A Liberal-Democratic case for the Two-Parent Family' in Etzioni, A. (ed.), *The Essential Communitarian Reader* Lanham et al. Oxford: Rowman and Littlefield, 145–55.

Garner, R. (1993) *Animals, Politics and Morality* Manchester: Manchester University Press.

Gatens, M. (1991) '"The oppressed state of my sex": Wollstonecraft on reason, feeling and equality' in M. Shanley and C. Pateman (eds), *Feminist Interpretations of Political Theory* Cambridge: Polity, 112–28.

Gellner, E. (1983) *Nations and Nationalism* Oxford: Basil Blackwell.

Geras, N. (1994) 'Democracy and the Ends of Marxism' in G. Parry and M. Moran (eds), *Democracy and Democratization* London: Routledge, 69–87.

Gerth, H. and Mills, C.W. (eds) (1991) *From Max Weber* London and New York: Routledge.

Giddens, A. (1985) *The Nation-State and Violence* Cambridge: Polity Press.

Giddens, A. (1994) *Beyond Left and Right* Cambridge: Polity Press.

Giddens, A. (1998) *The Third Way* Cambridge: Polity Press.

Giddens, A. (1999) *Runaway World* London: BBC Reith Lectures 1–5, http://news.co.uk

Giddens, A. (ed.) (2001) *The Global Third Way Debate* Cambridge: Polity Press.

Giddens, A. (2002) *Where Now for New Labour* Cambridge: Polity Press.

Gilmour, I. (1977) *Inside Right* London, Melbourne, New York: Quartet Books.

Goodwin, B. (1997) *Using Political Ideas* 4th edn, Chicester, New York, Toronto: John Wiley and Sons.

Gray, J. (1999) *False Dawn* London: Granta Books.

Guibernau, M. (1996) *Nationalisms* Cambridge: Polity Press.

Hall, S. and Held, D. (1989) 'Citizens and Citizenship' in S. Hall and M. Jacques (eds), *New Times* London: Lawrence and Wishart, 173–88.

Hamilton, A. et al. (1961) *The Federalist Papers* New York: Basic Books.

Harding, S. (1990) 'Feminism, Science and the Anti-enlightenment critiques' in L. Nicholson (ed.), *Feminism/Postmodernism* New York and London: Routledge, 83–106.

Hayek, F. (1960) *The Constitution of Liberty* London and Henley: Routledge and Kegan Paul.

Heater, D. (1999) *What is Citizenship?* Cambridge: Polity Press.

Held, D. (1987) *Models of Democracy* Cambridge: Polity.

Held, D. (1995) *Democracy and the Global Order* Cambridge: Polity Press.

Held, D., Goldblatt, D. and Perreton, J. (eds) (1999) *Global Transformations* Cambridge: Polity.

Held, V. (1993) *Feminist Morality* University of Chicago Press: Chicago and London.

Hirshmann, N. (1992) *Rethinking Obligation* Ithaca and London: Cornell University Press.

Hirst, P. and Thompson, G. (1996) *Globalization in Question* Cambridge: Polity Press.

Hoffman, J. (1984) *The Gramscian Challenge* Oxford: Basil Blackwell.

Hoffman, J. (1986) 'The Problem of the Ruling Class in Classical Marxist Theory: Some Conceptual Preliminaries', *Science and Society* 50 (3), 342–63.

Hoffman, J. (1988) *State, Power and Democracy* Brighton: Wheatsheaf Press.

Hoffman, J. (1991) 'Capitalist Democracies and Democratic States: Oxymorons or Coherent Concepts', *Political Studies* 39 (2), 342–9.

Hoffman, J. (1995) *Beyond the State* Cambridge: Polity Press.

Hoffman, J. (1996) 'Antonio Gramsci: *The Prison Notebooks*' in M. Forsyth and M. Keens-Soper, (eds), *The Political Classics: Green to Dworkin* Oxford: Oxford University Press, 58–77.

Hoffman, J. (1998) *Sovereignty* Buckingham: Open University Press.

Hoffman, J. (2000) *Reconstructing Conflict as a Building Block of Diplomacy* Leicester: Centre for the Study of Diplomacy, University of Leicester.

Hoffman, J. (2001) *Gender and Sovereignty* Basingstoke: Palgrave.

Hoffman, J. and Mzala, N. (1990–91) '"Non-Historical Nations": a South African Perspective', *Science and Society* 54 (4), 408–26.

Hofstadter, R. (1967) *The American Political Tradition* London: Jonathan Cape.

Huntington, S. (1996), *The Clash of Civilizations* New York: Simon & Schuster.

Hutchings, K. (1999) 'Feminist Politics and Cosmopolitan Citizenship' in K. Hutchings and R. Dannreuther (eds), *Cosmopolitan Citizenship* Basingstoke: Macmillan, 120–42.

Independent (2003) 'Britain Today: A Nation still Failing its Ethnic Minorities', 8 May.

Isin, E. and Wood, P. (1999) *Citizenship and Identity* London: Sage.

Janoski, T. (1998) *Citizenship and Civil Society* Cambridge: Cambridge University Press.

Johnston, S. (1993) *Realising the Public World Order* Leicester: Centre for the Study of Public Order, University of Leicester.

Jones, K. (1990) 'Citizenship in a Women-Friendly Polity', *Signs* 15 (4), 781–812.

Jones, K. (1993) *Compassionate Authority* London and New York: Routledge.

Jordan, B. (1985) *The State* Oxford: Basil Blackwell.

Kant, I. (1959 [1785]) *Foundation of the Metaphysics of Morals* Indianapolis and New York: Bobbs-Merrill.

Kymlicka, W. (1995) *Multi-Cultural Citizenship* Oxford: Clarendon Press.

Laver, M. (1985) *Invitation to Politics* Oxford: Blackwell.

Leftwich, A. (1983) *Redefining Politics* London and New York: Methuen.

Lerner, G. (1986) *The Creation of Patriarchy* New York: Oxford University Press.

Linklater, A. (1999) 'Cosmopolitan Citizenship' in K. Hutchings and R. Dannreuther (eds), *Cosmopolitan Citizenship* Basingstoke: Macmillan, 35–59.

Lister, R. (1997a), *Citizenship: Feminist Perspectives* Basingstoke: Macmillan.

Lister, R. (1997b) 'Citizenship: Towards a Feminist Synthesis', *Feminist Review* 57, 28–48.

Lloyd, G. (1984) *The Man of Reason* London: Methuen.

Locke, J. (1927) *Two Treatises of Civil Government* London: Dent.

Löwy, M. (1998) *Fatherland or Mother Earth?* London and Sterling, Virginia: Pluto Press.

MacKinnon, C. (1989) *Toward a Feminist Theory of the State* Cambridge, MA: Harvard University Press.

Macpherson, C. (1977) *The Life and Times of Liberal Democracy* London, Oxford and New York: Oxford University Press.

Macpherson, W. (1999) *The Stephen Lawrence Inquiry* London: TSO.

Mair, L. (1962) *Primitive Government* Harmondsworth: Penguin.

Mannheim, K. (1991) *Ideology and Utopia* London: Routledge.

Marcuse, H. (1968) *One Dimensional Man* London: Sphere Books.

Marshall, T. and Bottomore, T. (1992) *Citizenship and Social Class* London: Pluto Press.

Marx, K. (1966 [1894]) *Capital Vol. 3* Moscow: Progress Publishers.

Marx, K. (1970 [1867]) *Capital Vol. 1* London: Lawrence and Wishart.

Marx, K. and Engels, F. (1967 [1848]) *The Communist Manifesto* Harmondsworth: Penguin.

Marx, K. and Engels, F. (1975a [1835–1843]) *Collected Works* vol. 1 London: Lawrence and Wishart.

Marx, K. and Engels, F. (1975b [1843–1844]) *Collected Works* vol. 3 London: Lawrence and Wishart.

Marx, K. and Engels, F. (1975c [1844–1845]) *Collected Works* vol. 4 London: Lawrence and Wishart.

Marx, K. and Engels, F. (1975d [1844–1895]) *Selected Correspondence* Moscow: Progress Publishers.

Marx, K. and Engels, F. (1976a [1845–1847]) *Collected Works* vol. 5 London: Lawrence and Wishart.

Marx, K. and Engels, F. (1976b [1845–1848]) *Collected Works* vol. 6 London: Lawrence and Wishart.

McKinnon, C. and Hampsher-Monk, I. (2000) 'Introduction' in C. McKinnon and I. Hamphsher-Monk (eds), *The Demands of Citizenship* London and New York: Continuum, 1–9.

Melucci, A. (1988) 'Social Movements and the Democratization of Everyday Life' in J. Keane (ed.), *Civil Society and the State* London: Verso, 245–60.

Melucci, A. (1989) *Nomads of the Present* J. Keane and P. Mier (eds), London: Hutchinson Books.

Miliband, R. (1973 [1969]) *The State in Capitalist Society* London, Melbourne and New York: Quartet Books.

Mill, J.S. (1974 [1859]) *On Liberty* Harmondsworth: Penguin.

Miller, D. (1995) *On Nationality* Oxford: Clarendon Press.

Miller, D. (1999) 'Bounded Citizenship' in K. Hutchings and R. Dannreuther (eds), *Cosmopolitan Citizenship* Basingstoke: Macmillan, 60–80.

Monbiot, G. (2002) 'The Rich World's Veto', *Guardian*, 15 October.

Mouffe, C. (1992) 'Feminism, Citizenship and Radical Democratic Politics' in J. Butler and J. Scott (eds), *Feminists Theorize the Political* New York and London: Routledge, 369–84.

Mouffe, C. (1996) 'Radical Democracy or Liberal Democracy' in D. Trend (ed.), *Radical Democracy* New York and London: Routledge, 19–26.

New Internationalist (1994) Special Issue, December.

Nicholson, P. (1984) 'Politics and Force' in A. Leftwich, (ed.), *What is Politics?* Oxford: Blackwell, 33–45.

Nimni, E. (1989) 'Marx, Engels and the National Question', *Science and Society* 53 (3), 297–326.

Novak, M. (1998) *Is There a Third Way* London: IEA Health and Welfare Unit.

Offen, K. (1992) 'Defining feminism: a comparative historical approach' in G. Bock and S. James (eds), *Beyond Equality and Difference* London and New York: Routledge, 69–88.

Ohmae, K. (1995) *The End of the Nation-State* New York: Free Press.

O'Leary, B. (1998) 'Ernest Gellner's Diagnoses on Nationalism: A Critical Overview or What is Living and What is Dead in Ernest Gellner's Philosophy of Nationalism' in J. Hall (ed.), *The State of the Nation* Cambridge: Cambridge University Press, 40–88.

Oliver, D. and Heater, D. (1994) *The Foundations of Citizenship* New York and London: Harvester Wheatsheaf.

Oommen, T. (1997) *Citizenship, Nationality and Ethnicity* Cambridge: Polity Press.

Osler, A. and Starkey, H. (2001) 'Citizenship Education and National Identities in France and England: inclusive or exclusive?', *Oxford Review of Education* 27 (2), 288–305.

Parekh, B. (1990) 'When Will the State Wither Away?', *Alternatives* 15, 247–62.

Petit, P. (1997) *Republicanism* Oxford: Oxford University Press.

Pettman, J.J. (1996) *Worlding Women* London and New York: Routledge.

Philp, M. (2000) 'Motivating Liberal Citizenship' in C. McKinnon and I. Hampsher-Monk (eds), *The Demands of Citizenship* London and New York: Continuum, 165–89.

Plato. (1955 [380 BC) *The Republic* Harmondsworth: Penguin.

Poggi, G. (1978) *The Development of the Modern State* London: Hutchinson.

Pringle, R. and Watson, S. (1992) Women's Interests and the Post-Structural State' in M. Barrett and A. Phillips (eds), *Destabilizing Theory* Cambridge: Polity Press, 53–73.

Reiss, H. (ed.) (1970) *Kant's Political Writings* Cambridge: Cambridge University Press.

Ross, K. (2000) *Woman at the Top* London: Hansard Society.

Rousseau, J.J. (1968) *The Social Contract* Harmondsworth: Penguin.

Runyan, A.S. and Peterson, V.S. (1991) 'The Radical Future of Realism: Feminist Subversions of IR Theory', *Alternatives* 16, 67–106.

Sader, E. (2002) 'Beyond Civil Society' *New Left Review* 17, Sept./Oct., 87–99.

Sandel, M. (1982) *Liberalism and the Limits of Justice* Cambridge: Cambridge University Press.

Sandel, M. (1992) 'The Procedural Republic and the Unencumbered Self' in S. Avineri and A. De-Shalit (eds), *Communitarianism and Liberalism* Oxford: Oxford University Press, 12–28.

Saunders, P. (1995) *Capitalism: A Social Audit* Buckingham: Open University Press.

Schumpeter, J. (1947) *Capitalism, Socialism and Democracy* 2nd edn, New York and London: Harper.

Selznick, P. (1998) 'Social Justice: a Communitarian Perspective' in A. Etzioni (ed.), *The Essential Communitarian Reader* Lanham et al. Oxford: Rowman and Littlefield, 61–71.

Shanley, M. and Pateman, C. (eds) (1991) *Feminist Interpretations and Political Theory* Cambridge: Polity Press.

Sharp, P. (2001) *Making Sense of Citizen Diplomats* Leicester: Centre for the Study of Diplomacy, University of Leicester.

Smith, A. (1998) *Nationalism and Modernism* London and New York: Routledge.

Sorensen, G. (2001) *Changes in Statehood* Basingstoke: Palgrave.

Soysal, Y. (1994) *The Limits of Citizenship* Chicago and London: University of Chicago.

Sperling, L. (2001) *Women, Political Philosophy and Politics* Edinburgh: Edinburgh University Press.

Spragens, T. (1998) 'The Limits of Libertarianism' in A. Etzioni (ed.), *The Essential Communitarian Reader* Lanham et al. Oxford: Rowman and Littlefield, 21–40.

Squires, J. (2000) 'The State in (and of) Feminist Visions of Political Citizenship' in C. MacKinnon and I. Hampsher-Monk (eds), *The Demands of Citizenship* London and New York: Continuum, 35–50.

Steans, J. (1998) *Gender in International Relations* Cambridge: Polity Press.

Stepan, A. (1998) 'Modern Multinational Democracies: Transcending a Gellnerian Oxymoron' in J. Hall (ed.), *The State of the Nation* Cambridge: Cambridge University Press, 219–39.

Stiglitz, J. (2002) *Globalization and its Discontents* London: Allen Lane, Penguin.

Sylvester, C. (1994) *Feminist Theory and International Relations in a Postmodern Era* Cambridge: Cambridge University Press.

Sylvester, C. (2002) *Feminist International Relations* Cambridge: Cambridge University Press.

Taylor, C. (1998a) 'Nationalism and Modernity' in J. Hall (ed.), *The State of the Nation* Cambridge: Cambridge University Press, 191–218.

Taylor, C. (1998b) 'The Dangers of Soft Despotism' in A. Etzioni (ed.), *The Essential Communitarian Reader* Lanham et al. Oxford: Rowman and Littlefield, 47–54.

Tickner, J. (1992) *Gender and International Relations* New York: Columbia University Press.

Tickner, J. (1995) 'Re-visioning Security' in K. Booth and S. Smith (eds), *International Relations Theory Today* Cambridge: Polity Press, 175–97.

Tocqueville, A. de (1966 [1835 and 1840]) *Democracy in America* London and Glasgow: Fontana.

Touraine, A. (1981) *The Voice and the Eye* Cambridge: Cambridge University Press.

Touraine, A. (1995) 'Democracy: From a Politics of Citizenship to a Politics of Recognition' in L. Maheu (ed.), *Social Movements and Social Classes* London: Sage, 258–75.

Tully, J. (2000) 'The Challenge of Reimaging Citizenship and Belonging in Multi-cultural and Multinational Societies' in C. McKinnon and I. Hampsher-Monk (eds), *The Demands of Citizenship* London and New York: Continuum, 212–34.

Turner, A. (2002) *Just Capital* London: Pan Books.

Turner, B. (1986) *Citizenship and Capitalism* London: Allen and Unwin.

Turner, B. (1994) 'Postmodern Culture/Modern Citizens' in B. Van Steenbergen (ed.), *The Condition of Citizenship* London: Sage, 153–68.

United Nations (1993) *Charter of the United Nations and Statute of the International Court of Justice* United Nations, New York.

Van Creveld, M. (1999) *The Rise and Decline of the State* Cambridge: Cambridge University Press.

Van Steenbergen, B. (1994) 'Towards a Global Ecological Citizen' in B. Van Steenbergen (ed.), *The Condition of Citizenship* London: Sage, 141–52.

Vincent, A. (1987) *Theories of the State* Oxford: Basil Blackwell.

Viroli, M. (2000) 'Republican Patriotism' in C. McKinnon and I. Hampsher-Monk (eds), *The Demands of Citizenship* London and New York: Continuum, 267–75.

Voet, R. (1998) *Feminism and Citizenship* London, Thousand Oaks, New Delhi: Sage.

Vogel, U. (1994) 'Marriage and the Boundaries of Citizenship' in B. Van Steenbergen (ed.), *The Condition of Citizenship* London: Sage, 76–89.

Walker, R.B.J. (1999) 'Citizenship After the Modern Subject' in K. Hutchings and R. Dannreuther (eds), *Cosmopolitan Citizenship* Basingstoke: Macmillan, 171–200.

Weldon, T. (1953) *The Vocabulary of Politics* Harmondsworth: Penguin.

Williams, R. (2002) 'Full text of Dimbleby lecture delivered by the Archbishop of Canterbury', http://www.Guardian.co.uk/religion, 1–9.

Yeatman, A. (1994) *Postmodern Revisionings of the Political* London: Routledge.

Youngs, G. (1999) *International Relations in a Global Age* Cambridge: Polity Press.

Yuval-Davis, N. (1997a) 'Women, Citizenship and Difference', *Feminist Review* 57, 4–27.

Yuval-Davis, N. (1997b) *Gender and Nation* London: Sage.

Yuval-Davis, N. (1999) 'The "Multi-Layered Citizen": Citizenship in the Age of "Glocalization"', *International Feminist Journal of Politics* 1 (1), 119–36.

Zalewski, M. (1995) 'Well, What is the Feminist Perspective in Bosnia?', *International Affairs* 71 (2), 339–58.

Glossary

Words as used in this book.

Abstraction
A conceptual and practical process that mystifies and conceals underlying social relationships.

Anarchism
A theory that seeks to abolish the state, but adopts statist tools of analysis and hence enjoys no success.

Atomistic
An approach that treats individuals and entities in purely discrete terms and ignores the relationships between them.

Capitalism
A system of production that divides society into those who can hire the services of others and those who are compelled to work for an employer.

Citizen
A person able to govern their own life. Citizenship is an emancipatory situation towards which we move, but can never actually reach.

Class
An identity that divides people based upon economic, social, regional, religious, gender, ethnic and other differences.

Coercion
A concept and practice that should be rigorously distinguished from force. Coercion embraces social pressures that deliberately punish those who harm a person or collectivity's interests.

Communitarianism
A theory which stresses that all people belong to communities and can only identify themselves in relations with others.

Conflict
A clash of interests that can be tackled through violence, but only resolved through non-statist pressures. Conflicts of the latter kind are inevitable and arise from the fact that we are all different from one another.

Constraint
A natural or social pressure ensuring that we do something which we had not intended to do. Unlike coercion, this pressure is unintentional and informal in character.

Deconstruction
The act of criticizing. Deconstruction involves pulling an argument to pieces, but in a way that works from the assumptions upon which this argument rests.

Democracy
A society in which people govern themselves.

Difference
Identifications that separate people and inevitably cause conflict to arise.

Division
Differences that undermine common interests and necessitate the use of force.

Emancipation
The capacity of people to act freely and thus govern their own lives.

Feminism
A theory that works toward emancipation of women.

Force
A pressure that undermines the agency of individuals by physically harming them.

Globalization
A linkage between peoples of the globe that enables them to understand and empathize with one another.

Government
The resolution of conflicts of interest. It can occur at every level in society; it is inherent in social relationships, and needs to be contrasted with the state.

Hierarchy
An assymetrical linkage inherent in relationships. It is normally assumed to be repressive, but it need not be.

Individual
A person who is separate from others but who finds their identity through relating to these others.

Liberalism
A theory which stipulates that individuals realize their freedom through the possession of private property and through the market mechanism.

Market
A mechanism enabling exchanges to occur, but in a way that conceals the real power that people possess.

Marxism
A theory whose potential for emancipation is undermined by notions of class war, revolution and dictatorship.

Momentum Concept
A concept that has a potential for freedom and equality, but whose progress is infinite, and therefore can never be realized.

Multi-culturalism
A respect for and a belief that we can learn from the cultural differences of others, provided these differences express themselves in a democratic manner.

Nationalism
A statist attitude and movement that arises when one nationality is privileged at the expense of others.

Nationality
An identity that arises from a sense of belonging to one or more nations.

Natural
A developmental process. What is natural is therefore susceptible to historical change.

Naturalism
A doctrine that treats the natural in a static and ahistorical way. It assumes that what exists at the present can never change.

Order
A stability in the possession of things; security against violence, and a trust in others that promises will be kept.

Patriarchal
A static concept and practice that enshrines male domination. Patriarchy can be pursued by women. It need not be pursued by men.

Politics
A public process that involves resolving conflicts of interest. Politics is undermined by force and is inherent at every level in all societies.

Post-liberalism
A theory that accepts liberalism but goes beyond it, by extending liberal values to all individuals, and thus challenging the need for a state.

Postmodernism
A theory that goes beyond modernism and therefore challenges the dualisms and one-sidedness expressed in the modernist tradition.

Pre-modern
A theory and practice that has yet to obtain the institutions and to support the values of liberalism (or modernism).

Private
The sphere of life in which conflict is imperceptible or embryonic.

Public
The sphere of life in which conflict is manifest and has to be resolved.

Reconstruction
The reworking of concepts so that an alternative to the status quo is charted.

Relational
An approach which stresses that individuals and collectives only find their identity in relationship with one another.

Relationship
A linkage that is vitiated by force but whose mutuality is necessarily hierarchical in character and sustained by coercion and constraint.

State
An institution that claims a monopoly of legitimate force for a particular territory. This claim makes it contradictory and paradoxical.

Static Concept
One which is divisive in character and cannot therefore be reconstructed.

Statism
An approach that creates or accepts divisions and thus the need for force to tackle them.

Violence
A synonym for force.

Index